Embroidery
A HISTORY

PAMELA WARNER

For Dee
Pamela Warner
Best wishes

B.T. Batsford Ltd, London

First published 1991

All rights reserved. No part of this publication
may be reproduced, in any form or by any means,
without permission from the Publisher.

Typeset by Tradespools Ltd
and printed in Great Britain by
Courier International Ltd, East Kilbride

Published by B.T. Batsford Ltd
4 Fitzhardinge Street, London W1H 0AH

A catalogue record for this book is
available from the British Library

ISBN 0 7134 6106 3

PHOTOGRAPHIC SOURCES

The author and publishers would like to thank the following for permission to reproduce illustrations:

Colour plates

Dean and Chapter of Durham Cathedral, 1 and 3; author, courtesy of the Embroiderers' Guild, Hampton Court Palace, 4, 5, 6, 7, 9, 10, 12; Victoria and Albert Museum, London, 2; author, courtesy of Westminster Abbey, 8, 11.

Black and white photographs

Author, 70, 76, 77, 97, 103, 104, 105, 107, 111, 113, 114, 115, 116; Birmingham City Council Museums and Art Gallery, 98; Dean and Chapter of Durham Cathedral, 8; E. Ryle-Hodges, 99; author, courtesy of the Embroiderers' Guild, Hampton Court Palace, 55, 60, 61, 67, 71, 72, 75, 78, 79, 80, 81, 82, 93, 101, 108, 109, 110, 122; Fitzwilliam Museum, Cambridge, 56; Kunsthistorisches Museum, Vienna, 32; National Museum of Scotland, Edinburgh, 38; Dr James Shapiro and Turner's Photography, 96; Victoria and Albert Museum, London, 3, 19, 21, 23, 30, 35, 39, 44, 62, 66, 94; Whitworth Art Gallery, Manchester, 64.

Front and back cover: panel, Britain c. 1840–1860. Canvas embroidered with wool and silk threads, applied velvet, glass and metallic beads. EG 304

CONTENTS

ACKNOWLEDGEMENTS

I would like to thank Moyra McNeill for many years of friendship and encouragement, and for giving me the confidence to undertake this venture. Thanks also to Nancy Kimmins for stimulating my initial interest in the history of embroidery. Thank you to Vanessa Stanfield for her proof reading and to Karen Finch for her translation from Danish of an article on needlebinding.

When making enquiries, I received the most generous help from the following people: Carol Humphrey, Fitzwilliam Museum; Paul Harrison and Howard Batho, Victoria and Albert Museum; Martin Ellis, Birmingham Museums and Art Gallery; Naomi Tarrant, National Museums of Scotland; Blanda Winter, Museum für Angewandte Kunst; Dr Rotraud Bauer, Kunsthistorisches Museum; and Dr Jennifer Harris, Whitworth Art Gallery. My thanks also to Sir Andrew Morritt and Mrs Patricia Yeats, the administrator, of Rokeby Park for allowing me to research the needlepaintings.

My grateful thanks go to Lynn Szygenda, the curator of the Embroiderers' Guild, for making available items from the Guild's collection for photography, to my editor, Sandra Winfield, for her help and, finally, to my husband for his generous support and practical help.

Pamela Warner, 1991

INTRODUCTION

This book has been written to provide a concise, non-academic and easy-to-read historical background for students and all who are interested in embroidery. It covers the requirements for students studying for the City and Guilds Embroidery examination, and for those interested in related textile crafts.

This volume covers mainstream embroidery and its influences from early textile structures, through medieval techniques, to the embroidery of later centuries. The development of, and changes in, embroidery techniques are related to the living conditions, outside influences and fashions of the period, setting them within the context of their time.

The aim of this volume is to provide the student with a knowledge of the history of embroidery and details of important historical examples. A guide to further reading and a list of museums and collections is included to lead the reader into areas of special interest.

There is not enough space here to cover the ethnic techniques of the world; these will be dealt with in a later volume. However, where relevant, the influences of imported ideas and techniques, and trade, are noted.

Diagrams and sketches have been used to illustrate many of the examples included. The best way to understand and remember a piece is to make your own sketches and notes – not necessarily as beautiful drawings, but as a memory aid. An overall impression of the whole item, with details of small areas and added colour, will keep the image in your mind. You will almost certainly have to sketch from memory in an examination. Where possible the photographs included show details of a piece, to show the techniques and materials used.

Embroidery is a beautiful, stimulating and exciting area of study – I hope you enjoy exploring it with me.

Coptic roundel, *The Annunciation and Visitation*.
Egyptian, seventh to eighth centuries AD. Linen
with silk in satin stitch, stem stitch and long and
short stitch. 814–1903.

(By courtesy of the Board of Trustees of the Victoria
and Albert Museum, London)

1

EARLY TECHNIQUES

Ancient Egyptian Textiles

The Ancient Egyptians were skilled builders and craftsmen. By 2700 BC they had built the Great Pyramids at Giza. Their religion and beliefs were based on the safe passage of the spirit and soul of the dead into the next world, and mummification developed because the spirit needed a body. Much of their art and textiles survived because of the practice of providing the dead with all their requirements for the next world, and also because of the dryness of the climate.

Early Egyptian art shows a great sense of design and included all the essential parts, whether they could be seen or not. Faces were drawn with great care; men were depicted with a darker skin than women. A figure drawn in profile would have two shoulders, two left or right feet and a 'full-face eye'. There was a lack of perspective; a pond would be drawn as a circle with fish shown sideways on.

Egypt perfected the manufacture of linen and honoured the fabric, attributing the invention of flax to the goddess Isis. Linen was regarded as a symbol of purity, so it was used for burial cloths, often adorned with embroidery.

In the Cairo Museum there is an early specimen of patchwork and appliqué, the funeral tent of Queen Istemkeb, c. eleventh century BC. Recent research suggests that the pieces actually belong to two canopies. They are made from many pieces of gazelle hide, the outer edges bound with twisted pink leather cord sewn with a pink thread. There is a central flat top with four sides that hang down (*Figure 1*).

There are many references to early pieces. A corselet of Aramis, King of Egypt, 672–525 BC is described by Herodotus: 'It was made of linen, ornamented with numerous figures and animals, worked in Gold and Cotton, each thread of the corselet was worthy of admiration.' Gold thread was known at an early date, being beaten with hammers into shreds, which were then rounded. Silver wires have also been found in tombs, and there are many references to textiles and needlework in the Book of Exodus, for example, 'They did beat the gold into thin plates and cut it into wires, to work in the blue and the purple, and in the scarlet and in the very fine linen, with cunning work' (Exodus 39:3).

Fabrics with woven patterns date from 945–745 BC, and were very expensive. Contemporary embroidery relates to these woven designs, as the less wealthy copied them by embroidering them.

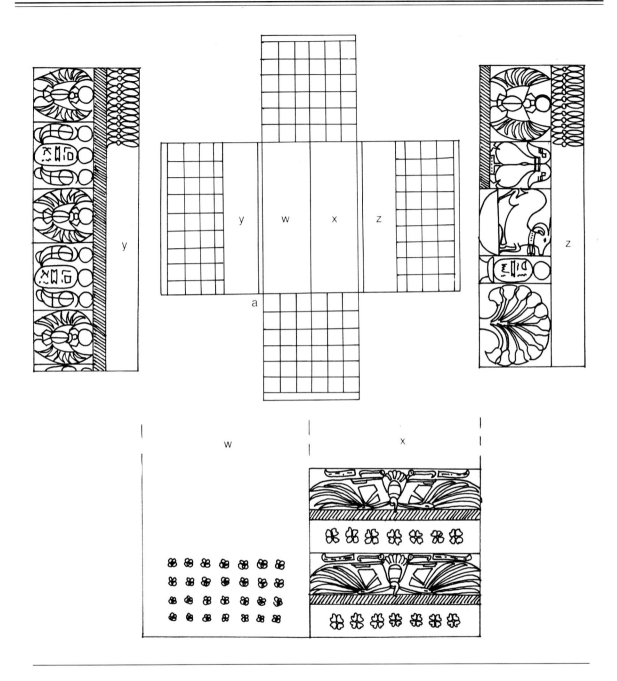

Figure 1
The funeral tent of Queen Istemkeb, *c.* eleventh
century BC, consists of a central flat top and four
sides which hang down (*a*). The top is divided down
the middle, one half pink and yellow rosettes on a
blue ground, the other six vultures and hieroglyphic
text (*w* and *x*). The four side flaps are of alternate
squares of pink and green with decorative borders
including kneeling gazelles and lotus blossom on the
two longer sides (*y* and *z*). Patchwork and appliqué
on fine leather. 26276.
(Cairo Museum)

Coptic Art and Embroidery

The Copts were Egyptian Christians who as a persecuted minority fled into the desert and there set up their own communities, which became important centres for textiles and weaving. Coptic art had two branches, provincial Greek and Coptic, both of which were influenced from the sixth century by Byzantine art.

Decoration on early Coptic textiles is basically tapestry weaving and small-scale needleweaving. The designs are usually circles or medallions, bands and borders, the positioning of which denoted the social status of the wearer. When the basic garment was woven, the area to be decorated was left unwoven. The weft threads were either taken across the back of the fabric, or turned back to weave the next row, thus leaving the warp threads exposed within the woven cloth to receive the needle- or tapestry weaving (*Figure 2*). The areas of decoration were

Figure 3
Part of an altar cover or hanging, fourth to seventh centuries. Linen embroidered in wool using chain and stem stitches. The tree motifs are about 18 cm (7 in) high. Egyptian, found at Shaikh Shata, near Damietta. T233–1917.
(Victoria and Albert Museum, London)

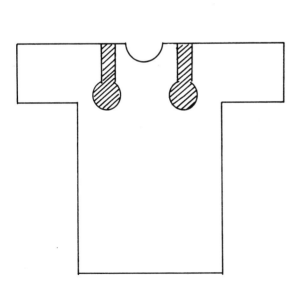

Figure 2
Coptic tunic. The shaded areas show where the weft would be omitted to receive the design.

stronger than the plain fabric and were often re-applied to later garments, as can be seen in many museum examples. Early pieces were of limited colour, but later examples have many colours and show great skill in shading. Examples of embroidered roundels date from around the fourth century, and include satin stitch, stem stitch, and long and short stitch (see page 6). On larger items motifs tended to be in rows, copying the woven fabrics. Designs

included figures, birds, animals, flowers and plant forms. An example is the Damietta Hanging, thought to be an altar hanging or cover, which is worked in wools on linen in chain and stem stitches (*Figure 3*).

Greek and Roman Textiles

Many of the early textiles of Greece and Rome came from Asia, being the spoils of victory. Homer, writing *c*. 900 BC, refers to embroidery many times, stating that expert embroideresses were brought from Sidon to Troy. He relates how a picture representing the Trojan Wars was embroidered by Helen of Troy, and describes Ulysses wearing a mantle embroidered with a hunting scene. The later imported embroidered cloths in Rome were very costly and worn only by the very rich.

Oriental Embroidery

Oriental art is based on beliefs and symbols used to please the gods and to show status and rank. Embroidery is a very ancient craft in China. The written characters that represent the word belong to the earliest picture forms in the language. It is thought that embroidery was an established craft by 2000 BC and developed to a very high standard, alongside the decoration of ceramics and bronzes.

Sericulture – the breeding of silkworms to produce silk – and the use of silk has been known in China for at least 4,000 years. Silk was used for beautiful brocaded fabrics and fine tapestry weaving, *k'o-ssu*, as well as for embroidery. The production of silk was a closely guarded secret, until some eggs were smuggled out of China in the mid-sixth century to Byzantium, by two Nestorian monks who had learned the process.

The earliest evidence of Chinese embroidery

is the impression of chain stitch on a Shang wine vessel, 1523–1027 BC. Also in chain stitch is a surviving fragment found in a Huang tomb dated 481–221 BC. Embroidered clothes and bedding, with beautifully executed tigers and birds in chain stitch, have survived in good condition from the fourth to third centuries BC. Chain stitch seems to be the dominant stitch on these early pieces. Later embroideries show the use of satin stitch, Peking knot, Pekinese stitch, cross stitch, couching and counted thread work. The designs often feature a form of voiding, leaving a tiny band of fabric showing between the blocks of embroidery, almost like a stencil.

The embroidery of Japan is similar to that of China, but the work is more likely to be padded. A Japanese dragon would appear far more ferocious than a Chinese one. The Japanese made beautiful covers for gifts, *fukusa*, that were exquisitely embroidered. Some late Japanese pieces were worked in soft greys and mauves to satisfy the European taste.

Korea has a recorded history of embroidery from the fourth century, and Koreans travelling in China wore embroidered costumes. More embroidery was done by the common people here than in China or Japan. Modern embroidery in Korea is very free and the designs of gift covers have a bright, naive feeling.

Byzantine Art

In the Byzantine Empire in the fourth century, images were considered holy in their own right, and were made in an attempt to show exactly what the saints should look like. The figures were stiff and rigid, with limbs showing through the drapery. The use of figures without landscapes against a plain gold background is typical of Byzantine art. Probably the best-known examples are the mosaics in San Vitali in Ravenna, which date from the sixth century.

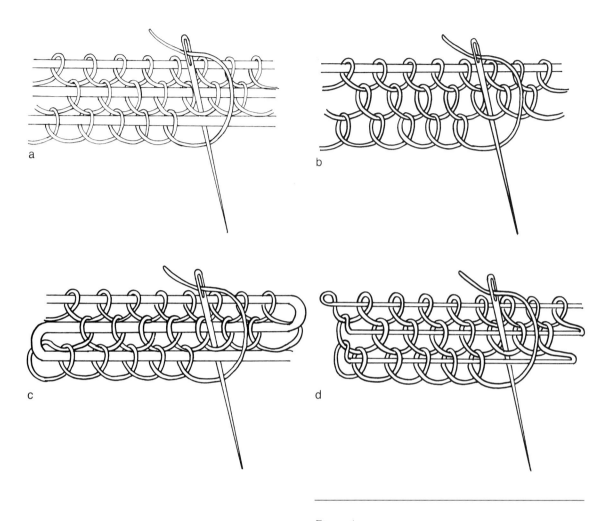

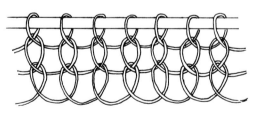

Figure 4
Techniques for needlemade fabrics (*see overleaf*).
(*a*) Needlebinding with a transverse thread,
   worked in the round.
(*b*) Needlebinding, without a transverse thread,
   worked in the round, as found in Egypt, first
   century AD.
(*c*) Needlebinding worked flat, with a separate
   transverse thread.
(*d*) Needlebinding worked flat, but with a single
   thread.
(*e*) Needlemade fabric which resembles knitting,
   found in South America.
Note that all these variations reappear in later
embroidery and needlemade lace.

Celtic Art in Britain

The change in climate, which resulted in Central Asia becoming drier, caused a major westward drift of people across northern Europe and eventually into Britain. The Celts came as colonists, building hilltop villages, having already virtually colonized the whole of the northern areas of Europe. They brought with them great skill in metalwork and intricate interlacing and elaborate designs, and were driven into the north and west of Britain.

The Romans came to Britain in 55 BC but they did not mix racially with the people already here, and were mainly town-dwellers. Their great legacy was the building of hard-surfaced roads and garrison towns. They left Britain around AD 450 and took their skills with them.

Christianity reached Britain via the Celtic missionaries of Ireland in the fourth century. For about a hundred years three religions fought for supremacy: the pagan worship of Woden; Celtic Christianity in Wales, Ireland, Scotland and Northumbria; and Roman Christianity in Kent.

The Angles, Saxons and Jutes came as pirates and then claimed the land for farming, killing a large proportion of the population. Norsemen from Scandinavia and Vikings from Denmark came, settled and intermarried. They were skilled woodcarvers and brought intricate, interlaced designs.

In AD 664 the Synod of Whitby pronounced against the Church of Iona, and Celtic Christianity gave way to the Roman Church, although pagan ideas survived for many centuries. Christianity brought books and learning, music, law and organizing ability. However, in spite of the dictates of Rome, the Celtic style of art persisted in manuscripts, with elaborate interlacing and scrolling executed with incredible skill, as the Lindisfarne Gospels show.

Early Needlemade Fabrics

Needlebinding, or knotless netting, was a very early way of making fabrics and small articles of clothing. Pieces of fabric, plaited ropes and cords have been excavated near Tybrind in Denmark, and have been dated scientifically to 5200–4000 BC. Fragments that pre-date this find by about a thousand years have been found in Syria. The Danish fragments are made from vegetable fibres and are stitched using the needlebinding method (*Figure 4a*). The technique was used mainly for hats, gloves and socks, although larger garments have been known, and it has also been used as a decorative feature on costume items. Variations of needlebinding have been found in Europe and Egypt (*Figure 4b*). Similar techniques are to be found in South American textiles (*Figure 4e*).

Needlebinding was also worked in wool, or wool mixed with animal hair. Pieces of yarn about one metre long were joined, as required, by spinning the ends together. True needlebinding has a transverse thread to make it thicker and warmer, and the item was made oversized and then 'fulled', or shrunk to size, making it a virtually wind- and waterproof fabric.

Needlebinding was popular until the sixteenth century, when knitting took over, but it survived in a few places until recently.

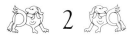 2

EARLY ENGLISH EMBROIDERY

During the Middle Ages there was little comfort and little in the way of soft furnishings and therefore there was not a lot of opportunity for embroidery in the home.

Later, the main buildings were of stone, and the feudal castle or manor house developed, serving as a school for the sons and daughters of the gentry. The girls learned to spin, sew and weave, and many hours were spent in needlework and in prayer. As life became more settled, the arts, manuscript illumination, metalwork and needlework reached a high standard, and the reputation of English needlework spread throughout Europe.

Most embroidery was designed by the monks, who illustrated the manuscripts, and by stained-glass artists, who were familiar with the iconography. The stories and events illustrated on the church vestments acted as visual aids to those who could not read. Women of high birth went to live in nunneries and worked embroideries there. The religious houses were the first workshops, initially providing for their own needs but later realizing the potential for outside trade.

Early References

Many records have references to the skill of Englishwomen in needlework. Inventories and wills provide us with details of pieces that have not survived. Many were wantonly destroyed and much was burned to recoup the small quantities of precious metal that they contained.

The first wife of King Canute, Aelgitha or Elgifa, is recorded as having made embroideries for the Abbeys of Croyland and Romsey. His second wife, Aelgiva or Emma, presented to Ely 'a purple banner she had made, surrounded on every side by a border of gold embroidery, and adorned with magnificent embroidery of gold and precious gems . . . for her needlework seems to excel in work even her materials' (*Liber Elienses*, pp. 196–97). Aelgiva's daughter, Aelthelswitha, 'rejected marriage, and was assigned Coveney, a place near the monastery [Ely], where in retirement she devoted herself, with her maids, to gold embroidery. At her own cost, and with her own hands, being extremely skilled in the craft, she made a white chasuble' (*Liber Elienses*, pp. 207–8).

William of Malmsbury records that Eadgyth, or Edith, Queen to Edward the Confessor, embroidered robes for him. A reference in the Domesday Book tells us that Alwid the Maid, of Buckinghamshire, was granted land by the Sheriff 'in return for which she would teach embroidery in gold to his daughter'. William of Poitiers, chronicler to William the Conquerer, wrote, 'the splendour of the State robes, rich with embroidery of gold, wrought by English hands, taken back by Chief William and his

nobles, made all that France and Normandy had beheld of the same seem mean by comparison'.

It was common for royalty to give State garments to the Church to use as vestments. The will of Queen Matilda, wife of William the Conqueror, says: 'I give to the Abbey of the Holy Trinity [at Caen] my tunic, being embroidered at Winchester by Alderet's wife, and the mantle embroidered with gold, which is in my chamber, to make a cope. Of my two golden girdles I give that which is ornamented with emblems for the purpose of suspending the lamp before the great altar.' She also left her horse trappings together with the above 'with the consent of my husband'.

Much English needlework was sent out of the country. Matthew Paris records the Abbot of St Alas taking 'an offering of three mitres . . . of wonderful workmanship, embroidered by Christina, Prioress of Markgate', to Pope Adrian IV (1154–59) in Rome. Paris also records how Pope Innocent IV saw gold-embroidered vestments from England, and sent messages to the abbots of the Cistercian order in England that he desired to have some sent to him.

Guilds were set up to monitor the quality of workmanship, and they had the power to destroy that which they found inferior.

THE MAASEIK FRAGMENTS

Two very early surviving important fragments of Anglo-Saxon work, eighth to early ninth centuries, were made in the south of England and are to be found at Maaseik, Limburg, in Belgium. (There are some earlier examples of embroidery in wool on linen from garments found in graves.) The fragments were discovered in a shrine at St Catherine's Church, Maaseik late in the sixteenth century, with relics of the early eighth-century saints, Harlandis and Relindis, but were originally from the church at Aldeneik. They were probably taken from England as a gift to the Court of Charlemagne. Early references suggest that they are a *casula* (chasuble), and two *velamen* (veils), one almost whole and decorated, the other plain linen cloth.

The *casula* (*Figure 5a*) is made up from many fragments of different silk textiles of various dates. The fragments have been re-arranged several times over the centuries and many repairs were worked by nuns during the late nineteenth century. In addition to the embroidered pieces, there are tablet-woven braids, and two types of woven patterned

fabrics, one showing King David. There are eight pieces of embroidery in gold and silk: two long strips (x in *Figure 5a*), with a series of arches with interlaced designs with animals and birds in geometric shapes (*Figure 5b*); two short strips, each with ten roundels containing an animal or bird (y in *Figure 5a*); and four monograms, one at each corner, possibly M and A, or Alpha and Omega, decorated with scrolling stems (z in *Figure 5a*). The embroidery is in surface-couched gold thread, flattened pure gold wire wound on a single horse hair, worked on a closely woven linen ground. There are blocks of silk embroidery in six colours – red, beige, green, yellow, light and dark blue – in split and stem stitches. Originally there were pearls which have now disappeared, and some of the gold appears to have been removed deliberately.

The decorated *velamen* are also made from various pieces: appliquéd coloured brocaded silk, tablet-woven braids and a later velvet. They are decorated with gilded copper bosses, glass beads and pearls.

The fragments were mounted and displayed

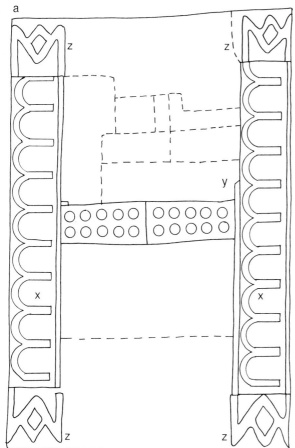

after the Second World War, following the first detailed study made, in Brussels. A second study was undertaken by visiting British experts in 1982–83, prior to the conservation work which was begun in 1984. When conservation work has been completed the fragments will be displayed in a new museum in Maaseik.

Figure 5
The casula (*a*), Maaseik fragments, ninth century AD, mounted on joined fragments of different silk textiles, indicated by the broken lines.
(*x*) Two long embroidered strips of arches with interlaced designs (*b*).
(*y*) Two short strips each with ten embroidered roundels.
(*z*) Four embroidered monograms decorated with scrolling stems.
Surface-couched gold thread and coloured silks in split and stem stitches on linen.
(Maaseik, Belgium)

THE DURHAM RELICS

Two other important examples of Anglo-Saxon work are the exquisite stole and maniple of St Cuthbert in the Cathedral Treasury in Durham (*Figure* 6). An inscription on both pieces – AELFFLAED FIERI PRECIPIT PIO FRIDESTANO – tells us that they were made at the command of Queen Aelfflaed (d. 916), wife of King Edward the Elder, for Fridestan, Bishop of Winchester from 909, and they can thus be dated. The work was probably executed in Winchester, the Saxon capital.

The embroidery is of the highest standard and is worked in surface couching in pure gold wound around a silk core and laid straight to cover the ground, there being sixteen threads to 3 mm ($^1/_8$ in). The figures and lettering are worked in stem stitch and split stitch in two thicknesses of coloured silks, now discoloured. Within the haloes, the gold is laid with diaper patterns and at right-angles to the main ground; the drapery on the figures is outlined with gold thread couched directionally (*Plate 1*).

The silk foundation has almost entirely disappeared. The red silk fringes that were evident when the pieces were lifted from the tomb in 1827 have now decayed. The red silk backing was probably added at the time, together with a resinous varnish, which was removed in 1936 by the British Museum when fungoid growths were discovered.

The design shows full and half figures of prophets and saints issuing from clouds, with a foliate canopy above. Each is identified with an inscription, and the gold background shows a strong Byzantine influence (*Figures 6, 7a* and *7b*). The stole (*Figure 7c*) is in five pieces and is incomplete. It has been mounted on a fine white gauze for display, and in this form measures 182.9 × 4.5 cm (6 ft × 1$^3/_4$ in). The maniple (*Figure 7d*) is in better condition and shows popes with their attendant deacons. It measures 82.2 × 4.5 cm (32$^3/_8$ × 1$^1/_4$ in).

Also found in the tomb was a girdle

Figure 6
St Cuthbert's stole (909–916), detail showing *Jonah the Prophet*. Surface couching in gold thread with a diaper pattern within the halo. The draperies are worked in coloured silks in split and stem stitches, with directional couching in gold thread. The horizontal threads that are visible at intervals are filaments used for conservation.
(With the kind permission of the Dean and Chapter of Durham Cathedral)

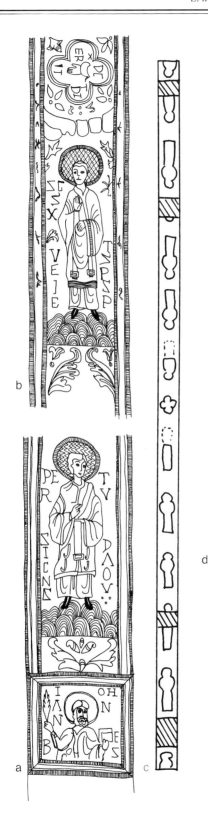

Figure 7

The stole and maniple of St Cuthbert (909–916).

(*a*) Peter, Gregory's deacon, and St John the Baptist, one end of the maniple.

(*b*) The Dextra Dei and Pope Sixtus II, from the maniple.

(*c*) The stole, from the top:
St Thomas the apostle with PIO EPISCOPO FRIDESTANO on the reverse, a gap with Ezekiel and Malachi missing, Zachariah, Jonah, a gap with the top of a halo belonging to Habakkuk, Joel, Hosea, Isaiah, the Agnus Dei, Jeremiah, Daniel, Amos, Obediah, Naham, a gap with Zephaniah, Micah and Haggai missing, and St James the apostle with AELFFLAED FIERI PRECIPIT on the reverse.

(*d*) The maniple, from the top:
St John the Baptist with PIO . . . on the reverse, Gregory's deacon, Peter, Pope Gregory I, the Dextra Dei, Pope Sixtus II, Sixtus's deacon, Laurence, and St John the Evangelist with AELFFLAED . . . on the reverse.
Surface-couched gold thread on a silk core using coloured silks in split and stem stitches.

(*e*) Detail of St John the Baptist, end of maniple.

(Treasury of Durham Cathedral)

decorated with foliage designs in gold thread and coloured silks, worked in stem stitch and surface couching. The design closely relates to the manuscripts of the early tenth century. Three tablet-woven fragments associated with these pieces have a silk warp and a weft of gold thread, and are described as a girdle and two bracelets.

St Cuthbert (d.687) was the last of the Irish bishops at Lindisfarne and his remains were revered and laid to rest at Chester-le-Street in 833. It is recorded that King Athelstan, the stepson of Aelfflaed, visited the shrine in 934 and offered a stole and maniple. A century later the body was moved to Durham until 1069–70, when the monks fled briefly to Lindisfarne to escape William the Conqueror. The body was returned to Durham where it remained, the relics being discovered in 1827 by James Raine.

THE BAYEUX TAPESTRY

The most famous surviving piece of Norman embroidery is, of course, the Bayeux Tapestry. The title is misleading as tapestry is a woven technique. Hangings depicting heroic deeds and battles were not unknown, and a reference exists to a piece worked in the previous century that has not survived. It depicted the deeds of Brithnoth, an Ealdorman of the East Saxons, killed fighting the Danes in 997. The hanging was embroidered by his wife, Aedelfleda, for a church in Ely. There is also an Icelandic 'tapestry', *c*.1000, in the National Museum in Copenhagen, depicting the life of the Virgin Mary and worked in the same technique as the Bayeux Tapestry.

The Bayeux Tapestry is 68.38 m (221 ft) long and 45.7–53.6 cm (18–21 in) wide, worked on a linen ground. There is a length missing from the end. It was worked in separate panels, and the eight surviving panels are joined almost invisibly.

The embroidery is in wool, probably English worsted, in eight colours: terracotta red, bluish-green, sage green, dark green, yellow, buff, blue and dark blue. The colours are not used in a naturalistic way – some horses, for example, have 'odd' legs. The solid shapes are worked in laid and couched work (*Figure* 8), a technique that was widely used in Europe until the sixteenth century, and which is used in Iceland to the present day. All the details are in stem stitch. These two techniques are used throughout. On the representation of Mont St Michel there appears to be some chain stitch, but this is probably a later incorrect repair mistaking two rows of stem stitch. The actual drawing is very simple and cartoon-like, but closer inspection reveals the quality of design in the placing of the birds and animals, the interlacing of the trees, and the sense of pattern and movement of the horses.

The Bayeux Tapestry was probably commissioned by Bishop Odo of Bayeux and is thought to be a secular piece, which found its way into the cathedral where it is known to have been hung. The embroidery is mentioned in an inventory of Bayeux Cathedral in 1476. It was not always on display and was stored folded in a press, which would account for the vertical areas of damage that can be seen.

The scenes tell the story of the invasion and conquest of England by William of Normandy in 1066, and the work was carried out in English workshops, probably at Winchester, between the event and 1082 when Odo was imprisoned. The greatest value of the embroidery is in the content, providing us with an accurate social document of the time. A series of scenes telling the story form the main design, with an inscription providing a commentary. The interlaced trees divide each scene. There is a narrow decorative border top

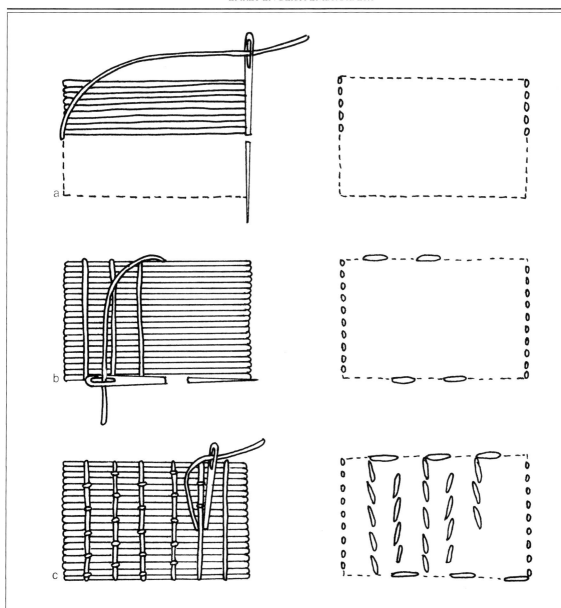

Figure 8

Laid and couched technique as used on the Bayeux Tapestry, also showing the reverse side.

(*a*) Thread laid side by side to cover the ground taking a tiny stitch at each end.

(*b*) Second layer of threads laid about 5 mm apart at right-angles to the first.

(*c*) Second layer secured with couching stitches. Note the economy of thread with little wasted on the reverse side.

and bottom, consisting mainly of birds, animals and small domestic scenes (*Figure 9*), although the lower border is sometimes included in the main story. Within the scenes we find reference to the costume of all classes, vestments, armour and weapons. Tools and methods of boat-building can be seen. Buildings of all kinds, the preparation and serving of food, the use of horses and their trappings all give us an insight into life in the eleventh century (*Figure 10*).

Figure 9
Detail, the Bayeux Tapestry, eleventh century. A bird, animals and an agricultural scene from the upper and lower borders. Laid and couched work and stem stitch on linen.
(Centre Guillaume le Conquerant, Bayeux)

A paper was read in Paris in 1724 which renewed interest in the piece. Detailed drawings were made and the deterioration and damage recorded. During the French Revolution the tapestry came close to being destroyed; it was found covering a wagon and rescued. It was displayed in Paris in 1803 when Napoleon studied the comet and pondered its omens. The tapestry was returned to Bayeux in 1804 and was repaired and re-lined in 1842. The embroidery was viewed by winding it from one roller to another, which caused more damage. The tapestry was displayed again in Paris after the Liberation in 1944.

It is now on display at the Centre Guillaume le Conquerant in Bayeux, after a careful study was made recording all the holes, stains, patches and repairs. A copy of the Bayeux tapestry was made by the Leek Embroidery Society in 1885–86, and can be seen at the Reading Art Gallery. This copy was cleaned by Karen Finch when her conservation workrooms were in Ealing.

Figure 10
Detail, the Bayeux Tapestry, eleventh century.
Drawings from the main narrative, worked in laid
and couched work and stem stitch on linen.
(Centre Guillaume le Conquerant, Bayeux)

THE TAPESTRY OF THE CREATION

The cathedral in Gerona, Spain, was consecrated in 1038 by Bishop Roger. The Tapestry of the Creation, which is on display within the cathedral, is an embroidery worked in coloured wools, dating from between the second half of the eleventh century and the early twelfth century. The hanging is rectangular, now measuring 4.7 m (15 ft 5 in) long × 3.65 m (12 ft) high, but it is thought to have been originally some 6 m (19 ft) long. It was restored and assembled in its present form in 1952.

In the centre of the hanging is a circle within a circle, the inner one showing the Creator giving His blessing. The outer circle is divided into eight segments which show aspects of the Creation and the Spirit of God. The perimeters of the circles contain inscriptions in Latin. The inner one translates: 'And God said let there be light and there was light.' The outer inscription can be translated, 'In the beginning God created the heavens and the earth, the sea and everything in them and God saw that all that he had done was good.'

Along the top edge and to the two sides is a border with nineteen further scenes and a fragment of one more. These show the months of the year (although three are missing), the seasons, scenes from Paradise, the sun and moon, Samson and Abel. Within the rectangle formed by this border, the four winds of the earth appear with an angel in each corner. Finally, along the lower edge is an incomplete panel depicting the story of the finding of the Holy Cross by St Helena.

It is difficult to identify the stitches, which are used as a filling with outlines, but they could be split, chain or stem stitches.

There are also some fourteenth-century vestments in this cathedral.

THE GIPON OF THE BLACK PRINCE

The Gipon, or Jupon, of the Black Prince, Edward Plantaganet, Prince of Wales (1330–76), was hung together with his heraldic achievements over his tomb in Canterbury Cathedral for nearly 600 years. The Gipon, shield, sword, helm and gauntlets would have been borne, as was the custom, before him at his funeral.

This type of garment varied in style in different ages and had various names. During the fourteenth and fifteenth centuries the gipon, jupon, paltock or pourpoint was a high-necked, hip-length tunic, padded for protection. Later it became a shorter waist-length garment.

The original achievements were taken down during the Second World War, after which they were cleaned and repaired, the gipon being covered with a coarse nylon net for protection. A replica of the gipon was made at the Royal School of Needlework and presented to Canterbury Cathedral in 1954, where it now hangs above the tomb. During the cleaning process, careful note was taken of the fragments of colour found in the seams, which showed that the linen base, padded with lambswool, was originally covered with red and blue velvet.

This heraldic garment (*Figure 11*) would have shown the then English royal arms: the ancient French (gold fleurs-de-lys on blue) quartering the leopards (lions) of England (three gold leopards on red), and showing the label of the first son. In early heraldry lions were termed 'leopards' when their heads faced outwards.

Gipons usually had elbow- or full-length sleeves, which suggests that the lower sleeves

are missing. The embroidery would have been in gold and silk thread, but only the outlines remain on the original. The garment is gamboised – quilted with vertical parallel lines – and eyelet holes down the front show the method of fastening with a lace.

In his will the Black Prince left a set of black tapestries bordered with crimson, with a design of ostrich feathers and swans with ladies' heads.

Figure 11
The Gipon, or Jupon, of the Black Prince, 1376. Originally gold and silk embroidery on velvet over linen padded with lambswool. Gamboised quilting in vertical parallel lines.
(Canterbury Cathedral)

3

OPUS ANGLICANUM

Opus Anglicanum means 'English work', but is used to refer to the work produced by the professional embroidery workshops from the eleventh to the fourteenth centuries. England had a high reputation for embroidery, the quality of which we have already seen in the earlier example of the St Cuthbert stole and maniple. Some workers are known by name – Mabel of Bury St Edmunds, a famous embroideress of the thirteenth century, is mentioned in the Issues of the Exchequer of Henry III between 1239 and 1244.

The standard of excellence reached its height in the great period of Opus Anglicanum from around 1250 to 1350. The inventories of many cathedrals show that an amazing number of embroidered vestments dated from this time, and Opus Anglicanum was much sought after. An inventory of St Paul's Cathedral, dated 1295, gives us an insight into the types of embroidery being worked at this time. It lists the following technical processes: *opus plumarium* (feather or plumage stitch); *opus pectineum* (embroidery that looked like weaving techniques); *opus pulvinarium* (canvas stitches); *opus consutum* (cutwork); and *opus Saracenum* (probably Eastern embroidery or that which resembles or imitates it).

The early Opus Anglicanum, until the end of the twelfth century, was dominated by the Romanesque style, with stiff, rigid-looking figures and often incorporating the Dextra Dei,

the hand of God. This period was influenced by the development of the monasteries as centres of learning and the arts, particularly embroidery. The large numbers of men travelling to and from the Crusades brought an exchange of ideas and goods. Pilgrims made contacts, and spread ideas in their search for sacred relics. Abbeys were built to house the relics and to act as resting places for the pilgrims. A fashion for sculpture spread to England from France and the figures used in the embroidery followed the style, often distorted to fit the shape to be filled. By the thirteenth century master craftsmen were designing for arts and crafts other than their own. Embroidery was designed by goldsmiths, stained-glass and manuscript artists.

Opus Anglicanum figures have rather large heads with staring eyes and exaggerated expressions and gestures. The hair is emphasized by being worked in two colours of silk, giving a striped effect, often in unnatural colouring – blue and white or yellow and green. In English work, bearded figures would have a shaven upper lip.

It is, however, the treatment of the faces that is the main characteristic of the best examples of Opus Anglicanum. The faces are in a fine split stitch worked directionally, with spirals from the centre of the cheeks, the chin, and above the lips (*Figure 12*). This gives a three-dimensional appearance which is

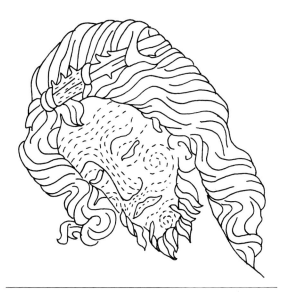

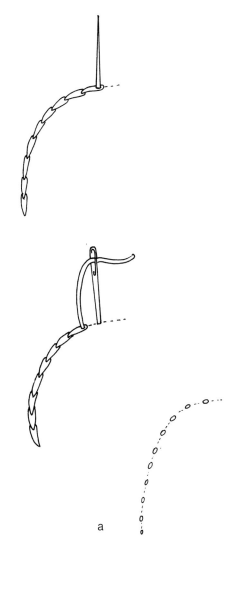

Figure 12
The directional use of split stitch in the face and hair of Opus Anglicanum figures. From the Melk chasuble.
(Museum für Angewandte Kunst, Vienna)

a

Figure 13
Methods of working split stitch and underside couching.
(a) Split stitch. Rows are worked closely together to cover the ground. The needle is brought up through the previous stitch to give a tiny stitch on the reverse.
(b) Underside couching. The upper thread is pulled through to the reverse side of the fabric to form a loop. The linen thread, shown in black, on the reverse side must pass up and down through the same hole. By placing the couching stitches carefully, a diaper, or all-over, pattern can be created.

b

accentuated by the physical distortion of the fabric. Split stitch is worked by taking a small stitch and returning the needle back up through the previous stitch, and so on. Hardly any silk is wasted on the reverse side of the fabric (*Figure 13a*). The needle is not taken back down through the previous stitch, as this gives a long stitch on the reverse and disturbs the play of light.

In addition to split stitch and surface couching, the use of underside couching is a dominant feature of Opus Anglicanum. Although it was also used in France and Italy, but not in Germany, it was mainly an English technique. Anyone who has worked with metal threads will know how stiff and rigid the completed embroidery is. One can imagine the problems this would create on a large item such as a cope. By using underside couching the metal thread is pulled through to the reverse side of the fabric with each stitch, thus forming a tiny hinge which allows the embroidery to be flexible. Underside couching differs from surface couching in that the thread to be laid is sewn with a strong linen thread. The needle is brought through the fabric, over the laid thread, and returned through the same hole to enable the laid thread to be pulled to the reverse side (*Figure 13b*). Underside couching gradually gave way to surface couching by the end of the fourteenth century.

Many examples of Opus Anglicanum are worked on a ground of linen. When the embroidery completely covers the vestment the linen is double, a fine layer over a coarse one. Some pieces are worked on a twill-woven silk lined with linen, or on velvet mounted on linen which would have been overlaid with fine linen or silk, through which the embroidery would be worked. The excess linen or silk was then cut away.

The coloured silk threads were mainly floss, but some examples, like the Syon cope, also include twisted silks. The metal threads were flattened strips of silver-gilt (gold-plated silver), or silver wound round a core of silk. The art of drawing wire was known in early times and has not changed a great deal. The wire is drawn back and forth through successively smaller holes in a metal plate, gradually becoming finer. The gold, plated onto the silver, would remain uniform throughout the process and this silver-gilt was used to replace gold wire. The wire was flattened before being wound around the core thread.

By the middle of the thirteenth century the styles had changed owing to the Gothic influences of France. Cathedrals were lighter with larger windows and slender columns. Fan-vaulting gave an almost lace-like effect, and a lighter feeling came into the embroidery designs, featuring foliated scrolls and softer figures.

The comparatively large number of references and surviving examples of Opus Anglicanum is an indication of the prestige and output of the English workshops. Originally situated within the religious, royal and noble houses, by the middle of the thirteenth century demand led to centralized workshops, the greatest number of which were centred in and around London.

THE MITRES OF ST THOMAS À BECKET

At the end of the twelfth century, four mitres, representing the Martyrdom of St Thomas à Becket and St Stephen, were sent to Europe, probably as propaganda. One of these mitres (see below), now to be seen in the Bayerisches Nationalmuseum in Munich, is thought to have been given to Kloster Seligenthal by the Duchess Ludmilla (c.1170–1240). It is dated 1180–1210 and shows St Thomas of Canterbury on one side, and St Stephen on the other, with crescents and inscriptions. The lappets are missing.

Figure 14
Mitre of St Thomas à Becket, 1180–1210. Depicts the saint's death, with the Dextra Dei (hand of God) above. Silver-gilt thread in underside couching, with dark silk outlines, on a white silk twill. It measures 23 × 28 cm (9 × 11 in). (Bayerisches Nationalmuseum, Munich)

THE WORCESTER FRAGMENTS

Fragments of vestments were found in a tomb at Worcester Cathedral, thought to be that of William de Blois, Bishop of Worcester (1218–36). The fragments are thought to pre-date the Bishop, being early twelfth century. The stole would originally have shown the twelve apostles, and the maniple four prophets.

Fragments from a pair of buskins are of silver-gilt thread and silk in underside couching and stem stitch, worked on a brown silk. One of the larger fragments, 13.5 × 29.5 cm (5¼ × 11½ in), is in the British Museum (*Figure 15*), and a smaller fragment, 13.5 cm (5¼ in) high, is in the Victoria and Albert Museum. They show kings and saints seated within scrolled foliage.

Some of the fragments bear the inscriptions ADELBUTUS (King Ethelbert), NICO[LA]VS (St Nicholas), and TO (St Thomas of Canterbury?).

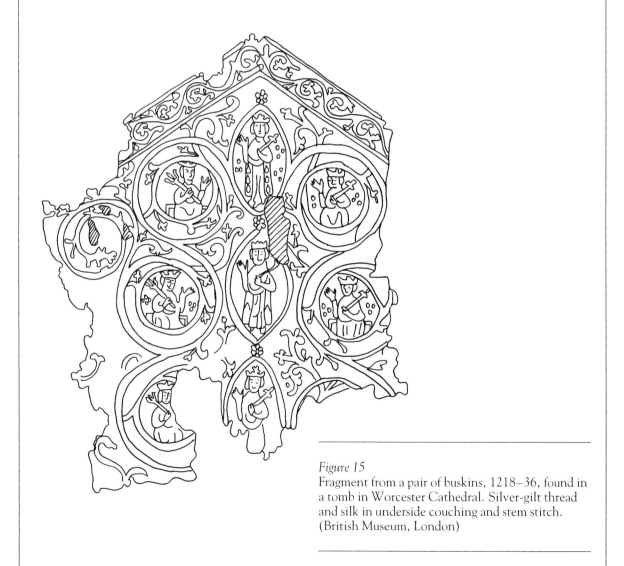

Figure 15
Fragment from a pair of buskins, 1218–36, found in a tomb in Worcester Cathedral. Silver-gilt thread and silk in underside couching and stem stitch. (British Museum, London)

THE CLARE CHASUBLE

The Clare chasuble (1272–94) is one of the earliest surviving examples of Opus Anglicanum to show the use of directional split stitch on the faces. The vestment has been cut down from a larger chasuble. Early chasubles developed from a circular cloak-like garment with a hole in the centre for the head. Gradually the garment became less cumbersome, as the sides were cut away to allow the arms to be raised when elevating the Host (*Figure 16b*). Decoration usually appears on an orphrey, a vertical band on the front and back.

The ground of the Clare chasuble (*Figure 16a*) is of blue silk satin, with embroidered lions and griffins within foliated scrolls. It is worked in silver-gilt, silver thread and coloured silk in underside couching, split stitch and laid and couched work. The back measures 119 × 81.5 cm (3 ft 11 in × 2 ft 8 in), the front 94 × 62.5 cm (3 ft 1 in × 2 ft ¹/₂ in). An orphrey down the back, 36 cm (1 ft 2 in) wide, contains four barbed quatrefoils with scenes of the Crucifixion, the Virgin and Child, St Peter and St Paul, and the Stoning of St Stephen. Records from 1786 show that a stole and maniple were probably made from the pieces that were cut away. Four heraldic shields on these items suggest that Margaret de Clare commissioned the chasuble. She was, from

1272 to 1294, the wife of Edmund Plantaganet, Earl of Cornwall, nephew of Henry III. The four shields bore the arms of Clare, Lacy (for her mother), Cornwall and England.

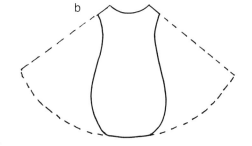

Figure 16
Clare chasuble, 1272–94. Cut down from an earlier shape as shown in *(b)*. Silver-gilt and silver thread and coloured silks in underside couching, split stitch, and laid and couched work on a ground of blue silk twill. The blue and gold lace on the front of the chasuble is sixteenth century. 673–1864. (Victoria and Albert Museum, London)

OPUS ANGLICANUM COPES

There are a number of copes surviving from the great period of Opus Anglicanum. A cope is a large semi-circular vestment with the centre of the straight edge to the back of the neck, which is fastened at the front by a morse, an oblong tab. The orphrey on a cope, if it has one, is laid along the straight edge.

There are three main types of design to be found but, in all styles, the scenes and figures within the various shapes always radiate so that they appear in a vertical position when the cope is worn (*Figure 17a*). The most important scenes appear down the centre back. The three types are as follows:

1   The main area is divided regularly by geometric shapes (*Figure 17*).

2   The design shows the Tree of Jesse with scrolling stems and branches growing from the reclining figure of Jesse (*Figure 18*).
3   This type features architectural, or Gothic, arcading with radiating divisions of architectural canopies (*Figure 19*).

COPES WITH GEOMETRIC DIVISIONS

The copes described on pages 30–34 are all worked in silver-gilt and silver thread and coloured floss silks in underside couching, split stitch and laid and couched work, together with any additional techniques related to individual copes.

THE SYON COPE

The Syon cope (1300–20) is one example of the geometrical division design, and is to be found in the Victoria and Albert Museum (*Figure 17a*). The cope was associated with a monastery at Syon, built and endowed by Henry V for the Bridgetine nuns in 1414–15. The nuns hid the cope at the time of the Dissolution of the Monasteries, taking it to Flanders, France and finally Portugal. They returned to England in 1810, and in 1864 the cope became the property of the Museum.

The body of the cope is divided with interlaced, barbed quatrefoils containing a faded red background within the shapes, and green in the intervening spaces. The entire background is embroidered in silk using underside couching giving a chevron pattern (*Figure 17b*). The scenes are worked in silver-gilt and silver thread and silks in underside couching, split stitch, and laid and couched work on a linen base. It measures 147 × 295 cm (4 ft 10 in × 9 ft 8 in).

The cope has been cut and re-made, and the alterations can clearly be seen around the semi-circular edge. Originally the scenes would have included all twelve apostles but only nine remain intact. The main scenes at the centre-back are the Coronation of the Virgin, the Crucifixion with the Virgin and St John, and the archangel Michael overpowering the dragon. The remaining scenes show Christ appearing to St Mary Magdalene, the Funeral and Assumption of the Virgin, the Death of the Virgin, the Incredulity of St Thomas, and the nine remaining apostles. The compartments between the quatrefoils contain six-winged angels.

The cope, when altered, was given an heraldic orphrey 24.5 cm ($9^3/_4$ in) wide, and an heraldic stole and maniple 8 cm ($3^1/_8$ in) wide was added to the curved edge. The orphrey was made from three apparels, and the morse from three narrow apparels. The orphrey also contains cross and plait stitch.

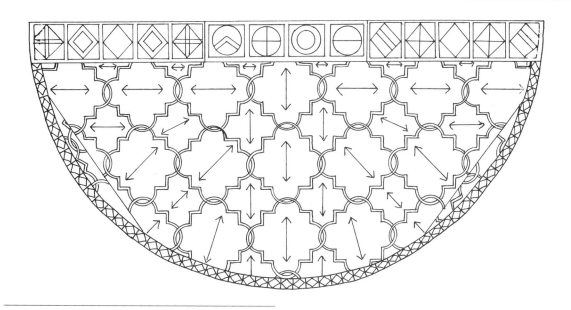

Figure 17a
The Syon cope. Embroidered silk background on a linen ground with interlaced barbed quatrefoils. The arrows indicate how the figures within the scenes radiate. The orphrey and edgings are worked in underside couching, cross and plait stitches. (Victoria and Albert Museum, London)

b

Figure 17b
The Syon cope. Detail of *The Incredulity of St Thomas*. Silver-gilt and silver thread and coloured silks in underside couching, split stitch, and laid and couched work. This figure is very similar to a wall painting in Westminster Abbey, which is dated a little earlier. Note the chevron pattern created by the underside couching on the background, and the striped hair in split stitch. 83–1864. (Victoria and Albert Museum, London)

THE DAROCA COPE

The Daroca cope in the Madrid Museum is thought to be a little later than the Syon cope (c.1300) and has subjects enclosed by barbed quatrefoils, joined by dragons. Scenes include the Crucifixion, the Annunciation, and the story of the Creation, with angels in the intervening spaces. An illustrated manuscript, dated early fourteenth century, in the library of the Earl of Leicester at Holkham Hall in Suffolk has subjects that appear on this cope.

The cope is worked in coloured silks on a patterned ground of gold underside couching. The embroidery is very worn, showing the use of split stitch and laid work, and originally included pearls. The orphrey contains royal personages and saints, under canopies decorated with lions' heads. It measures 297.5 × 141 cm (9 ft 9 in × 4 ft 7½ in).

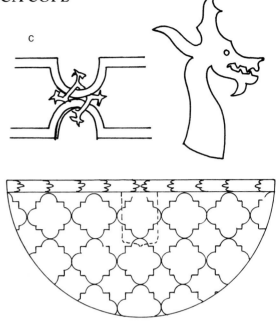

Figure 17c
The Daroca cope, metal thread ground on linen. Quatrefoils linked with dragons' heads. (Madrid Museum)

THE ANAGNI AND THE ASCOLI COPES

The Anagni cope, late thirteenth century, was a gift to Anagni Cathedral by Pope Boniface the VIII (*Figure 17d*). It is divided by circular compartments containing scenes from the history of our Lord and of the Virgin Mary, with angels in the intervening spaces. The orphrey and hood are missing and the cope is badly disfigured as it was cut into many pieces to make two dalmatics. The background is in gold underside couching giving a chevron pattern. The embroidery is in silver-gilt and silver thread and coloured silks. It measures 160.5 × 356 cm (5 ft 3 in × 11 ft 8 in). There is also a chasuble that is very similar.

Another cope (1275–80) at Palazzo Comunale at Ascoli Piceno, also has circular compartments (*Figure 17e*), enclosing the head of our Lord, the Crucifixion, the Virgin and Child, and saints and popes. Within the circles the underside couching goes round and round, following the shape. Normally it would be straight. Knotwork patterns appear between the circles. The embroidery is worked on a linen ground with silver-gilt and silver thread and silks in underside couching, split stitch and laid work. Originally there were pearls which were stripped to pay a war levy in the Napoleonic Wars. It measures 164 × 341 cm (5 ft 4½ in × 11 ft 2 in). The orphrey, 20.5 cm (8 in) wide, is in gold embroidery with interlaced circles and lozenges, and has a small triangular hood.

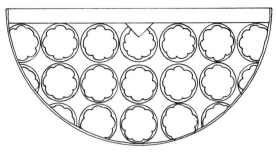

e

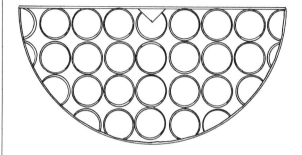

d

Figure 17d
The Anagni cope, metal thread ground on linen,
with circular divisions.
(Anagni Cathedral)

Figure 17e
The Ascoli cope, metal thread ground on linen.
Divisions are circles with an inner shallow octofoil.
The orphrey is decorated with interlaced circles and
diamonds.
(Palazzo Comunale, Ascoli)

THE VATICAN COPE

The Vatican cope (1280–1300) in the museum
and treasury in the Vatican Library in Rome
has compartments in the shape of eight-
pointed stars, reminiscent of mosaics and
tilework. The iconography is related to that on
the Syon cope. The scenes depicted are the
Coronation of the Virgin, the Crucifixion, the
Virgin and Child, and sixteen saints. Six-
winged angels fill the intervening spaces. It is
worked on a ground of red silk twill, in silver-
gilt thread and silks in underside couching,
split stitch, and laid and couched work. It
measures 138.5 × 310 cm (4 ft 6½ in × 10 ft
2 in).

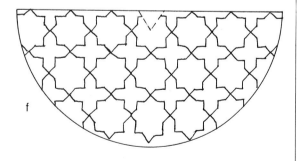

f

Figure 17f
The Vatican cope, with a ground of red silk twill
and divisions of eight-pointed stars.
(Vatican Library Museum, Museo Sacro, Rome)

THE STEEPLE ASTON COPE

This early fourteenth-century cope has been cut and re-made into a frontal and dossal, which are to be found in the Victoria and Albert Museum. The compartments are of barbed quatrefoils heavily foliated with oak and ivy leaves, linked by masks. (*Figure 17g* shows the original form of the cope.) The scenes are of the Passion of Christ and the martyrdom of saints. The original morse has been used at the top centre of the dossal, and is in raised embroidery.

The scenes on the frontal show the martyrdom of various saints. At either end is a piece of the original orphrey, each showing an angel on horseback with a musical instrument. One of the horses is beautifully dappled, interpreted by tiny spirals of split stitch (*Plate 2*). The orphreys also show barbed quatrefoils enclosing animals, birds and fishes (see below). The orphrey, 20 cm (7³/₄ in) wide, and the morse have a gold-embroidered background in underside couching, giving a pattern of diagonal wavy bands, and are on a base of linen. The main cope is worked on a ground of pale fawn twill silk, in silver-gilt thread and silks in underside couching and split stitch, with some raised embroidery. The metal underside couching on the stems of the foliated divisions is directional, as is the working of the dragon with St Margaret. The dossal measures 141 × 157.5 cm (4 ft 7¹/₂ in × 5 ft 2 in), and the frontal 80 × 218.5 cm (2 ft 7¹/₂ in × 7 ft 2 in).

g

Figure 17g
The Steeple Aston cope, with a ground of pale fawn silk twill and foliated barbed quatrefoils. Orphrey and morse, metal ground on linen. Details show the foliated divisions, masks and a barbed quatrefoil from the orphrey containing animals and birds. (Steeple Aston, Oxfordshire, displayed in the Victoria and Albert Museum)

THE TREE OF JESSE

The traditional Tree of Jesse design shows the tree with scrolling stems and branches growing from the figure of Jesse. Good examples are shown below and overleaf.

THE JESSE COPE

The Jesse cope (1295–1315) in the Victoria and Albert Museum is typical of the Tree of Jesse design, a vine springing from the body of Jesse. The vine shelters prophets and the ancestors of Christ within its branches. This cope has been cut and re-used at some time, but the remaining pieces have been remounted in their original positions. Some figures are missing, together with the orphrey and hood. Jesse lies at the bottom centre-back of the cope with the branches forming circular compartments, worked on a ground of rose-coloured silk twill (*Figure 18b*). The cope is embroidered in silver-gilt and silver thread and coloured silks in underside couching and split stitch, with laid work. The remaining re-assembled fragments measure 135 × 183 cm (4 ft 5 in × 6 ft).

Copes of red samite with the Tree of Jesse design are frequently mentioned in documents from the reigns of Henry III and Edward I.

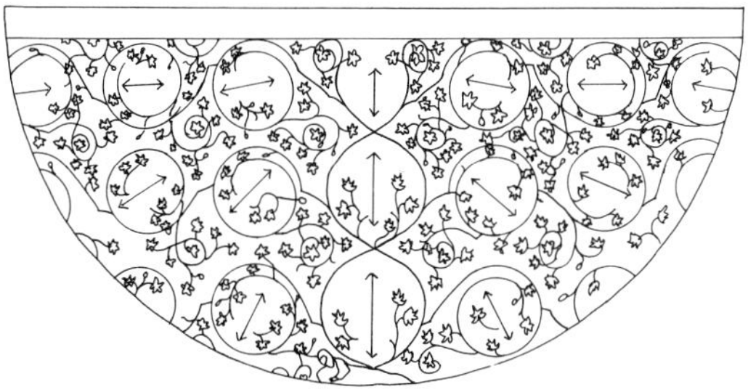

b

a

Figure 18a
The Jesse cope, silver-gilt and silver thread and coloured silks in underside couching and split stitch, with laid and couched work, on a ground of rose-coloured silk twill.
(Victoria and Albert Museum, London)

Figure 18b
Detail of the Jesse cope, showing Abia (ABIAS REX). Note the missing areas where the cope was cut. 175–1889.
(Victoria and Albert Museum, London)

THE SALZBURG COPE

Another Tree of Jesse cope is to be found at the Abegg-Stiftung, Bern, Thun, and is known as the Salzburg cope (1290–1310). This cope is said to have been presented by Emperor Charles IV (1316–78) to a shrine on the road from Salzburg to Rome near Maria Pfarr, Lungan, Austria.

The cope has been cut but shows a vine with the ancestors of Christ. The whole of the centre panel is missing. The background is worked in underside couching in silver-gilt thread, and the figures and details are in coloured silks in split stitch, laid and couched work on linen. It measures 117 × 269 cm (3 ft 10 in × 8 ft 10 in).

COPES WITH ARCHITECTURAL ARCADING

The third type of cope design features Gothic or architectural arcading forming decorated compartments which radiate within the semi-circle of the cope. This design closely reflects the decoration to be found in the illuminated manuscripts of the time. All the designs are worked in silver-gilt and silver thread and coloured silks in underside couching, split stitch and laid and couched work, together with additional techniques relevant to individual copes mentioned on the following pages.

THE COPE OF THE VIRGIN

The earliest existing example of this type of design is the Cope of the Virgin (1300–20) which is associated with the Cathedral de St Bertrand de Comminges, Haute Garrone, Southern France. The scenes and figures show Christ, the Virgin and Child, and the twelve apostles, within arches that are decorated with lion and leaf masks entwined in sprays of ivy, oak and vine. The original hood and orphrey are missing and the cope has been cut away

Figure 19a
Cope of the Virgin. Right: detail of the arcading with foliated masks.
(Cathédrale de St Bertrand de Comminges)

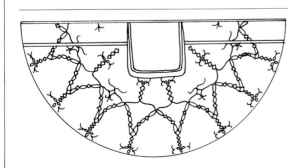

around the lower edge. The embroidery is worked on a ground of rose-coloured silk twill, in underside couching, split stitch, and laid and couched work using silver-gilt and silver thread and coloured silks. The cope measures 142 × 295 cm (4 ft 8 in × 9 ft 8 in).

A second vestment associated with the same cathedral is the Cope of the Passion, *c.* 1300. This cope has a gold-embroidered background, the patterns of which resemble those on the Coronation chair in Westminster Abbey, the work of Master Walter of Durham.

THE BOLOGNA COPE

Two splendid examples of Opus Anglicanum are the Bologna and the Pienza copes, both dated 1315–35. The Bologna cope is in the Museo Civico Medievale, Bologna. It has two main rows of arcading divided by narrow bands; the hood and orphrey are missing.

The scenes in the outermost band are the Annunciation, the Visitation, the Nativity, the Annunciation to the Shepherds, the Flight into Egypt, the Massacre of the Innocents, the Presentation at the Temple, the Three Kings consulting Herod, the Journey of the Kings, the Adoration of the Kings, the Dream of the Kings, and the Martyrdom of St Thomas of Canterbury. The spandrels are occupied by angels playing musical instruments. The narrow band above contains twenty-three heads of saints within eight-pointed stars.

The second arcaded row shows the Entry into Jerusalem, the Betrayal, the Flagellation, the Crucifixion, the Resurrection, the Harrowing of Hell (depicted with a splendid monster) and Christ appearing to St Mary Magdalene. The next narrow band contains

the heads of Christ and eight saints. The uppermost area contains two censing angels on either side of the missing hood. The two wider bands are 51 cm (20 in) high, and the narrow bands are 14 cm (5½ in) high.

The background is in silver-gilt thread in underside couching, and the scenes also use silver thread and silks in split stitch and laid work. The cope measures 322.5 × 147 cm (10 ft 7 in × 4 ft 10 in).

Where the embroidery has worn away, it is possible to see a design drawn underneath the background area, which the embroiderers have not followed, working a simple plain background instead.

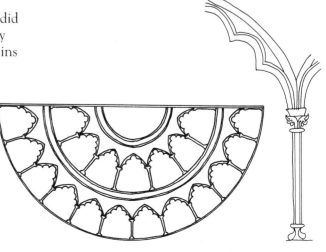

Figure 19b
The Bologna cope, background of metal thread on linen. Right: detail of the simple arcading.
(Museo Civico Medievale, Bologna)

THE PIENZA COPE

This cope, in the Capitolo della Cattedrale di Pienza, is very well preserved, and dates from the second quarter of the fourteenth century. It has three rows of arches decorated with foliage and animal and human heads, with the apostles, the ancestors of Christ, and angels and birds in the spandrels. Within the arches are scenes from the lives of the Virgin, St Margaret and St Catherine.

The gold background is worked with foliated scrolls, fleurs-de-lys, heraldic beasts, squares, quatrefoils, lozenges, etc. The embroidery is worked in silver-gilt and silver thread and silks in underside and surface couching, split, tent, satin and overcast stitches on a linen ground. The cope measures 162.5×850.5 cm (5 ft $4^{1}/_{2}$ in $\times$ 11 ft 6 in).

The hood shows two six-winged seraphs. The orphrey, 18 cm (7 in) wide, has interlaced quatrefoils with birds, beasts and plants. The cope originally had a large number of pearls which are now missing.

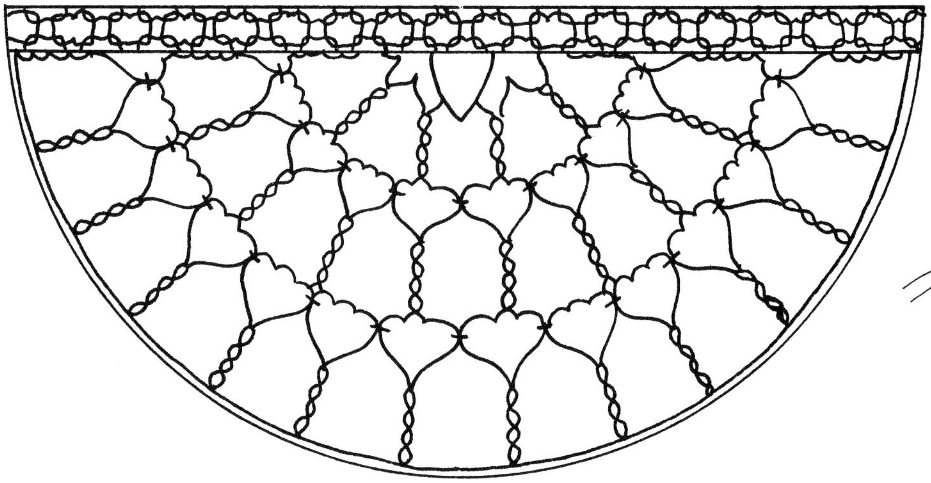

Figure 19c
Pienza cope. Background of metal thread on linen. Also surface couching, tent and satin stitches.
Right: detail of the arcading.
(Capitolo della Cattedrale di Pienza)

THE BUTLER-BOWDEN COPE

The Butler-Bowden cope (1330–50) in the Victoria and Albert Museum has three rows of arcading containing sacred scenes, apostles and saints (*Figure 19e*). The arcading is decorated with oak sprigs, lions and lion masks, and in the spandrels are seated angels. The orphrey, which is incomplete, shows kings and bishops and archbishops with heraldic lions and griffins. The main scenes are the Coronation of the Virgin, the Adoration of the Kings (see below) and the Annunciation.

The cope was severely cut to make another garment but has been re-assembled for display. The design and technique resemble the Chichester-Constable chasuble (see page 42), so closely that they may have been part of the same set of vestments. The embroidery is worked on a ground of red velvet, in silver-gilt and silver thread with coloured silks in underside and surface couching, split stitch,

Figure 19d
The Butler-Bowden cope. Detail of *The Adoration of the Kings*. T36–1955.
(Victoria and Albert Museum, London)

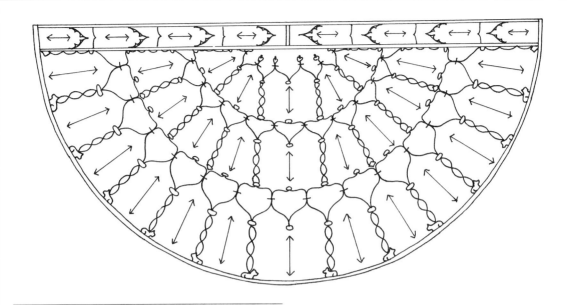

Figure 19e
Butler-Bowden cope. Arrows show how the figures within the divisions radiate.
(Victoria and Albert Museum, London)

laid and couched work, raised work, knots and satin stitch, with pearls and green beads and small gold rings. It measures 168×345.5 cm (5 ft 6 in $\times$ 11 ft 4 in).

THE VICH COPE

Figure 19f (see opposite)
Vich cope. Raised work. Right: detail of the arcading.
(Museo Episcopal de Vich, Spain)

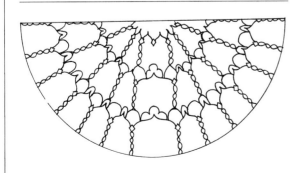

The Vich cope (1340–70) is in the Museo Episcopal de Vich, Spain. Three rows of arcades show sacred scenes, the apostles and saints, and are adorned with leaves and leaf masks, and angels playing musical instruments within the spandrels. The hood and orphrey are missing. The main subjects are the Coronation of the Virgin, the Nativity, and the Adoration of the Kings.

The cope is embroidered in silver-gilt and silver thread and silks in underside and surface couching, split stitch, laid and couched work, and raised work. The underside couching on the drapery is accentuated by a thread underlay which raises the embroidery. It measures 320 × 132 cm (10 ft 6 in × 4 ft 4 in); it has been cut into pieces at some time, and has been re-assembled.

THE ST JOHN LATERAN COPE

This cope is to be found in the Pinacoteca Vaticana in Rome, and is dated 1340–60. It displays scenes of the Passion of Christ, the Life of the Virgin, and the martyrdom of various saints within three rows of ogee arches decorated with stars and birds. Within the spandrels are seated angels playing musical instruments. A pair of rampant griffins are shown within the area of the hood.

The orphrey, 24 cm (9½ in) wide, has alternate ogee arches and barbed quatrefoils, with bishops, archbishops and kings in the arches. The quatrefoils contain Christ in Judgement, and seated angels with the symbols of the four evangelists.

The gold background is worked with small lattice patterns. Silver and silver-gilt threads are used together with coloured silks in underside couching, split stitch and tent stitch, and raised work on linen. A few pearls remain. It measures 159 × 336.5 cm (5 ft 2½ in × 11 ft ½ in).

Figure 19g
St John Lateran cope. Metal thread background on linen, also tent stitch and raised work. Right: detail of the arcading.
(Pinacoteca Vaticana, Rome)

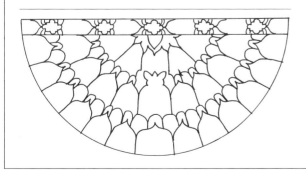

THE TOLEDO COPE

Dating from the beginning of the fourteenth century, this cope can be found in the Treasury of the Cathedral in Toledo. The main scenes show the Annunciation, the Nativity and the Coronation of the Virgin, together with a number of saints.

Silver-gilt and silver thread and coloured silks in underside couching and split stitch are used, and the background is of patterned gilt thread depicting foliage, fleurs-de-lys, lions, etc. It measures 168 × 328 cm (5 ft 6 in × 10 ft 9 in).

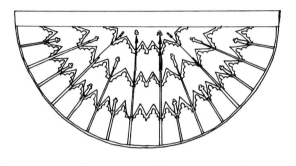

Figure 19h
Toledo cope. Background of metal thread on linen. (Cathedral Treasury, Toledo)

OTHER EXAMPLES OF OPUS ANGLICANUM

Arcading features on many other surviving examples of Opus Anglicanum.

THE CHICHESTER-CONSTABLE CHASUBLE

Dated 1330–50, this can be found in the Metropolitan Museum of Art, New York, and relates closely to the Butler-Bowden cope in the Victoria and Albert Museum, London (see page 39). Sacred scenes, apostles and saints are depicted within ogee arches decorated with oak sprigs and lion masks, with seated angels holding stars in the spandrels. The scenes on the back are the Annunciation, the Adoration of the Kings, and the Coronation of the

Virgin. On the front are four saints. The chasuble has been severely cut down and parts used for a stole and maniple.

The embroidery is worked on a ground of red velvet, using silver and silver-gilt thread and coloured silks in underside couching, split stitch, laid and couched work, and some raised work. A few pearls remain. The front measures 99 cm (3 ft 3 in) high × 74 cm (2 ft 5 in) wide, and the back 118 cm (3 ft 10½ in) high.

Two surviving examples of Opus Anglicanum are unusual, with figures much larger than those normally found.

THE JOHN OF THANET PANEL

The first example is a panel (1300–20) in the Victoria and Albert Museum. It is thought to be part of a cope because of the triangular shape at the top where a hood may have been. It shows Christ enthroned beneath an arch, on a dark blue ground which is powdered with rampant lions, with his hand on an orb inscribed EVROPA, AFFICA, ASIA. The sun and moon are shown in the spandrels with lions and wyverns. The inscription IOHANNIS DE THANETO appears above the arch, and beneath a scene of the Annunciation (*Figure 20a*). John of Thanet was a monk at Canterbury, skilled in mathematics and music, who died in 1330 aged ninety-two years.

The panel is worked in silver-gilt and silver thread, coloured silks and pearls in underside couching and split stitch on a dark blue silk twill ground. The panel measures 100.5 × 42 cm (3 ft 3½ in × 1 ft 4½ in). The seated figure is 68.5 cm (2 ft 3 in) high, and is the largest Opus Anglicanum figure to be found in Britain.

Figure 20a
The John of Thanet panel.
(Victoria and Albert Museum, London)

THE MELK CHASUBLE

The second example is the Melk chasuble (1300–20) from a Benedictine monastery at Melk in Austria, now in the Museum für Angewandte Kunst in Vienna. The bell-shaped chasuble shows Christ crucified, with the Virgin and St John, and the sun and moon above. The figure of Christ closely resembles a mural depicting the Crucifixion in St Faith's Chapel in Westminster Abbey. The figure of the Virgin is similar to a stained-glass window originally in the cathedral in Vienna Neustadt, but now in the Nuremburg Museum. The background, within the area of the figures, is powdered with fleurs-de-lys, and the rest of the vestment has a lattice of barbed quatrefoils and cruciform compartments, with roses and vine leaves. Roundels containing the symbols of the four evangelists are placed at the four ends of the cross. The underside couching on the bird forms a pattern of scallops. Tablet-woven braids with geometric patterns were used at the neck. The slits for the arms were cut at a later date.

The vestment is of lilac silk twill, which has deteriorated badly, and is embroidered in silver-gilt and silver thread, on a silk core, and coloured silks in underside couching, split stitch and laid and couched work. The underside couching in metal thread is very close bricking and looks rather like the Chinese style of satin stitch. The folds in the garments are well defined with sharp lines where the underside couching stitches have been repeated closely. The green shades of silk are still a very good colour and they appear on the garments, the cross and the crown of thorns. The areas of cream silk are very badly worn.

The standing figures on the back of the chasuble are 68.5–76 cm (2 ft 3 in–2 ft 6 in) high, with an almost identical scene on the front, but smaller. The front of the chasuble measures 117 cm (3 ft 10½ in) high, and the back 141 cm (4 ft 7½ in) high.

Figure 20b
The Melk chasuble. Note the openings for the arms cut into the chasuble.
(Museum für Angewandte Kunst, Vienna)

PART OF AN ALTAR FRONTAL

A fragment in the British Museum dated 1315–35 shows scenes from the Passion of Christ within ogee arches, with half-length seriphs in the spandrels. One of the foliate capitals shows the inscription MCCCXC ROMA. The drapery on the figures shows an incredibly fine use of split stitch in Opus Anglicanum.

The gold background is worked in a pattern of quatrefoils and foliate crosses, with eagles and wyverns. The whole is embroidered with silver-gilt thread and silks in underside couching, split stitch, and laid and couched work on linen. It measures 51 × 60 cm (1 ft 8 in × 1 ft 11¾ in).

APPARELS FROM AN ALB

Figure 21 (see overleaf)
Detail of apparel from an alb, depicting *The Annunciation to the Shepherds* and *The Journey of the* *Kings*. The dappled horses are worked with tiny spirals of split stitch.
(Victoria and Albert Museum, London)

Smaller items of Opus Anglicanum include apparels from albs. An alb is the white linen garment worn under the vestments. Where the alb showed beneath the vestments, apparels were applied. These were small panels of embroidery to match the vestments, and could be removed when the linen was washed. The remains of one such set are to be found in the Victoria and Albert Museum. Dated 1320–40, they show scenes from the Life of the Virgin and her parents, delightfully depicted beneath ogee arches, with heraldic shields in the spandrels. Each apparel should have five scenes, but two of the three apparels are incomplete. The Annunciation to the Shepherds is particularly charming, and the Journey of the Kings shows dappled horses (*Figure 21*) as on the Steeple Aston cope (see page 34).

The embroidery is worked on red velvet in silver and silver-gilt thread and silks in underside couching, split stitch, and laid and couched work, with some small details in raised work. The size of the one complete apparel is 84 × 26.5 cm (2 ft 9 in × 10$^{1}/_{2}$ in).

FRONTLET FOR AN ALTAR

A piece in the Victoria and Albert Museum dating from the late thirteenth to early fourteenth centuries has two main claims to fame: it is the only signed piece of English embroidery from the medieval period, and it is the work of an amateur. It has three shields, at either end the arms of Vescy and, in the centre, the arms of Henry de Lacy (d.1311). An inscription appears on the front, each letter set within a frame: IN HORA MORTIS SVCCVRRE NOBIS DOMINE (*see below*). On the reverse it is signed in a form of running stitch: IOHANNA BEVERLAI MONACA ME FECIT ('made by Johanna Beverlai, a nun'). The piece is basically counted thread work (*Figure 22b*), with some couching. It is worked in silver-gilt thread and coloured silks in tent, satin, and long and short stitches, on linen. It is 9 cm (3$^{1}/_{2}$ in) wide × 264 cm (104 in) long.

Figure 22a
Detail, frontlet for an altar.
(Victoria and Albert Museum, London)

Figure 22b
Counted thread work patterns. Couching in silver-gilt thread and coloured silks on a linen ground, in tent and satin stitches and long and short stitch.
Signed by Johanna Beverlai.
(Victoria and Albert Museum, London)

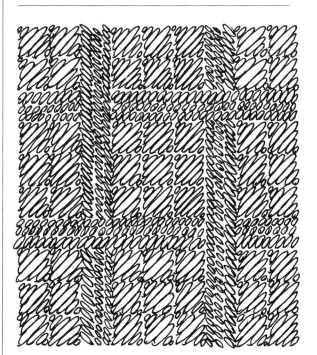

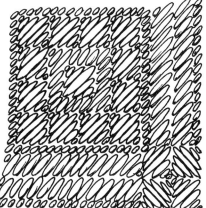

Many vestments were re-used for smaller items.

THE CATWORTH CUSHIONS

A cope orphrey (1329–54) was cut up, probably during the seventeenth century, to make a set of kneeling cushions. Now in the Victoria and Albert Museum, they were originally in St Leonards Church, Catworth, Huntingdonshire. The cushions depict saints beneath arches, with the heraldic arms of the Clinton and Leybourne families, which were united by marriage in 1329. They are worked on buff silk twill damask using silver-gilt and silver thread and silks in underside couching, split stitch, and laid and couched work. They measure between 35.5–41 cm (14–16 in) high × 16 cm (6¼ in) wide.

THE FELBRIGGE PSALTER

A fragment has been made into a book-cover for a thirteenth-century psalter known to have belonged to Anne Felbrigge, a nun in the late fourteenth century. It is from the Sloane Collection (MS2400) in the British Museum.

The embroidery is badly damaged and shows the Annunciation on the front, and Christ crucified on the back. It is worked in silver-gilt thread and coloured silks in surface couching and split stitch on linen. It is unusual to find only surface couching in English embroidery of the fourteenth century, and this may indicate that this piece was actually made for a book-cover to avoid bulk on the back. The panels are 21 × 14.5 cm and 21.5 × 15 cm ($8^1/_4$ × $5^3/_4$ in and $8^1/_2$ × $5^7/_8$ in).

THE CLUNY CHASUBLE

Two pieces from a larger collection of fragments (1330–40) showing surface couching, have been used to make a chasuble from what was originally probably a horse trapper (*Figure 23a*). The heraldic embroidery shows the leopards of England amid foliated stems, with small figures of men and women, similar to those found in the Luttrell Psalter (*Figure 23b*). It is thought that the original trapper was taken to Coblenz in 1338 by Edward III, when visiting his brother-in-law the Emperor Ludwig. The chasuble is now in the Musée National des Thermes et de l'Hotel de Cluny in Paris.

The embroidery is in silver and silver-gilt thread and coloured silks in split, stem, running and satin stitches, with couching. The surface couching on the leopards is very lively, depicting the waves of the mane. Features like the eyes, ears and mouth are emphasized with a heavier twisted metal thread, and the eyes are covered with cabochon crystals (*Figure 23c*). It is worked on red velvet in two pieces, each 59.5 × 130 cm ($23^1/_2$ × $51^1/_8$ in).

Figure 23a
Cluny fragments made into a chasuble. Leopards of England amid foliated stems with figures. (Musée National des Thermes et de l'Hotel de Cluny, Paris)

a

Figure 23b
Detail of a figure.
(Musée National des Thermes et de l'Hotel de Cluny, Paris)

Figure 23c
Detail of a leopard's head.
(Musée National des Thermes et de l'Hotel de Cluny, Paris)

THE STONEYHURST FRAGMENT

This small fragment (1320–40) consists of a knight on his charger with heraldic trappings, showing the Cross of St George. The horse is dappled with spirals of split stitch. The embroidery is in silver and silver-gilt thread and silks in underside couching and split stitch, applied to a ground of green velvet. The fragment, approximately 21.5 cm (8$^{1}/_{2}$ in) high, is in Stoneyhurst College, Whalley, in Lancashire.

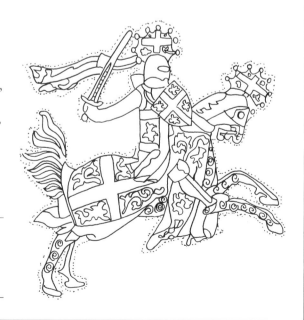

Figure 24
Stoneyhurst Fragment.
(Stoneyhurst College, Whalley, Lancashire)

FUNERAL PALLS

Used to cover the coffin at a funeral or laying in state, these are important items of late Opus Anglicanum. Most of the guilds or fraternities had a funeral pall. The Fayrey Pall (1490–1538) in the Victoria and Albert Museum has a central panel of Italian cloth of gold, woven in a pattern of flowers and leaves, in red velvet pile of two heights with gold loops. This would have been a prestigious fabric. The four side panels are deep violet velvet, each showing St John the Baptist preaching. Two of the sides depict John and Mary Fayrey. The two long sides have groups of standing figures. Four heraldic shields show the arms of the Merchants of Staple, Fayrey, the Mercers' Company and Butler. The embroidery is in silver-gilt and silver thread and silks in split stitch and couched work on linen, applied to velvet. It measures 264 × 142 cm (8 ft 8 in × 4 ft 8 in).

Other similar palls to survive are the First (1490–1512) and Second (1512–38) Palls of the Merchant Taylors, the Brewers' Pall (1490–1538), the Saddlers' Pall (1490–1538), and the Fishmongers' Pall (1512–38). All are held by the appropriate Worshipful Company.

The Decline of Opus Anglicanum

The great era of Opus Anglicanum came to an end; workmanship declined as a result of a series of events and changes. Probably the most dramatic influence was the devastation of the Black Death in 1348, when one-third of the population died. Many embroiderers and craftsmen were lost, and the guilds were weakened.

The outbreak of wars in Europe affected the demand for vestments as money had to be spent on men and weapons. There was also an increase in the manufacture and availability of rich fabrics such as damasks and brocades, which became very popular and were highly valued. Vestments did not then require the same quantity of embroidery, which was often restricted to the orphrey.

The signs of decline came with a loss of fineness and precision in both the drawing and the technique. Although faces continued to be worked in split stitch, it was no longer directional, but simply straight up and down with the features added afterwards. Figures were badly drawn, and the emblems of the saints were omitted. The foliated canopies became clumsy and degenerate, often obscuring the spandrels which previously contained angels, etc.

With the decline of English work there was an increase of skills in Europe. Or nué was developed in the Low Countries, and some English workers went to learn the technique, but the industry in England had lost its prestige.

THE ERPINGHAM CHASUBLE

An example of late Opus Anglicanum is the Erpingham chasuble (1400–30) now in the Victoria and Albert Museum. The ground fabric is quite magnificent, a red brocade from northern Italy; the silver-gilt thread that was used would have been very costly. The exotic design is of camels laden with flower baskets.

The orphreys are English needlework depicting the Crucifixion. There are two embroidered heraldic shields showing the arms of Sir Thomas Erpingham and an eagle, his adopted device. The drawing of the figures is inferior to the earlier work; the faces are not executed with the same skill or care. The orphreys have a ground of silver-gilt thread in underside couching, and coloured silks in split stitch.

THE STONEYHURST COPE AND CHASUBLE

Two later, but unusual, vestments of cloth of gold are preserved at Stoneyhurst College, Whalley, in Lancashire, and are dated 1485–1509. The cope is of cloth of gold in a red velvet pile with gold loops, and the design has been woven to the shape of the cope. The chasuble has been made from pieces of the same fabric. The cope design is two rose trees with three crowned portcullises, the badge of the Tudors. The embroidered hood and orphrey were probably not originally part of the vestment and were heavily restored in the nineteenth century. The orphrey shows saints beneath canopies, and the Annunciation appears on the hood. The embroidery on the chasuble dates from the sixteenth to seventeenth centuries.

These vestments appear to be among those bequeathed to Westminster Abbey by Henry VII (d.1509), whose will says they were 'bought and provided at Florence in Italy'. The cope measures $152.5 \times 366\,cm$ ($5 \times 12\,ft$), and the chasuble $114.5 \times 68.5\,cm$ ($3\,ft\ 9\,in \times 2\,ft\ 3\,in$). There is also a challis veil.

THE NEVILLE FRONTAL

A mid-sixteenth century frontal in the Victoria and Albert Museum has embroidery applied to red stamped velvet. A central scene shows the Crucifixion. On the left is the kneeling figure of Ralph Neville with his seven sons behind him, and on the right his wife, Lady Caroline Stafford, with their thirteen daughters. Beside her is a swan, the Stafford badge. The heraldic shields are thought to be later in date. The embroidery is in silver-gilt and silver thread and silks in couching and split stitch. There are marks on the velvet indicating that the embroidery has been re-positioned at some time.

European Examples of the Period

Although English work dominated throughout the period there were, of course, examples made in Europe that have survived.

THE IMPERIAL MANTLE OF HENRY II

An early example is the Imperial Mantle of the Emperor Henry II, to be found in the Diocesan Museum, Bamburg, Germany. It has a ground of blue silk and is embroidered in gold. The whole cope is powdered with motifs of various sizes, mostly circular, or figures and symbols within eight-pointed stars. There is also one square motif in the upper centre and some isolated figures. In the intervening spaces between the motifs are inscriptions, a feature very common in German work. The embroidery is Ottonian, and dated *c.* 1000, but the motifs appear to have been re-mounted at a later date.

THE CORONATION MANTLE OF ST STEPHEN

A second example is the Coronation Mantle of Stephen, now to be found in the Hungarian National Museum in Budapest.

A later wall painting of the coronation scene, showing the mantle in use, can be seen in St Matthias Church, Budapest. Originally a chasuble, the mantle bears an embroidered inscription in Latin, 'this chasuble was ordered to be made and given to the Church of St Mary situated in the city of Alba by King Stephen and Queen Gisela in the 1031st year of Christ's incarnation, in the 14th indiction'.

The ground fabric is silk, now faded, in a pattern of green and purple rosettes. Most of the embroidery is in gold thread, laid in solid areas, couched with red thread, with small areas of vivid indigo blue silk and green, which has sadly faded. The mantle is divided into three main areas of figures with an additional inverted triangular shape (*Figure 25a*). A victorious Christ is shown above a seated Christ, both within ovals, at the centre-back. Angels appear either side of Christ inside the triangular area, with evangelists, carrying towels, in the uppermost semi-circular area, beneath which appears the inscription. Saints are shown within shapes formed by simplified buildings in the next area, with small figures believed to be pilgrims. Kings in circles divided by pairs of bird-like creatures and scrolling stems appear around the outer edge. There is a collar and morse which is decorated with pearls.

The embroidery is thought to be by German workers who migrated to Hungary, and is dated by the inscription to 1031. The mantle shows many signs of repair, it being the custom for the future queen and her female relations to repair the mantle before a forthcoming coronation. The mantle measures 284×136 cm (111×53 in), the collar 65×20 cm ($25^{1}/_{2} \times 8$ in).

Figure 25a
Coronation Mantle of St Stephen, Hungarian, by
German workers. Couched metal threads and
stitchery in coloured silks. Pearls on the collar.
(Hungarian National Museum, Budapest)

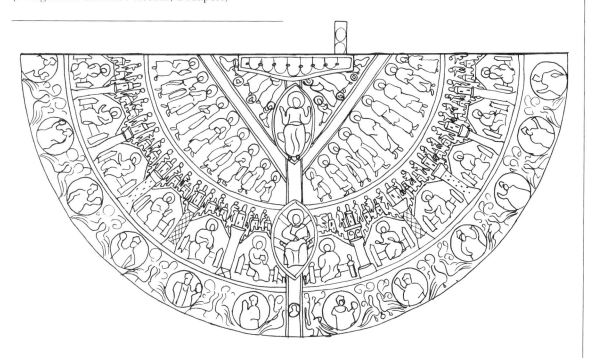

Figure 25a
Coronation Mantle of St Stephen, Hungarian, by
German workers. Couched metal threads and
stitchery in coloured silks. Pearls on the collar.
(Hungarian National Museum, Budapest)

THE CORONATION MANTLE OF KING ROGER II

Another example was made in the Royal
Workshops in Palermo, Sicily, by Arabic
workers (see overleaf). It is dated, by an
inscription around the hem, to 1112–33. The
Coronation Mantle of King Roger II was
worked on a beautiful red silk satin ground,
embroidered in couched gold and coloured
silks. The large design of a lion triumphantly
felling a camel is repeated symmetrically in
each half. The design fits the shape of the
vestment. There is a single stylized palm tree
with fruit hanging from it in the centre. The
animals are decorated with a scrolling stem
design and a linear pattern, which is
emphasized throughout with a double row of

pearls. Parts of the body, such as the lion's
mane, face and tail end, have a well-defined
double outline. The lion is decorated with
eight petalled rosettes in red, blue, yellow and
green silk in split stitch at the knee, brow and
bridge of the nose. The camel has little circular
flower-like motifs at the leg joints.

Most of the couched gold is laid to a close
bricking pattern giving a very smooth effect,
but on the head of each camel there is a
definite zig-zag pattern. There is an
embroidered border about 8 cm (3$\frac{1}{8}$ in) wide
along the straight edge and around the semi-
circular hem, with a generous use of pearls and
beautiful little enamelled plaques. Pearls,

Figure 25b
Coronation Mantle of King Roger II, Sicilian. Couched metal thread with stitchery in silks, enamel plaques and pearls. (Schatzkammer within the Hofburg, Vienna)

rubies, sapphires, garnets and semi-precious stones have also been used. The mantle measures 345 cm (11 ft 4 in) wide × 146 cm (4 ft 9½ in) high, and is in the Schatzkammer, within the Hofburg, in Vienna.

THE TRISTRAM QUILT

Another Sicilian example, *c.* 1400, is an early example of quilting. It is made of wool between two layers of linen, with scenes from the legend of Tristram depicted within square divisions, with a commentary in lettering. It is in two pieces; one is in the Victoria and Albert Museum, the other in the Palazzo Davanzati, Florence.

THE JACOPO DI CAMBI FRONTAL

An Italian altar frontal that relates much more closely to Opus Anglicanum is in the Museo degli Argenti, in Florence. Made in Florence in 1336 and signed by Jacopo di Cambi, it makes extensive use of gold-thread patterning and split stitch in silk on the drapery on the figures. A central scene shows the Coronation of the Virgin, with seven saints on either side, all beneath Gothic arcading. The spandrels are formed by the upper half and the wings of angels. The superfrontal also has arcaded divisions with alternating scenes and saints.

THE HINDERSHEIM COPE

A quite gruesome example of German embroidery is to be found in the Victoria and Albert Museum. The Hindersheim cope is divided by overlapping circles containing scenes of punishment and torture, designed to have a very sobering effect on the congregation!

The work has a simple cartoon-like quality as the figures are depicted with flat areas of diaper pattern in brick stitch, with some laid silver-gilt thread. Dating from the late thirteenth to early fourteenth centuries, it is a complete contrast to Opus Anglicanum.

Figure 26
The Hindersheim cope. Compare the flat treatment of the figures to those in Opus Anglicanum examples.
(Victoria and Albert Museum, London)

Opus teutonicum, German and Swiss professional whitework, was widely used, mostly for altar linen. Many different surface stitches were used including interlacing, brick stitch and satin stitch used in blocks.

During the fourteenth century the workshops of Paris specialized in small purses, worked in laid gold thread and silk in split stitch. These were small square or triangular purses associated with the East, hence the name 'Saracen' purses. They usually depict figures in scenes of romance or chivalry.

EMBROIDERY AND TAPESTRIES OF THE FIFTEENTH CENTURY

Or Nué

As Opus Anglicanum declined in England, the ecclesiastical embroidery of Europe reached new heights. The development of or nué allowed the embroiderers to interpret the

Figure 27
Or nué, surface-couched metal threads with coloured stitches placed at varying distances to give a tonal quality. Creates a three-dimensional effect on a completely flat surface.

designs of the artists very closely. Painters had discovered how true perspective worked and their paintings were more realistic than ever before. The technique was developed in the Low Countries (now Belgium and the Netherlands) and, by the late fifteeth century, was in use throughout Europe until the eighteenth century. The technique was possibly known in France by the mid-fourteenth century, as a reference is made in an inventory of 1352 to King John of France having a hat band of pictorial embroidery 'true to life' (Camille Enlart, *Manuel d'Archéologie Française*, Vol III, *Le Costume*, p. 167).

Or nué is a metal thread technique that completely covers the background fabric, often used with split stitch depicting the faces, hands and flesh areas and, sometimes, with decorative surface couching and raised work. The metal thread is laid, usually two strands at a time, horizontally from the bottom of the panel. The detailed drawing on the background fabric is followed closely, the image created by couching the gold thread with coloured silks. The closer the stitches are to one another, the denser the colour, and by grading the distance between stitches a complete tonal range can be achieved (*Figure 27*). Each row is completed before going on to the next, and the worker has a needle for each colour required throughout the row. It is essential to use a fine needle to allow the metal thread to lay closely.

VESTMENTS FOR THE ORDER OF THE GOLDEN FLEECE

Probably the finest set of surviving examples of or nué is the Vestments for the Order of the Golden Fleece (1425–75) comprising three copes, a dalmatic and tunicle, a chasuble, an altar frontal and a dossal. The frontal and the dossal are, however, both the same size and could both be frontals.

The Order of the Golden Fleece was founded by Philip the Good in 1429–30 and the embroideries are listed in the earliest inventory of the Order dated 1477. They were probably commissioned by the Dukes of Burgundy for use in their own chapel, but no reference to them is to be found in their accounts and inventories.

Seed pearls and gemstones were used and a great number still remain. Large areas are worked in or nué and decorative surface couching in metal threads, with the areas of flesh beautifully rendered in fine split stitch (*Figure 28*). The embroidery is worked on a ground of strong linen. The quality of the drawing and workmanship on these items are of the highest order. They are full of amazing and unexpected details.

One cope, the Mantle of the Virgin, depicts the figure of the Virgin on the hood, and apostles and prophets in arcaded divisions on the orphrey. Within three rows of radiating elongated hexagons appear the archangel Gabriel, holy women and women saints. The details on the figures are beautifully worked, each one placed on a tiled floor. One of the women saints has a child sitting at her feet and, on closer inspection, another child can be seen sheltering under each arm beneath the cloak. The Virgin appears on the hood, enthroned beneath a canopy. The pillars supporting the canopy are swathed with draped curtains edged with pearls, as is the Virgin's mantle. The cope measures 330 cm (10 ft 10 in) wide × 164 cm (5 ft 4½ in) high.

Figure 28
Detail, female saint from the cope of Mary, the Vestments for the Order of the Golden Fleece, second quarter of the fifteenth century. Or nué and decorative couching in metal thread and silks, with extensive use of pearls. The three-dimensional look of the drapery on the gown is due entirely to the closeness of the coloured stitches. Elongated hexagons in couched and laidwork as described in the text.
(With the kind permission of the Kunsthistorisches Museum, Vienna, displayed in the Schatzkammer)

Figure 29
Vestments for the Order of the Golden Fleece, second quarter of the fifteenth century, Low Countries.
(a) Diagram of a cope, showing the elongated hexagons, the orphrey and the pictorial hood.
(b) A detail of the laid and couched techniques used for the divisions.
Or nué and surface couching in silver-gilt thread with coloured silks in split stitch, stem stitch and decorative laid and couched work, with pearls. (Schatzkammer within the Hofburg, Vienna)

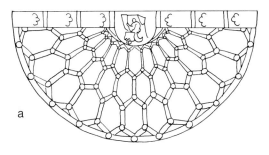

a

b

The copes are all of similar design (*Figure 29a*), the main difference being the scenes featured on the hoods, from which they take their names. The elongated hexagons containing the figures are formed with laid gold silk, overlaid with a trellis of metal thread. On either side is a band of red laid silk with a scalloped line of metal thread in chain stitch between two rows of straight chain stitch. This central band is enclosed on either side with bands of metal thread in brick stitch. At the junctions are circles outlined in pearls (*Figure 29b*). Within this is a six-petalled flower outlined in metal thread in chain stitch and filled with pearls. A scalloped line of chain stitch in metal thread lies between the central motif and the circle, on a ground of dark blue laid stitches. A great number of pearls are used on the orphreys of all three copes.

A second cope features St John the Baptist on the hood, with apostles and prophets on the orphrey. Within the body of the cope the archangel Raffael, patriarchs, prophets, monks and hermits appear in three rows of elongated hexagons. St John the Baptist is enthroned beneath a canopy, seated on a grass-topped cliff. The area of grass is scattered with plants, much in the manner of the tapestries of the time. On either side of St John is a tree, one of which supports a draped curtain from the canopy. The curtains and St John's mantle are

outlined in pearls. This cope measures 330 cm (10 ft 10 in) × 164 cm (5 ft 4¹/₂ in).

The third cope features God the Father enthroned on the hood. The figure is seated beneath a canopy with draped curtains lavishly edged with pearls. The orphrey contains prophets and apostles. The archangel Michael, cherubim, martyrs, bishops and clergy are shown in three rows of elongated hexagons on the body of the cope. The angels within the upper row are highly decorative with their six wings beautifully arranged, the lower two encompassing the legs. The angel to one end of the row has its back to the viewer and, as one looks along the row, the angels gradually turn until the centre one is facing outwards. Then they gradually turn again until the last one is

just peeping over its shoulder. The cope measures 330 cm (10 ft 10 in) × 164 cm (5 ft 4½ in).

The chasuble depicts the Baptism of Christ on the front, with angels in two rows of elongated hexagons. The Transfiguration of Christ is shown on the back with three rows of angels. There is an orphrey down the centre of the back and front of the chasuble. Some of the larger figures are applied and overlap the orphreys. It measures 149.5 cm (4 ft 11 in) long × 135.5 cm (4 ft 5½ in) wide.

The dalmatic depicts angels and holy men in three rows of elongated hexagons. There are two very narrow bands forming an outline to the central orphreys on the back and front. These bands obviously cover joins in the garment, as the rows of figures do not line up accurately. It is 128 cm (4 ft 2½ in) long × 161.5 cm (5 ft 4 in) wide, including sleeves. The tunicle is very similar except that it shows holy women. It is 125.5 cm (4 ft 1½ in) long × 160 cm (5 ft 3 in) wide, including the sleeves.

The altar frontal and dossal are thought to be the earliest of the set, dating from the second quarter of the fifteenth century, and are in the style of the workshops in Bruges, Ghent and Tournai. The frontal has a central panel depicting the Virgin and Child with St Catherine and St John the Baptist, with six smaller panels in two rows on each side showing prophets and apostles. On the crown of the Virgin there are gemstones and there is extensive use of pearls throughout the panel. The main three figures were worked separately as one piece and applied. The Virgin and St Catherine each have two little cords with tassels on, decorating the bodice of their gowns. St John the Baptist has a fleece emerging from his cloak, covering his arm. This is worked in shaded trailing over a twisted silk thread, worked in circles. All the figures in the smaller panels were also applied. The names of the prophets and apostles are worked into the framework above or below each figure. It measures 330 cm (10 ft 10 in) wide × 119 cm (3 ft 11 in) high.

The dossal has a main panel showing the Mercy Seat; God the Father holds the dead Christ with the Dove above His left shoulder, representing the Trinity. This also has six smaller panels either side, with prophets and apostles. Once again, the figures have been worked separately and applied, and there is extensive use of pearls. It measures 330 cm (10 ft 10 in) wide × 119 cm (3 ft 11 in) high.

The vestments can be found in the Schatzkammer, within the Hofburg in Vienna, together with the ceremonial robes of the Order and many heraldic tabards.

ANTONIO DEL POLLAIUOLO

Another set of nué panels, originally used on vestments, can be seen in the Museo di St Maria del Fiore in Florence. The twenty-seven panels, worked in Italy and designed by Antonio del Pollaiuolo, show scenes from the life of John the Baptist and are dated 1466–79.

They were removed from the vestments in 1730. Some of the finer detail is achieved by working over a single row of gold.

Unfortunately the panels are not in such good condition as the Golden Fleece examples.

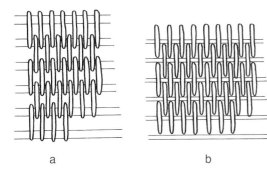

a   b

Figure 30
Burden stitch.
(*a*) Fine silk stitches spanning two laid threads,
       which can be metal thread or heavier silk. Used
       on a very fine scale for faces and flesh areas,
       particularly in Italian or Spanish work.
(*b*) Silk stitches over one laid thread, but
       extending to the edges of the two laid threads to
       either side. Often used to depict water or a
       background area.

Burden Stitch

A technique used with or nué, often to depict
water or the background of a panel, is burden
stitch. Two forms of this stitch were used. The
first consists of a gold thread or wire laid at
intervals with stitches in coloured silks
spanning from the edge of one gold thread,
over one, and to the edge of the next (*Figures
30b* and *31*). The second method was used in
early examples for flesh areas and worked in
two weights of silk. This time a silk thread is
laid and a finer matching silk thread is taken
over two laid threads (*Figure 30a*). This
method is worked on a finer scale than the first.
However, Edmund Harrison combined both
versions and or nué on his panels in the
seventeenth century (see chapter 6).

Figure 31
Spanish altar frontal, *c.*1530, detail of a roundel
showing a female saint within a landscape worked in
burden stitch. In addition, coloured silks in split
stitch and couched metal threads are used on a
ground of velvet.
(Victoria and Albert Museum, London)

Figure 32
Sixteenth-century applied motifs.
(a) Cope, early sixteenth century, Spanish. Applied rose motifs from the body of a cope, in silver-gilt, silver threads and silks in satin stitch and couching, on a ground of dark blue velvet. (Victoria and Albert Museum, London)

(b) Chasuble, early sixteenth century, English. Applied angels in metal thread and coloured silks. Originally a dalmatic, the ground fabric is black velvet with a deep red velvet orphrey. Probably used at Requiem Mass. (Victoria and Albert Museum, London)

a

b

Many painters like Pollaiuolo and Botticelli would have made designs for embroidery. By the fifteenth century the embroidery workshops were dominated by men, who were paid more than the women embroiderers, and only male signatures appear on pieces.

Extreme raised and padded work was added to the or nué in examples from Spain, southeast Germany, Austria, Hungary and Poland, the gold being mounted over wooden moulds or layers of cord.

Much of the rest of the ecclesiastical embroidery of the time and of the following centuries consisted of embroidered motifs applied to velvet or silk grounds, lacking the good drawing and design of earlier work (*Figure 32*).

During the fifteenth century there was a great increase in trading, both domestic and international, resulting in the creation of a new middle class. The tapestries give an insight into the lives of the people of the time.

Tapestry Weaving

Tapestry weaving differs from basic weaving in that the weft is beaten down to completely cover the warp threads. The weft was usually wool or wool and silk, on a strong linen warp. The tapestries were woven sideways on; the warp runs horizontally on the completed work. On some modern pieces where the warp is vertical, the heavy wool gradually slips down the warp, leaving gaps. A high warp means that the weaver has a tall loom and works with a vertical warp, and a low warp refers to a loom where the warp is horizontal to the weaver.

The weaver followed a cartoon, usually hung behind the loom, and worked from the reverse side of the tapestry so that the design was in reverse. Sometimes many tapestries would be woven from one set of cartoons, but the very wealthy could pay to have the cartoon destroyed so that their set would be unique.

THE DEVONSHIRE HUNTING TAPESTRIES

One set of tapestries that shows the activities and fashions of the times is the Devonshire Hunting Tapestries once hung at Hardwick Hall, home of Bess, the Countess of Shrewsbury, and the estate of the Dukes of Devonshire. The original owner is not known.

There are four tapestries, now restored and on display in the Victoria and Albert Museum. The costume, which is very accurately portrayed, has been used to date the tapestries; the *Boar and Bear Hunt* shows the current fashions for the 1430s; the *Falconry* and the *Otter and Swan* tapestries are a little later; and the *Deer Hunt* is from the 1440s.

The detail on the costume shows the beautiful woven silks of the time, decorated collars, jewellery, methods of fastening, fur linings, and an incredible array of headdresses. One can see the dress not only of the upper class, but also of the servants and workers.

When not at war, hunting was the main occupation of the nobility, and the tapestries show all its aspects in gruesome detail. The horses and their trappings are delightfully depicted, and we see the dogs and their handlers. Little intimate scenes are grouped to give an overall effect; conversations between ladies or ladies and gentlemen, the wooing of a lady complete with a very bored chaperone, and the seduction of a maid. We see the miller's daughter with a drop spindle, and the arrival of an Eastern gentleman and his servant. The houses that appear in each successive tapestry are also correct for the time.

The figures and animals almost cover the tapestries, but in the intervening spaces there are trees and flowers. In the later tapestries of the late sixteenth and seventeenth centuries we see more 'background' filled with multitudes of little flowers – the millefleur tapestries.

The Boar and Bear Hunt: 409 cm (13 ft 3½ in) high × 10.3 m (33 ft 6 in) wide.
The Falconry: 446 cm (14 ft 6 in) high × 10.86 m (35 ft 3½ in) wide.
The Otter and Swan: 428 cm (13 ft 11 in) high × 11.22 m (36 ft 5½ in) wide.
The Deer Hunt: 411 cm (13 ft 4½ in) high × 876 cm (28 ft 5½ in) wide.

The tapestries were woven either at Arras or at Tournai, when these two centres were supplying the Courts of France and Burgundy.

THE UNICORN TAPESTRIES

A slightly later set of seven tapestries (c. 1500) is housed in The Cloisters, New York. The central theme is the hunting of the unicorn, which was believed at the time to exist, and was first written about in 400 BC. The whole set shows 100 species of trees, flowers and shrubs, of which eighty-five have been identified. They are, however, portrayed without regard for the seasons. Two of the tapestries have millefleur backgrounds.

The first in the series, *The Start of the Hunt*, shows the hunters setting off. In the second we see *The Unicorn at the Fountain*, based on the belief that the unicorn had the magical power to remove the venom of serpents from the water, thus making it safe. *The Unicorn Leaps the Stream* is the third in the set, with the fourth showing *The Unicorn Defending Himself*. Only two fragments remain of the fifth tapestry, *The Unicorn is Captured by the Maiden*. *The Unicorn is Killed and Brought to the Castle* comes next in the set; the dead unicorn is shown with a wreath around his neck, symbolizing the crucified Christ. This is followed by *The Unicorn in Captivity*, representing the risen Christ.

The tapestries are thought to have been woven near Brussels, showing a French influence, and are probably the work of more than one designer. Unlike the Devonshire Hunting Tapestries, this set depicts symbolic images. Insignia and monograms on the tapestries associate them with Anne of Brittany, wife of Louis XII, and with the La Rochefouchauld family. An inventory of François VI de la Rochefouchauld of 1680 includes 'tapestries representing a hunt of the unicorn in seven pieces', used in his Paris house. The tapestries hung at Verteuil until the French Revolution, and later are known to have been used by the village peasants to protect their potatoes from frost! They were found in the 1850s and returned to Verteuil.

In 1922 the six large tapestries were exhibited in New York, and were purchased by John D. Rockefeller, who presented them in 1935 to The Cloisters, which opened in 1938. A year later the fragments of the fifth tapestry were found.

THE LADY WITH THE UNICORN

Another famous set of unicorn tapestries can be found in the Musée de Cluny in Paris, dating from the end of the fifteenth century. Each tapestry represents one of the senses depicted in a central scene with a red millefleur background, including many small animals. *Sight* shows the unicorn looking into a mirror held by the lady. *Hearing* is depicted by the lady playing a small organ, and in *Taste* the lady is offered fruit. To show *Smell* the lady weaves a garland of flowers and in *Touch* the lady gently touches the unicorn's horn. The meaning of the sixth tapestry is less clear, with the lady selecting a trinket from her jewellery case. The origin of the tapestries is not known.

During later centuries the style of tapestries changed, with the scenes appearing within ornate cartouches of flowers or scrolling 'sculpture'. Tapestries have always been a sign of wealth.

THE EMBROIDERY OF THE TUDOR ERA

The Tudor era brought forth the second great period of English embroidery, together with a blossoming of all the arts. There was a long period of peace and prosperity, with a rise in living standards. Those in the middle and upper classes had great wealth. The English Court set the pace for Europe during the reigns of Henry VIII and Elizabeth I.

Artists had begun to use oil paints, and the first School of Painting was set up by the Dutch. It was the time of Holbein, Hilliard and Isaac Oliver, whose portraits give us invaluable information about the costume of the time, and the great European artists Leonardo da Vinci, Michelangelo and Raphael. The language changed from medieval to modern; the world of literature was enhanced by Shakespeare, Bacon and Spenser. The arts were influenced by the Renaissance which began in Italy in the fourteenth century, and spread throughout Europe, finally blossoming in England in the sixteenth century. Musicians experimented with polyphony; it was the time of madrigals, and of Thomas Tallis and William Byrd. As at all times of wealth and abundance, there was time, money and inclination for much pageantry, masques, plays and firework displays.

There was a change too in the way in which people lived. Many of the great houses were built during this time. Dwellings used to be defensive, being built around a courtyard with windows on the inside. With the new style, many windows faced outwards and the great hall gradually became much smaller, as many more small separate rooms were used on several floors. This was also facilitated by the use of inside staircases and the fact that the builders were able to make the chimneys fireproof, allowing each room to be individually heated. No longer was there a single fire in the middle of the room. The walls were covered with panelling and often hung with tapestries. At all levels of society glazed windows added to the general comfort of the home.

Elizabeth I expected her ladies at court to have skills in Latin, Greek and modern languages, and to be able to spin, embroider, sing and play music.

The exploration and discovery of new countries brought new plants, vegetables and animals, creating a great interest in gardens and gardening. For the first time flower gardens were fashionable. The great houses had beautiful gardens, and everyone had to have the very latest plants. Artists recorded the new plants, and their illustrations were used by embroiderers for their designs.

The lady of a great house was responsible for overseeing the running of a considerable community, which needed to be virtually self-sufficient. She was responsible for feeding, baking, brewing, doctoring and directing a vast amount of needlework. Most large houses had a

resident seamstress and there were also journeymen embroiderers, professional draughtsmen, and dressmakers. All the ladies in the house were expected to be occupied with some form of needlework.

The major change that the sixteenth century brought was the almost total swing away from ecclesiastical embroidery to secular and domestic work. As we have already seen, embroidery for the Church was in decline in England, and the Reformation brought about its end. Embroidery was now predominantly on costume and on domestic items in the home.

The splendour of the reign of Elizabeth I brought a great variety of embroidery techniques, with many surface and knotted stitches. Braid and plaited braid stitches were common, as were Ceylon stitch and many forms of surface buttonhole stitch. Many composite stitches were used, often combining different types of thread. Much silk was used at this time, often together with metal threads (*Figure 51*). Inventories refer to metal threads called Venysse (Venice), or Damask (Damascus), named after the towns from which they were bought, not where they were made. Purls are also mentioned, together with spangles or 'O's (sequins).

Blackwork was a popular feature of the sixteenth century and was used in great quantities. Many examples have survived, but black silk is vulnerable, as the iron mordant used has an adverse effect on the thread over a period of time. There were three main ways in which blackwork was used:

1 Double running or Holbein stitch was used on cuffs, neck edges and anywhere that a reversible stitch was required because both sides showed (*Figure 48*).

2 Speckling, or seeding, stitches were used to indicate tonal shading (*Figures 49b* and *49c*), imitating the woodcut illustrations that were probably the most popular source of design. Sometimes these were worked just in black silk, as on the Shepherd Buss

(*Figure 43*), but elsewhere the black silk is twisted together with white and used as one. Blackwork was also worked in other colours – blue, red and green.

3 The third type was the use of counted diaper patterns to fill the spaces of the design, as in the Falkland Pillows (*Figure 44a*). Blackwork was also used together with metal thread work (*Figures 49a, 49b* and *50b*).

Needles were either made of drawn wire, or of steel. Originally these were imported from Germany, but by the end of Elizabeth's reign they were being manufactured in England.

A dominant design form was the scrolling stem, which developed from the early arabesques, and is reminiscent of the Tree of Jesse form found on the Opus Anglicanum copes. In the Elizabethan version the scrolling stem forms small compartments, which are filled with a multitude of flowers and embellished with insects, butterflies and tiny animals (*Figures 33, 49, 50* and *Plate 4*).

Gradually, as the century progressed, the work became more raised and, towards the end of the sixteenth century and into the early seventeenth century, the flower motifs were repeated instead of all being different. This scrolling stem design went on, as we shall see, to develop into the large crewelwork designs of the seventeenth century.

In addition to professional embroidery, many items were made by amateurs in their homes, often assisted by professionals with the drawing and preparation. Many ladies would also have help from their companions to 'fill in the background'.

Books were the source of many of the designs and were widely available. Artists and draughtsmen would prepare the work, either copying directly, or adapting, according to the wishes of the lady concerned. Sometimes the ladies actually pricked holes in the pages of the books to transfer their designs! Herbals, flower paintings, books on natural history, and wood

Figure 33
Detail from a large cover, late sixteenth century. A typical example of the scrolling stem design, worked in silk and metal thread on linen. Long and short stitch and plaited braid stitch, with spangles and metal purl. T222–1927.
(Victoria and Albert Museum, London)

engravings were used and also the decorative margins of deeds and charters. Pattern books especially for embroidery were published from the beginning of the sixteenth century. Some of the most widely used are the following:

1516 *Grete Herbal*, the first English printed herbal. Herbals were also essential for medical treatment within the household.
1525 *Bankes Herbal.*
1530 Lacis patterns from Germany, re-printed in England.
1542 Conrad Gesner, *Catalogue Plantarium.*
1557 Paradin, *Devises Heroiques.*
1560 Gesner, *Icones Animalium.*
1586 Jacques Le Moyne, *La Clef de Champs.*
1586 Witneys, *Choice of Emblems.*
1587 Vinciolo, *Les Singuliers et Nouveaux Pourtraicts, Renaissance Patterns for Lace, Embroidery and Needlepoint* (reprinted by Dover Publications, 1971).
1597 *Gerrards Herbal*, reprinted in 1633 and 1636.

Flowers and plants were treated naturalistically, the invention of the magnifying glass and microscope in the sixteenth century aiding the study of detail.

Vineyards were common, and the vine features in many designs. Knot gardens were also great favourites.

The love of emblems and allegory was strong in the sixteenth century and can be found not only in embroidery but in portraits and paintings, and in the hidden meanings in madrigals and plays.

It was common for princes to adopt a personal emblem, called an 'impresa', for example the portcullis of Henry VIII.

Elizabeth I granted the First Charter to the Broderers' Company in 1561, although there are fifteenth-century references in the City of London. The Charter granted rights to control the members of its trade, and the duty to look after their welfare. The Company controlled the quality of work sold, and burned any found to be substandard. Their records were lost in the Great Fire of London in 1666. (See also Edmund Harrison, chapter 6.)

THE FETTERNEAR BANNER

One important piece of ecclesiastical embroidery that has survived from the first quarter of the sixteenth century is the Fetternear Banner, now in the National Museum of Antiquities in Edinburgh. It is unfinished and only embroidered in silk, without any precious metal threads, and therefore escaped being destroyed.

It belonged to the Confraternity of the Holy Blood of St Giles Collegiate Kirk, Edinburgh, and was worked in Scotland about 1520. In floss silks on linen, the main stitches are satin stitch and double running stitch, both reversible. The design is of Christ depicted as the Man of Sorrows, his body covered with wounds, together with the symbols of the Passion. The heraldic arms of Gavin Douglas, Bishop of Dunkeld and Provost of St Giles (1501–21), and those of the Graham family appear on the banner. The banner was kept at the Scots Catholic College, Valladolid, Spain, and then from the early nineteenth century at the House of Fetternear in Aberdeenshire.

Figure 34
The Fetternear Banner, Scottish. Coloured silks on linen in reversible double darning and double running stitch.
(National Museums of Scotland, Edinburgh)

Vestments were used secretly in Catholic houses, at great risk to the family. There is a set of vestments in white quilting at Traquair House, Innerleithen, Peeblesshire in Scotland. They were folded and kept in the linen cupboard to avoid detection. However, Articles drawn up in 1571 permitted the use of chalice veils.

Domestic Embroidery

Embroidery was very important in wealthy households, whilst the poorer houses would at most use the galloon, or braid, 'laid about' a curtain or cover. All affluent young girls were educated in the use of the needle.

BED FURNISHINGS

Until the beginning of the eighteenth century the most important item of furnishing was the bed and its hangings. The actual bed would have been a simple wooden structure, but the hangings were very expensive items and reflected the wealth of their owners. Important people received their guests in the bedroom, and there would have been a set of matching chairs and stools. The tester, or roof, and head piece of the four-poster bed was often embroidered, together with the valances and curtains. The valances were the main field for pictorial work and many have survived in good condition, as they were not handled in the same way as the curtains and lower valances. Quite often they were in canvaswork, mostly tent stitch (known as 'petit point' in France), and they depicted hunting scenes, fables, Bible stories and mythology.

Many of these valances showed the French influence, and no matter which story is illustrated, the figures are dressed in the costume of the French Court (see below). They are a reliable source of research for students of costume. Some English examples also show pastoral scenes. Valances can also have applied slips or panels on a ground of velvet or silk, or be tapestry-woven.

Figure 35
Valance, detail, late sixteenth century, English. The story of Jephthah. Tent stitch on linen canvas in wools and coloured silks. Note how well the costume is depicted, contemporary with the valance, not with the story. T141–1969. (Victoria and Albert Museum, London)

Bed hangings continued to be focal points for embroidery throughout the seventeenth century, mainly in crewelwork. Many of those imported from India were specially made for the European market. In addition to the bed hangings, there were 'pillow-beeres' or embroidered pillow covers. For daytime use these were often rich with silk and metal thread, nearly always on a linen ground which distinguishes them from cushion covers. Whitework covers were used at night.

In the Victoria and Albert Museum there is a large late sixteenth century cover which is typical of the techniques used. Worked on linen with coloured silks and silver-gilt and silver thread, it shows the scrolling stem design enclosing flower heads. The stitches used include couching, chain, square, double chain, stem, and buttonhole. There are also areas of detached chain. This combination of stitches appears on many examples.

The dressing-table would have a coverlet of linen, often cutwork with needlepoint fillings and edges of needlemade lace. (For details of this work, see chapter 7.) The bedroom walls would have been hung with tapestries, or embroidered hangings like the Oxburgh Hangings (see page 81). Small window carpets were hung at the bottom of the windows to keep out draughts.

TABLE CARPETS

Carpets were another symbol of extreme wealth. They were not used for the floor, except on a dais under a throne. When we see a portrait from this time of someone other than royalty standing on a carpet, this is a form of compliment by the artist. Velvet carpets can be seen in paintings, edged with richly embroidered and fringed borders. These borders also appear on bed hangings, curtains and heraldic trappings, but very little of this work has survived.

The importing of woven and tufted carpets began during the reign of Henry VIII and only the most wealthy owned them. The design and layout of these carpets influenced the designers of embroidered table carpets, and the large size of these items would suggest professional work. The carpets used on cupboards were narrower.

The following three table carpets, all in the Victoria and Albert Museum, are typical of the three main types of design.

THE GIFFORD TABLE CARPET

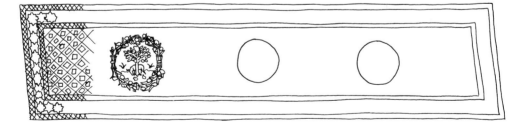

Figure 36a
Gifford table carpet. Tent stitch in wool on linen. Border composed of small bands of pattern, closely resembling the tufted carpets, with a central area of geometric diaper pattern. Three roundels of flowers and acorns surmounted by Tudor roses. This style of carpet sometimes has a centre of geometric shapes, or heraldry on a foliate background. T151–1930. (Victoria and Albert Museum, London)

A good example of a carpet that closely follows the design of a woven or tufted one is the Gifford table carpet. Dated *c.* 1550, it is the earliest surviving example. It measures 554 × 142 cm (18 ft × 4 ft 8 in), and is in tent stitch, 400 stitches to 1 sq in (2.5 cm). It has a border made up from several geometric borders, with a centre of intricate geometric patterns. There are three roundels, each within a garland of flowers; the central roundel shows the Gifford arms and the outer two show a stag, the Gifford badge, lying under a tree.

Figure 36b
Detail of the Gifford table carpet showing border.

THE BRADFORD TABLE CARPET

Figure 37a
Bradford table carpet. Tent stitch in wool and silk on linen. The centre shows a vine trellis with a pictorial border (see page 72).
Above: detail from the border. T134–1928.
(Victoria and Albert Museum, London)

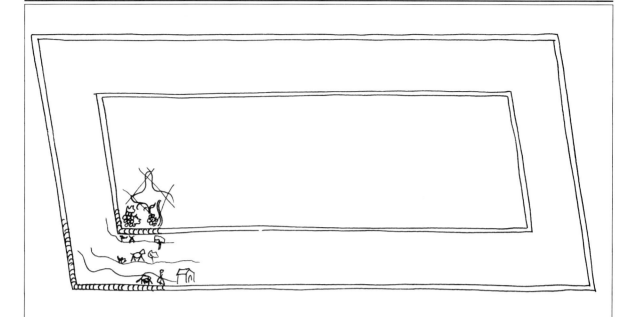

Figure 37b
Outline sketch of design layout of the Bradford table carpet. Motifs from woodcut illustrations. Sixteenth century. T134–1928.
(Victoria and Albert Museum, London)

Figure 38b (below)
'Lucretia's Banquet' table carpet. Coloured wools and silks in tent stitch on linen. Figures from an engraving by Philip Galle. T125–1913.
(Victoria and Albert Museum, London)

THE BRADFORD TABLE CARPET

This late sixteenth-century table carpet has a central area with a trellis and vine, and a border of pictorial scenes of the period (*Figure 37a*). The whole table carpet is misshapen (*Figure 37b*), which could suggest that the border was worked by the amateur ladies of the house; there are also changes in the colours used on opposite edges. It is probable that the centre was worked professionally. The scenes in the borders are typical of woodcut illustration in books and there is a total disregard for the size and scale of related motifs. You can imagine the ladies excitedly choosing the content for the professional draughtsman to make some sense of. This carpet also has 400 tent stitches to 1 sq in (2.5 cm) and measures 396×175 cm (13 ft $\times$ 5 ft 9 in).

THE 'LUCRETIA'S BANQUET' TABLE CARPET

This late sixteenth century carpet appears to have been made to be hung on the wall, as the design is basically a large central picture of the banquet. The costume and style show French influence. However, it is thought that there were workshops in Scotland producing this kind of work, the French influence having been imported by Mary Queen of Scots. It has a decorative strapwork border containing fruits and trees (*Figure 38*). The carpet is worked in tent stitch and has four heads, one at each corner, each embellished with surface stitchery to depict their elaborate lace ruffs, and jewels in their hair. These heads would appear upside down if the carpet were used on a table.

CUSHION COVERS

Chairs were rare. Generally stools and benches were used; these would have sets of cushions for added comfort, ranging in shape from square to a long and narrow rectangle. Small square cushions were used to support precious books, and small square and rectangular cushions, possibly to pin jewellery to, were often richly worked in raised embroidery. Pincushions, also small and rectangular, were essential items of everyday living, as all costume was either pinned together or laced.

Cushions survive in a great number of shapes and sizes, often embroidered, on a ground of velvet, silk or canvaswork. Many cushions are 51–56 cm (20–22 in) wide, the normal loom width of handwoven fabrics.

Various techniques were used for the cushions. Many were of canvaswork combining wool, silk and metal threads (*Figure 39*). Some used canvaswork slips, floral or botanical sprays, taken from books and herbals (*Figures 40 and 41*). (The word 'slip' is an early gardening term for a cutting.) Drawings for the slips would have been made on linen canvas by the draughtsman, who sometimes also outlined them in black silk tent stitch. Then the needlewoman would fill them in with tent stitch in coloured silks, and cut them out and apply them to satin or velvet, often with a couched outline of metal thread. They give the impression of being raised because of the contrast of the canvaswork and the flat surface to which they are applied, but some do actually have areas that are padded. Slips were a convenient method of working on a small frame, making it a favourite method for amateur embroiderers. Several examples of various-sized unused slips in their original colours can be seen at Traquair House, Innerleithen, Peeblesshire.

Figure 39
Cushion covers, sixteenth century.
(a) Cover of red velvet with applied silver cloth,
    worked in silver thread. The initials E and S are
    for Elizabeth Shrewsbury, Bess of Hardwick.
(Hardwick Hall, Derbyshire)
(b) Applied canvaswork slips in coloured silks and
    metal thread in two sizes of tent stitch, on a
    ground of cream silk satin, *c.* 1600. Motifs from
    herbals and woodcut illustrations.
(Victoria and Albert Museum, London)
(c) Metal thread embroidery on a red silk satin
    ground, late sixteenth century. Scrolling stems
    form heart-shaped divisions. T21–1923.
(Victoria and Albert Museum, London)

Figure 40
An unused slip, late sixteenth or early seventeenth century. Cross stitch on linen in coloured silks. The design shows both the fruit and the flower.
658–1927.
(Victoria and Albert Museum, London)

There are two excellent examples of this type of long cushion with slips in the Victoria and Albert Museum in London. One is on a ground of black velvet, with slips on linen, worked in silks and silver-gilt and silver thread in tent, cross, long-armed cross and stem stitches, and laid work. The second, on a ground of cream satin, shows three fruit trees, plants, animals and two figures on horseback (*Figure 39b*).

Some cushions are in silk or metal thread on satin (*Figure 39c*), and some use very raised embroidery.

Figure 41
Slips, late sixteenth to early seventeenth century. Typical designs from woodcuts, which were usually worked in coloured silks in tent stitch on linen canvas.
(Museum of Fine Arts, Boston. 49. 1898/7/9. Reproduced from *Historic and Floral Motifs for Embroiderers and Craftsmen*, Dover Pictorial Archive Series)

MARY QUEEN OF SCOTS CUSHIONS

A pair of square canvaswork cushions at Hardwick Hall bear the cypher of Mary Queen of Scots and are known to have been worked by her. The design is of interlocking compartments containing the lily of France, the thistle of Scotland, and the rose of England. There is a roundel in the centre of each cushion with emblems from Gabriel's *Faerno Fables* (1563) and Mary's cypher. The ground is in yellow cross stitch with gold thread running through, and the designs are in tent stitch with braid stitch for the stems.

Figure 42
One of the pair of cushions worked by Mary Queen of Scots.
(Hardwick Hall, Derbyshire)

A long canvaswork cushion bearing the arms of John Warneford of Wiltshire, and his wife Susanna Yates, is to be seen in the Victoria and Albert Museum. Worked on linen, it is embroidered in silks in tent stitch.

A later example dating from the early seventeenth century shows the work of an amateur needlewoman. There is a very large signature, MARY HVLTON. The cushion shows the arms of James I and the initials IR. It is worked on linen canvas and embroidered in silks and wools and silver-gilt thread using tent, plaited and long-armed cross stitches.

COVERS AND COVERLETS

Covers for small tables and chests were made of linen and silk and were richly embroidered. 'Coverlet' is also a name given to a counterpane.

THE SHEPHERD BUSS

Figure 43 (see overleaf)
The Shepherd Buss, English. Worked in black silk on linen, to imitate a woodcut illustration. Seeding, stem, back and satin stitches and couching. The piece contains allegory and emblems, and has a rebus. The oval bears the inscription: 'Di di in di vo cangiando il pelo e il mio miserabile viso.' T219–1953.
(Victoria and Albert Museum, London)

A late sixteenth century linen cover in the Victoria and Albert Museum illustrates several aspects of Elizabethan embroidery and design. It bears an inscription THE SHEPHERD BUSS, and is worked in black silk using speckling – seeding stitches to imitate the characteristics of a woodcut (*Figure 43*). Within a central oval there is a picture of a young man in the typical pose of the melancholy lover, a fashionable state much enjoyed at the time. It is very similar to the miniature by Nicholas Hilliard, 'Unknown Youth', thought to represent the Earl of Essex. The tree, in this example a vine, symbolizes constancy, and the eglantine was the Queen's flower. There are four popular emblems in the corners outside the oval:

A snake in a strawberry plant: 'the adder lurketh privily in the grass', which also appears on the Oxburgh Hangings.
The marigold and the sun, 'not having followed lower things', adopted by Mary Queen of Scots as one of her emblems.
A dog jumping from a sinking ship, 'a defence against dangerous waters'.

Finally, a fan made of peacocks' feathers with flies and bees, held by a hand, to 'take away the pricks of pleasure'.

All of these were capable of allegorical interpretation by the Elizabethans.

A border around the edge of the cover contains a message in the form of a *rebus*, a code of words and pictures. The capital letters represent the pictures:

False CUPID with misfortunes WHEEL hath wounded HAND and HEART,
Who SIREN like did LURE me withe LUTE and charmide HARP
The CUP of care and sorowes CROSS do (e)clips(e) mi STAR and SUN
Mi ROSE is blasted a(n)d mi BONES lo DEATH inters in URN.

Some of the emblems are from Paradin's *Devises Heroiques* (1557). The initials KB also appear. The cover is 117 × 102 cm (46 × 40 in), and is dated to the late sixteenth century.

THE FALKLAND COVER AND PILLOWS

Figure 44a
Details from the Falkland pillow cover. T81–1924. (Victoria and Albert Museum, London)

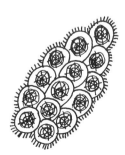

This is a set of two pillow covers and a long cover in blackwork using decorative all-over diaper patterns. The design is of a vine and is embroidered on linen in black silk in back, chain, cord, braid and buttonhole stitches.

Figure 44b
Falkland pillow cover, second half of the sixteenth century, English. T81–1924.
(Victoria and Albert Museum, London)

Embroidered Bookbindings

Books were treasured possessions, mostly being devotional books. Their bindings were usually of velvet and canvaswork. Although some later ones were made of silk, this was not such a practical material. A book would be kept in a drawstring bag for protection, and a cushion would be placed under it when in use. The embroidered book-covers were mostly professional work, but some amateur examples survive.

In the Bodleian Library at Oxford there is a book made by Elizabeth I for her stepmother, Katherine Parr, called *The Miroir of Glass of the Synneful Soule*. She translated it from the French and embroidered the cover (*Figure 45a*). The design is of strapwork enclosing the initials KP. It measures 18.5×13.5 cm ($7^1/_4 \times 5^1/_4$ in).

In the same library is a bible (1583) which has an embroidered red velvet cover with a pattern of interlacing rose stems. It is said to have belonged to Queen Elizabeth I (*Figure 45b*). Another bible, in metal thread work on green velvet, dated 1573, also a gift to Elizabeth I, can be found in the British Museum. Embroidered bookbindings continued to be popular into the eighteenth century, but were in greatest use in the seventeenth century (*Plate 3*).

a

b

Figure 45
Embroidered book-coverings.
(a) *The Miroir of Glass of the Synneful Soule*, worked
    by Elizabeth I in 1544, when she was still a
    princess. The ground is worked in heavy light-
    blue silk with the design in gold and silver braid.
(Bodleian Library, Oxford)
(b) A Bible, 1583, a gift to Elizabeth I. On a
    ground of red velvet, worked in metal threads and
    coloured silks. The original tiny seed pearls have
    almost rubbed away.
(Bodleian Library, Oxford)

Embroidered Wall Hangings

Many wall hangings were of tapestry weaving
and were owned only by the very rich. Some,
known as 'mock arras', were paintings on
canvas made to resemble tapestry; a good
example can be found in the chapel at
Hardwick Hall.

THE OXBURGH HANGINGS

Embroidered hangings were mostly in canvaswork, often worked in smaller pieces and applied to velvet. This method was used for the Oxburgh Hangings, which can be seen at Oxburgh Hall, Norfolk, and there is one in the Victoria and Albert Museum. Three pieces of embroidery from this set can also be seen in Holyroodhouse, Edinburgh. They bear the cyphers of Bess of Hardwick and Mary Queen of Scots, and were originally four hangings, two of which were later cut up and used as bed hangings. There are larger central square motifs in fine tent stitch, and smaller octagonal and cruciform motifs in a coarser tent stitch, mounted on a ground of green velvet (*Figure 46*). They depict animals, birds and mythological beasts, many taken from Gesner's *Icones Animalium* (1560).

Figure 46
Motifs from the Oxburgh Hangings. Worked by Mary Queen of Scots and Bess of Hardwick in tent stitch on linen canvas.
(a) An octagon, the marigold turning to the sun, with the motto NON INFERIORA SECUTUS [not following lower things].
(b) A BYRDE OF AMERICA on the Marian Hanging, from Gesner's *Icones Animalium*, 1560. (University of Edinburgh)
(c) A SEA MOONKE on the Marian Hanging, from *La Nature et Diversité des Poissons*, Paris 1555.
(National Library of Scotland, Edinburgh. All three embroidered motifs are in the collection of the Victoria and Albert Museum, on loan to Oxburgh Hall)

a

b

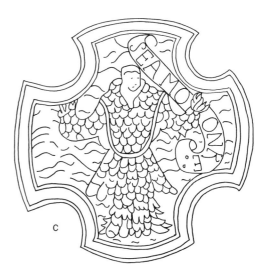

c

THE VIRTUE HANGINGS

These are a series of five large hangings, dated 1573, at Hardwick Hall, home of Elizabeth Shrewsbury, Bess of Hardwick. The hangings depict figures representing the Virtues under classical archways. The interesting feature of these hangings is that they contain some medieval ecclesiastical embroidered fabrics, that were seized by Bess's husband during the

Dissolution of the Monasteries. They are in patchwork and appliqué and include velvets, cloth of gold and silver thread; the faces and hands are of painted linen.

Figure 47
One of the Virtue Hangings. Patchwork and appliqué with various fabrics, including ecclesiastical embroidered fabrics.
(Hardwick Hall, Derbyshire)

Other embroidered items have survived in small numbers, or are referred to in inventories. They include the following:

Bucklers: the lining to a shield.
Canopies: cloths of state that were carried in the baggage of the Queen, to be erected where required. One can be seen in the Burrell Collection, Glasgow.
Hand screens: one in the Middleton Collection is sconce-shaped and worked in double-sided metal thread work.
Screens: often curtains that have been re-used.
Saddle-cloths: usually appliqué on a ground of velvet or satin. A small fragment, now at the Victoria and Albert Museum, was originally from Cranbourne House in Wiltshire. The appliqué is outlined in yellow silk.

Although embroidered caskets, cabinets and mirrors are mentioned in inventories, none have survived that can be positively dated.

Banners from the sixteenth century are usually painted with gold leaf on silk. The Broderers' Company have some dated 1564, but Wingfield-Digby suggests that these are eighteenth-century banners. Painted velvet was popular; a screen at Hardwick Hall has roundels of white velvet painted with birds.

Costume of the Tudor Era

The costume of this time amalgamated the skills of the embroiderer with those of the jeweller, so rich was the decoration. The stiff, cumbersome costume was in itself an indication of extreme wealth, as it rendered the wearers incapable of doing anything for themselves. Even high-ranking servants would have their degree of 'stiffness' within the hierarchy.

We have to refer largely to the portraits of the time, as the very richness of the costume meant that the jewels were re-used and much costume was burned to recoup the precious metal. This was, of course, the fate of much of

the earlier ecclesiastical pieces seized during the Dissolution of the Monasteries, although some were re-used for clothing (the Butler-Bowden cope, for example), or cut up for other work (the Virtue Hangings at Hardwick Hall, for example).

During the early part of the Tudor era the embroidery on the costume was mainly on embroidered bands or strips, purchased from professional workshops and then made up by the tailor. See, for example, Holbein's portrait of Henry VIII in the Thyssen-Bornemisza Collection, or the cartoon by Holbein in the National Portrait Gallery. However, in the portraits of Elizabeth I it is quite clear that the embroidery fits the shape and design of the garment. Unfortunately the surviving pieces are not a true guide to the vast amount of embroidery that would have existed. Garments were not made in one piece as they are today, but each separate component was pinned or laced into position.

SHIRTS, SHIFTS AND CHEMISES

A shirt or shift made of fine linen was worn underneath everything else. This protected the rich outer garments from perspiration and soiling. The shirt, shift or chemise was seen extending from the neck edge, the sleeve ends,

and through any slits in the costume, only being decorated where it showed. The most usual form of embroidery was blackwork (not necessarily black), but some examples of silk and metal thread work do exist (*Figure 48*). The earliest dated shirt, 1545, has decorated seams.

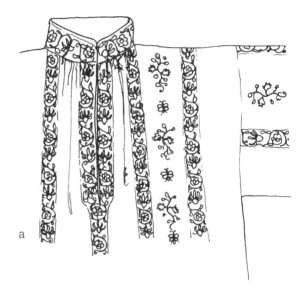

Figure 48
Linen shirts.
(*a*) Man's white shirt, late sixteenth century, English. Fine linen embroidered in black silk. Coiling stems, roses, oak leaves, birds and insects.
(Museum of Costume, Bath)
(*b*) Boy's shirt, 1540s, English. Fine linen with cross and double running stitches in blue silk. The edges are overcast and the seams are in knotted and buttonhole insertion stitches.
(*c*) Detail of collar.
(Victoria and Albert Museum, London)

THE PETTICOAT

The petticoat was worn under the skirt. It was often decorated and highly ornamental, and could match the skirt, making it difficult to distinguish the two garments. The forepart was a triangular piece worn over the petticoat, but under the skirt.

THE SKIRT OR KIRTLE

In earlier times the kirtle was a full-length garment worn under the dress, but in the sixteenth century it was divided into a doublet and skirt. The skirt itself was divided to show the petticoat.

SLEEVES

Sleeves were separate from the bodice, and were attached with pins, laces (points), or with early buttons. Laces mentioned in inventories of this time refer to sleeve laces. The term 'pin money' probably derives from the need for wealthy ladies to have servants just to pin them into their costume.

THE STOMACHER OR PARTLET

This is a triangular piece that fits into the front opening of the bodice or doublet. Earlier in the period it was called a partlet. Later in Elizabeth's reign it became longer and more pointed, and was called a stomacher. These items were nearly always richly embroidered, and were often made as part of a set comprising stomacher, sleeves and forepart.

JACKETS AND BODICES

In the late sixteenth century, jackets and bodices with sleeves came in, continuing well into the seventeenth century. They were worn under long, loose sleeveless coats, and were often decorated with scrolling stem designs worked in blackwork, blackwork with metal threads, and polychrome silks with or without metal threads. The jackets were often edged with metal lace trimmings.

COIFS AND FOREHEAD CLOTHS

A coif is a bonnet-shaped headdress, worn informally at home for leisure and for receiving guests, not at Court. Although sometimes referred to as nightcaps, they were not worn at night. They are often mentioned in the lists of New Year gifts given to Elizabeth I. They have survived in great numbers, possibly because they were worked by their owners and treasured for that reason. Coifs were embroidered using many techniques, mostly on linen, using polychrome silks and metal threads, blackwork with or without metal threads, and whitework techniques (*Figures 49b, 50a, 51* and *Plate 4*).

Forehead cloths were matching triangular pieces worn over the forehead with the point to the back. They were always worn at a time of illness, and were supposed to prevent wrinkles! They were also worn by babies. Hoods were worn by the elderly and considered very old-fashioned, although they remained in use until the reign of Charles I.

NIGHTCAPS

These were the male version of the ladies' coif. They were worn indoors informally, but not at night, when the biggin was used. The nightcap was a deep round cap with a turned-back brim, (*Figure 50b*). Most were embroidered linen, using the same techniques as were used for the coif, with the exception of whitework. The use of brocades and velvets became common later.

Many nightcaps survive, some unfinished, and from these we can see that they were embroidered on a straight piece of linen. The four shaped sections were embroidered on the right side of the fabric and the embroidery on the rim was worked on the reverse.

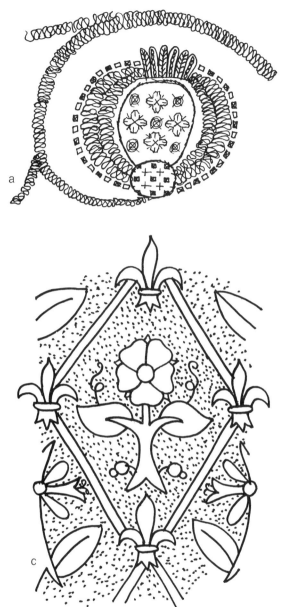

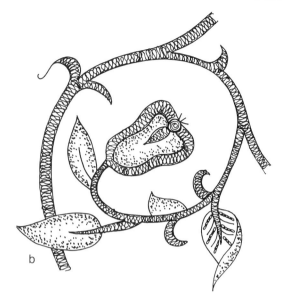

Figure 49
Blackwork designs.
(*a*) Long cover, *c.* 1600, English. Linen, worked in black silk and silver-gilt thread in stem, back, chain, plaited braid and buttonhole stitches. T531–1897.
(Victoria and Albert Museum, London)
(*b*) Coif, *c.* 1600, English. Gilt thread and black silk in plaited braid, ladder braid, chain and stem stitches, with speckling on linen. T28–1975.
(Victoria and Albert Museum, London)
(*c*) Costume panel, late sixteenth to early seventeenth centuries, English. Dark brown silk in back and double running stitches, with speckling on linen. T14–1948.
(Victoria and Albert Museum, London)

GLOVES

Gloves were mainly given as gifts, and were carried rather than worn, as a mark of rank. They were given as love tokens by ladies. The early gloves were like mittens with a slit for the thumb. Later, gloves were of fine doeskin and cut to have seams from the fingers that extended well onto the back of the hand, giving the impression of long fingers. The fingers were often padded and perfumed. Both the mittens and the gloves had beautifully embroidered, elaborate cuffs, embellished further with metal lace and ribbons. The embroidery, in silks and metals threads, was usually worked on silk, then applied to the leather.

a

b

Figure 50
Coif and nightcap.
(*a*) Coif, late sixteenth century, English. Brown
     silk in braid, stem and double running stitches on
     linen, edged with bobbin-made lace. Detail of
     insect. T12–1948.
(Victoria and Albert Museum, London)
(*b*) Man's nightcap, late sixteenth century,
     English. Linen with coloured silks and metal
     thread, edged with metal bobbin lace.
     2016–1899.
(Victoria and Albert Museum, London)

HANDKERCHIEFS

Like gloves, handkerchiefs were given as gifts.
They were of fine linen decorated with
embroidery and lace, but very few have
survived. The borders were often in Holbein
stitch or blackwork, in black or colours, or in
cutwork or reticella.

COLLARS

Collars date from the last few years of
Elizabeth's reign, and are thought to have been
used at the dressing-table to protect clothes.

BAGS AND PURSES

Little embroidered bags and purses, sometimes
with matching pincushions, were very popular
as receptacles for gifts and sweets. A great
many have survived with their highly
decorative and elaborate embroidery. They
were made of silk, satin or canvaswork, using
a variety of stitches. The embroidery was
worked in metal threads, coloured silks, pearls
and spangles. The bags were usually
10–12.5 cm × 7.5–10 cm (4–5 in × 3–4 in).
The canvaswork bags were in tent stitch or
gobelin stitch, often with a ground of metal
thread. Bags worked on silk or satin were
usually in raised embroidery, using detached
buttonhole stitch, perhaps with petals
completely standing above the ground, the
forerunner of stumpwork.

A feature of these little bags are the
trimmings. They had a drawstring top with
multicoloured cords, either made on a lucette,
which makes a square cord, or using a plaited
technique. In addition there are ornamental
tassels and fringes. Most bags were lined with
coloured silk taffeta. As with gloves and
handkerchiefs, bags are mentioned regularly in
the lists of gifts given to Elizabeth I. Decorated
bags were also made for devotional books, and
for ceremonial items like the Chancellor's
Purse for the Great Seal.

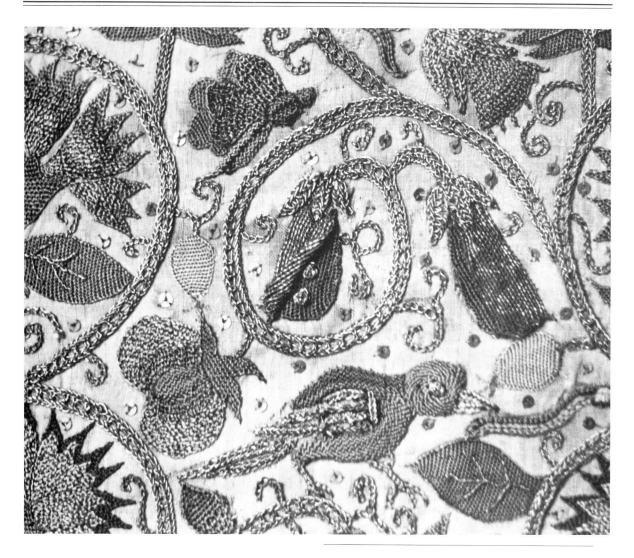

SCARVES, CROWNS AND HAWKING GEAR

Scarves are also mentioned in the list of gifts to the Queen. A surviving example can be found in the Middleton Collection. It is embroidered on white silk, in silk and gold thread in double-sided satin stitch, and is therefore reversible. The floral stems are couched on both sides. The scarf is about 305 cm (10 ft) long.

The City Livery Companies had crowns embroidered on velvet, for the ceremonial crowning of the Masters in the Courts of Livery. These were professionally worked.

Figure 51
Detail from a coif, early seventeenth century, English. Various forms of raised and detached buttonhole stitch, chain and double chain stitches, darning over detached laid threads and plaited braid stitch in coloured silks and metal thread. The ground is dotted with spangles. EG 79–1982. (Embroiderers' Guild, Hampton Court Palace)

Hawking gear was embroidered, usually in metal thread on velvet, with embossed leather. Once again, it features tassels and strings.

Personalities of the Sixteenth Century

ELIZABETH I (1533–1603)

The Queen set the style and fashion of the age. She was splendid, handsome and vain, constantly rejecting the advance of old age. The use of cosmetics became common among the aristocracy during her reign, and she wore auburn wigs to hide her grey and thinning hair. She undoubtedly had tremendous magnetism and excelled in her use of magnificent clothes and jewellery. She was very fastidious for the time; her acute sense of smell must have been a great disadvantage in the sixteenth century! The Queen was very well educated, as were her companions, and embroidery numbered among her accomplishments. She was a patron of the arts. From the inventories of her possessions, and lists of gifts, we gain much information about the embroidered costume and accessories of the time.

MARY QUEEN OF SCOTS (1542–87)

Mary wrote copious letters from which we derive much information; she also produced a large number of embroidered pieces.

The third and only surviving child of James V of Scotland, she was born at Linlithgow Palace, her father dying when she was only a few weeks old. She became Queen of Scotland with her mother, Mary of Guise, as Regent. Mary was sent to France for her education, and her needlework was supervised by Catherine de Medici, for whom Vinciolo compiled a book of lace, embroidery and lacis designs.

In 1558 Mary was married to the Dauphin, and it was at this time that the throne of England was claimed for her. The King of France, Henry II, was killed in 1559 and Francis and Mary became King and Queen. However, Francis died in the following year and Mary returned to Scotland in 1561.

Mary married Henry Darnley in 1565, and her son James was born in the following year.

She was taken prisoner by her nobles and placed in Lochleven Castle. A year later, in 1568, she escaped to England where she was subsequently imprisoned in Tutbury Castle, and placed in the care of the Earl and Countess of Shrewsbury (Bess of Hardwick).

Bess and the Queen were friends during the early years of her imprisonment, and worked a large amount of embroidery, but later they quarrelled. They had a draughtsman embroiderer to draw and prepare their work, as was the common practice in large establishments, and together they planned and worked the Oxburgh Hangings (*Figure 46*), one of which is dated 1570. The two cushions at Hardwick are the only other authenticated pieces of Mary's work (*Figure 42*).

In 1587 Mary Queen of Scots was executed. A full account of her life can be read in *Mary Queen of Scots*, by Antonia Fraser (World Books 1969).

THE COUNTESS OF SHREWSBURY,
BESS OF HARDWICK (152?–1608)

Bess was a remarkable woman of her time. Her father was a country squire and she rose from the middle class to be the richest woman in England, second only to Queen Elizabeth I. Her exact date of birth is not known but was between 1520 and 1525. She was the daughter of the estate manager of Old Hardwick, and was put into service in another Great House, as was the custom. Her brief one-year marriage to Robert Barlow, several years her junior, and her widow's penure of one-third of his estate, left her in the position of being able to enter service in a wealthier house. On 20th August 1547 (at two in the morning), she married Sir William Cavendish, Commissioner for the Dissolution of the Monasteries. In 1549 they bought Chatsworth and began the rebuilding. Bess was very close to Court life: Queen Mary and the Princess Elizabeth were godparents to her children.

In 1557 Sir William died and left Bess the life interest of Chatsworth, together with a large proportion of his property. Bess, now a very wealthy woman, married Sir William St Loe in 1559, and he settled all his lands on her. He was close to Queen Elizabeth I, and Bess became Lady of the Bedchamber. St Loe died in 1564.

Bess's final husband (m. 1568) was George Talbot, Earl of Shrewsbury. This marriage was like two companies merging together. Bess set the seal on her fortune by marrying her daughter Mary to the Earl's second son, and his daughter married Bess's eldest son Henry.

A year later Bess and her husband became responsible for confining Mary Queen of Scots, which placed a great strain on their marriage. Bess secretly married her daughter Elizabeth to Charles Stuart, which infuriated Elizabeth I and the Earl, resulting in Bess spending a winter in the Tower of London.

The daughter of this union was Arabella. Bess openly groomed her as heir to the Throne, thus angering Mary Queen of Scots. Arabella brought much trouble to Bess during her later years. In 1590 Bess was widowed again, having lived apart from the Earl for many years. She was now extremely rich.

It was at this time that she re-built Hardwick, next to the Old Hall. It was there that she died in 1608. Hardwick has the finest collection of Elizabethan embroidery, mostly dating from the 1570s, and most of it made for one of Bess's houses.

6

SEVENTEENTH-CENTURY
EMBROIDERY

During the seventeenth-century the continued enclosure of land caused many people to move to towns and cities to find work. It was an age of scientific awakening and the questioning of earlier teachings. The most notable advances were in the fields of mathematics and astronomy. Galileo put forward the idea that the earth moved around the sun. The circulation of the blood was discovered by Harvey.

Travellers were returning with many new plants – the tulip, nasturtium and laburnum. There were new herbs available for medicinal purposes. The Huguenot refugees brought gardening knowledge with them, together with the skills of lacemaking, glassmaking and weaving.

Gardens in the seventeenth century were on a larger scale than the Elizabethan knot gardens, and there was a great interest in water gardens and fountains. Gardens became yet another measure of wealth and status, judged by their size, unusual features and whether they contained the latest plants.

Palladian houses were being built, houses of solid mass without a courtyard and with all the windows facing outwards. The earlier great hall was reduced almost to a vestibule. Rushes gave way to carpets on the floor, and this led to a cleaner environment with fewer fleas to carry the plague. Tapestries gave way to panelling and smaller pictures, and there was a fashion for sculpture in the house. Benches and stools

were gradually replaced with upholstered chairs and stools, which were often embroidered. Life was generally more comfortable.

Beds were still the most valuable item in the house, with much money spent on lavish hangings. The headboards and canopies were often deeply carved with scrolls and spirals. These would be covered with fabric, sometimes embroidered, like the bed in Calke Abbey, Derbyshire, with its beautiful Chinese hangings. Alternatively, the mouldings were covered in silk and trimmed with rich fringes and tassels, like the Melville bed in the Victoria and Albert Museum. In addition to embroidered hangings, the newly available cut velvets were much sought after.

The seventeenth century divides into three distinct periods: the early Stuart period; the Commonwealth with its austerity; and the Restoration with its excesses. Social life changed. The ladies did less embroidery and engaged in more frivolous pastimes. Costume altered little at first. Anne of Denmark, the wife of James I, is known to have worn the clothes of Elizabeth I, some 3,000 items, until 1625. The richly embroidered costume of Elizabeth's reign eventually gave way to rich, plain fabrics decorated with much lace and metal braids. The portraits of the time give us an excellent source of information. The artists were highly skilled in depicting satins, silks, velvets and the beautiful lace of the period.

The fashion for tea-drinking began in the seventeenth century. The lady of the house would brew tea for herself or her guests in the drawing-room wearing an elaborate apron of embroidered silk or muslin. Tea-drinking was one result of the enormous interest in the Far East which was fashionable throughout Europe. Records show that the first tea, brought to Woburn Abbey, Bedfordshire, in 1685, cost 23 shillings to 25 shillings for a pound weight. Each member of the family would have had their own tea-drinking set and a caddy with a lock. The growth of this fashion encouraged more merchants to go to China, thus increasing trade. Among the many things they brought back was the chrysanthemum.

Chinoiserie

The influence of the Far East on Western art forms is apparent from the fourth century BC. The Silk Road was well established by the first century, and during the sixth century some silkworms were smuggled out of China, resulting in the virtual closure of the borders. This caused the Chinese to remain almost isolated until the twelfth century, when the land routes were re-opened.

People believed that beyond the mountain ranges of India lay the mythical land of 'Cathay'. The ideas and images that grew from what the Europeans thought was Chinese bear no resemblance to Chinese art.

True Chinese art and artefacts, made for Chinese use, were hardly known in Europe until comparatively recent times. The vision of Cathay was fabricated by European writers in the seventeenth and eighteenth centuries. Accurate accounts did not arrive until early in the nineteenth century. The chinoiserie style continued to be popular into the eighteenth and nineteenth centuries and influenced the design of pottery, china, furniture, paintings and textiles. Notable examples include the furniture of Thomas Chippendale (1718–79), the pagoda in Kew Gardens (1763) and the Royal Pavilion at Brighton. Hand-painted Chinese wallpapers were a feature in houses of note, and many commissioned complete services of porcelain to be made and decorated in China. The influence of chinoiserie can be seen too in the embroidery of the seventeenth and eighteenth centuries.

THE THURSTONE QUILTS

This pair of quilts, worked by two sisters, are very good examples of embroidery in the chinoiserie style. Worked by Sarah and Mary Thurstone, they show flowers, birds and people in a central scene with a garland. At the base of each garland the quilts are signed and dated 1694. The arms of Thurstone of Challock quartering Woodward appear at the top of the garland. Both quilts are worked in coloured silks and metal thread on a ground of cream satin. The quilt worked by Sarah is in the Victoria and Albert Museum, and that of Mary in the Fitzwilliam Museum, Cambridge.

Figure 52 (overleaf)
Detail, central motif of a quilt embroidered by Mary Thurstone. Coloured silks and metal thread on silk satin. A good example of the influence of Indian and chinoiserie styles on English embroidery. Note the joins in the fabric running vertically to each side of the motif, showing the loom width of handwoven silk. 51 to 56 cm (20 to 22 in).
(Reproduced by permission of the Syndics of the Fitzwilliam Museum, Cambridge)

The Baroque Style

The definition given, in retrospect, by the compiler of an eighteenth-century dictionary describes baroque as 'the superlative of the bizarre, the excess of the ridiculous'. It was indeed an extravagant artistic excess which began in Rome in the late sixteenth century and spread throughout Europe, reaching its peak in the seventeenth century.

In painting it is shown in the use of excessive light and shade and in creating bold three-dimensional images. *Trompe-l'oeil*, for example, is a style of painting that depicts architectural features and the scenes therein to give the impression of three-dimensional reality. A later, but very famous, example of this style of painting, is of a violin hanging on a door in the music room in Chatsworth House, Derbyshire. From a distance it is difficult to believe that it is a painting.

The baroque style is bold, elaborate and theatrical, and it flourished particularly in Roman Catholic countries. The term 'baroque' was used initially in a derogatory sense. The style pervaded all areas – architecture, painting, music, embroidery and costume. From the middle of the century, dress fabrics with very large designs were woven, and these were known as 'bizarre silks'. Genoese velvets were much used for upholstery and beds, the designs being very sculptural.

The fashion for the use of large pieces of

Figure 53
The scrolling stem design in the early seventeenth century.
Two covers, English, silks and metal thread. Both from the Elizabeth Day McCormick Collection. Museum of Fine Arts, Boston. 43.271 and 43.256. (Reproduced from *Historic Floral and Animal Designs for Embroiderers and Craftsmen*, Dover Pictorial Archive Series)

sculpture in the house has already been mentioned. Furniture was ornately carved and gilded. The walls and ceilings of main rooms were painted with scenes within gilded and carved cartouches, with simulated pillars, balconies, niches and doorways.

Design Sources

Many books were popular with ladies and were used by them to provide illustrations for embroidery. Among the most notable are the following:

Thomas Moufet's *The Insectorum* published in 1607.

The illustrations of Peter Stent, issued between 1640 and 1662, of birds, beasts, flowers, emblems and personages.

Quarles's *Emblems*.

Simpson's *Flowers, Fruits, Birds and Beasts*.

Edward Topsell's *Historie of Four-Footed Beasts*, 1607.

Figure 54
Detail from a crewelwork bed, *c.* 1680, English. The alternating leaf and honeysuckle motifs form the main body of the hangings and the edging of the valance. Red wool on linen.
(Cotehele House, Cornwall)

Figure 55
Hanging, late seventeenth to early eighteenth centuries, English. Worked in worsted wools on a linen and cotton twill. EG 1282.
(Embroiderers' Guild, Hampton Court Palace)

Two well-known technical books were:

The Schole House of the Needle by Richard
Shorleyker, published 1624.
The Needle's Excellency by John Taylor,
published in 1640, and subtitled 'A new
book wherein are divers admirable works
wrought with the needle for the pleasure and
profit of the industrious'.

The scrolling stem design which featured in the
embroidery of the sixteenth century continued
to be popular well into the seventeenth
century. Though largely unchanged at first
(*Figure 53*), the design gradually opened to a
larger scroll, with more open areas of fabric
showing (*Figure 54*). The next step was for it to
develop into the Tree of Life form, growing
from a little hillock or mound and becoming
more and more elaborate and clumsy (*Figure
55*). This style echoes the baroque fashion for
the ornate.

All manner of exotic birds and animals were
displayed within the branches and leaves,
without any regard for scale. Eventually, in the
eighteenth century, the tree form reverted to
being more open and airy, followed by the later
fashion for placing the stem in a pot or urn.

EDMUND HARRISON

A professional embroiderer of high reputation,
Edmund Harrison was a member of the
Broderers' Company. He presented a silver cup
to the Company in 1628 inscribed as follows:

'THE GIFT OF EDMUND HARRISON, INBRODERER
TO OUR LATE SOVEREIGN KING JAMES, DEC'D,
AND UNTO OUR SOVEREIGN LORD KING
CHARLES THAT NOW IS. 24TH JANUARY 1628,
THEN BEING WARDEN OF THE COMPANY OF
BRODERERS.'

On the foot of the cup, engraved after he died:
'Edmund Harrison o.b. [died], 9th January 1666
aged 77 years, parishioner of Cripplegate and 21
children were born to him.' His epitaph at St
Giles Cripplegate says that he served three kings
– James I, Charles I and Charles II – and, in 1660,
the Broderers' Company considered him the
most able worker living. He is known to have
done much heraldic work, costumes for pageants
and masques, and also to have embroidered coats
for the yeomen of the chamber. A record states
that he preserved the 'King's best cloth of state
and his rich carpet embroidered with purl'.

His only known surviving works, dated
1637, are six religious panels representing
scenes from the life of the Virgin and the
infancy of Christ. They were made for William
Howard, Lord Stafford (1611–80), who lived
at Corby Castle, Carlisle. The six panels
remained in the possession of the family until
1922, when they were auctioned. *The Visitation*
and *The Betrothal* were sold again in 1959.

The extensive use of or nué on these panels
would suggest that Edmund Harrison did some
of his training in Europe, especially as he used
the technique in its true form, i.e. with the
gold thread laid in straight lines horizontally.
Burden stitch in both its forms also features on
these pieces. The faces and flesh areas are in
split stitch, and there is good use of decorative
metal thread work, couching over padding.
The embroidery is worked on a ground of
linen, the figures being worked separately and
applied.

One panel, *The Adoration of the Shepherds*, is
in the Victoria and Albert Museum in London.
It is inscribed on the back: EDMUND HARRISON
IMBRODERER TO KING CHARLES MADE THEIS
ANNO DONI. 1637. 67.5 × 105.5 cm
(26$\frac{1}{2}$ × 41$\frac{1}{2}$ in).

The Adoration of the Magi forms a pair with

the above and is the same size, but does not have an inscription. The location of this panel is not known.

A third panel, *The Betrothal of the Virgin*, originally called *The Marriage of the Virgin*, is to be found in the Fitzwilliam Museum in Cambridge. It is also inscribed on the back: EDMUND HARRISON, IMBRODERER TO KING CHARLES, MADE THEIS, 1637. 56 × 67.5 cm (22 × 26½ in).

The fourth panel, *The Visitation*, originally called *The Virgin and St Anna*, is in the National Museum of Scotland in Edinburgh (formerly the Royal Scottish Museum). It bears the same inscription as *The Betrothal*. 58.5 × 67.5 cm (23 × 26½ in).

The Annunciation of the Virgin measures 53.5 × 62.5 cm (21 × 24½ in). Its location is not known.

The Circumcision of Christ has some damage to one of the lower corners and is in the National Museum of Scotland, Edinburgh (formerly the Royal Scottish Museum). 68.5 × 109.5 cm (27 × 43 in).

Samplers

The earliest surviving dated English sampler is that of Jane Bostocke, 1598. It is rectangular and has motifs at the top, an alphabet and inscription, followed by blocks of patterns. It is worked in metal thread, pearls, beads and silks on linen. There is a great variety of stitches including back, satin, chain, ladder, buttonhole, detached buttonhole, cross, interlacing, patterned couching, coral and two-sided Italian cross stitches with speckling, bullion and French knots. It measures 43 × 38 cm (17 × 15 in).

Most seventeenth-century samplers are long and narrow, unlike that of Jane Bostocke. They contain three main types of work, sometimes combined on one sampler. First there are rows of patterns in coloured silks and metal thread, featuring a great variety of stitches including Holbein (*Figure 56*), and raised embroidery (*Plate 5*). By the 1660s these patterns were obviously schoolroom exercises, as they were no longer used in contemporary work. Secondly there is an area of whitework using counted satin stitch, forming borders and edgings. The third type of embroidery was the reticella needlelace of the previous century (*Figure 57*).

Figure 56
Sampler, seventeenth century, British. Double running stitch in coloured silks on linen. EG 3881. (Embroiderers' Guild, Hampton Court Palace)

1   St Cuthbert's Maniple, detail of St John the
Baptist, 909-916, English.
Surface couching in gold thread, with coloured silks in
split and stem stitches.
(By kind permission of the Dean and Chapter of
Durham Cathedral).

2	The Steeple-Aston cope, now a frontal and dossal, early fourteenth century, English.
Detail of an angel on horseback from the orphrey, which now appears on the frontal.
Silver-gilt thread and silk in underside couching and split stitch with raised work on pale fawn silk twill.
(By kind permission of the Rector and Churchwardens of Steeple Aston, Oxfordshire.
On loan to the Victoria and Albert Museum London).

3	Embroidered book cover, 1630's. Book of Common Prayer with the Arms of the See of Durham. Raised metal thread work on a ground of red velvet.
(By kind permission of the Dean and Chapter of Durham Cathedral).

4	Panel, probably originally a coif, early seventeenth century, English.
Linen embroidered in coloured silks, metal thread and spangles. Stitches include plaited braid, chain, detached buttonhole, double chain and detached darning.
(With the kind permission of the Embroiderers' Guild, Hampton Court Palace).

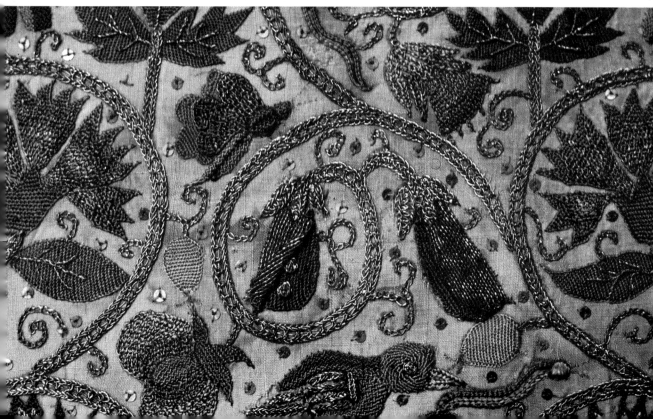

5　Detail, sampler, seventeenth century, English.
Coloured silks and metal thread on linen, raised
embroidery.
(With the kind permission of the Embroiderers' Guild,
Hampton Court Palace).

6　Panel, The Finding of Moses, mid-seventeenth
century, English.
Linen embroidered with coloured silks in tent stitch,
with drawn, but unworked, faces. Motifs from pattern
books by Peter Stent and John Overton. EG5860.
(With the kind permission of the Embroiderers' Guild,
Hampton Court Palace).

7　Detail, gentleman's coat, eighteenth century,
English.
Embroidery in coloured floss silk, metal thread and
silver purl on a ground of navy and green patterned
velvet. M443.
(With the kind permission of the Embroiderers' Guild,
Hampton Court Palace).

8　Detail, altar frontal, 1905, designed and worked by
Harriet Wyatt.
Laid and couched work, couching, split and satin
stitches on linen. The embroidery completely covers
the ground.
(With the kind permission of Westminster Abbey).

9 Detail, cushion front, Berlin wool work, nineteenth century, Britain.
Wools and beads on canvas in cross and plush stitch. 4134.
(With the kind permission of the Embroiderers' Guild, Hampton Court Palace).

10 Sampler, art nouveau style, c. 1910-20, worked by Katherine Powell.
Coloured silks on pale green linen. 96-1982.
(With the kind permission of the Embroiderers' Guild, Hampton Court Palace).

11 Roundel from a dalmatic, 1910, worked by Christine Angus.
Applied embroidered panels worked in coloured silks in buttonhole, chain, stem and satin stitches which almost cover the ground of linen. The faces and flesh areas are outlined but not worked.
The panels show the children of the family of Sir Peter Scott, who appears as a small child on the panel at the back hem. A similar panel decorates the front hem.
The roundel shown appears on the back of the dalmatic, with two smaller panels on each shoulder showing a baby as an angel, with their limbs bound, being those who died in infancy.
The embroidery shows the style of the late Arts and Crafts Movement and was shown in the 1916 exhibition. Originally, the panels were mounted on damask, but are now on a deep turquoise velvet.
(With the kind permission of Westminster Abbey).

12   Tea cosy, c. 1910-20, Britain.
Silk embroidery on linen, showing the influence of art nouveau. 154-1983.
(With the kind permission of the Embroiderers' Guild, Hampton Court Palace).

Figure 57
Sampler, second half of seventeenth century, British. Reticella, pulled thread with the design re-woven and counted whitework in linen thread on a linen ground, with an alphabet and a coloured band, which is worked in Italian two-sided cross stitch in coloured silks. EG78–1987.
(Embroiderers' Guild, Hampton Court Palace)

Stumpwork

The raised embroidery of the sixteenth century gradually became more exaggerated and, by the middle of the seventeenth century, took the form we now know as stumpwork. The name, given by the Victorians in the nineteenth century, was intended as a derogatory term, probably taken from 'embroidered on the stamp'. This reference first appears in the *New and Complete Dictionary of Arts and Sciences*, published in 1754.

Stumpwork was fashionable for only a short period, reaching a peak from about 1650 to 1680. The highly raised nature of the embroidery corresponded with the fashion for ornate carving within the home. Stumpwork was mostly carried out by young girls and formed part of their education in needlework. Their first task was to complete their coloured and whitework samplers, described opposite, followed by the panels and fittings for a casket, and finally a beadwork jewel box.

Raised embroidery, or stumpwork, was popular throughout most of Europe, being worked in considerable quantities for the Church in France, Italy, Spain and southern Germany. It was also produced in England for ceremonial use, for example the purse for the Great Seal. There had been highly raised work on the ecclesiastical vestments of northern Europe from the fifteenth century.

The designs were pictorial, either one complete picture or a series of scenes telling a story. They nearly always included people wearing contemporary Stuart costume, even if the story was biblical. Among the personages would be one or two people under a canopy, suggesting royalty (*Figure 58*). Sometimes the curtains hanging from the canopy are on a rail, allowing them to be opened and closed. The proportion and scale is often wrong, suggesting that the motifs were selected from a variety of sources and copied willy-nilly. In the spaces between the main items, all manner of flowers, animals, birds and insects were scattered.

Many examples take the form of small pictures, usually on a ground of cream satin. The design was drawn with ink for the worker to follow. This can be seen on unfinished pieces. Shading and raised areas were

Figure 58
Stumpwork panel, *Esther and Ahasuerus*, 1686,
British. Coloured silks and chenille on a ground of
cream satin, which has been completely overworked
in long and short stitch. The panel shows most of
the features of stumpwork. The windows in the
buildings are of mica and some of the fruit is worked
over wooden moulds. T17–1946.
(Victoria and Albert Museum, London)

indicated. Some of the embroidery was worked
directly on to the ground fabric, but much was
worked separately and applied in the same
manner as the slips in Elizabethan work,
although much smaller in size.

A great variety of threads was used; all forms
of metal threads, purls and plates, which were
often coloured and sometimes bound round
with coloured silks. Silks of many textures and
weights, both floss and twisted, were widely
used. Crewel wools, chenille, cords, braids and
gimps, seed pearls, beads, spangles, feathers,
tinsel and paste jewels were included for some
features. Transparent talc or mica was used,
with embroidery behind, for windows and
water.

Many different types of padding were
employed: wool, tow (short fibres of flax, hemp
or jute), hair, horsehair, or scraps of fabric. For
faces and hands, carved wood, bone or wax was
used. On some examples the hands are very
clumsy, being made out of wire which was
bound with silk.

The stitches used in examples of stumpwork
were numerous, but the most common was

surface buttonhole in its many forms
(*Figure* 59). There were three main forms:

1   All in one direction, giving a smooth
    twilled surface, the thread being brought
    back as a transverse thread or taken behind
    the fabric.
2   Worked in alternate directions giving a
    broken surface.
3   Up-and-down buttonhole stitch, which
    gives a firm knotted surface.

These could be used to create many variations
by grouping stitches together and leaving
spaces. Couching was used, sometimes with a
knotted thread, or in conjunction with
laidwork. Grass was achieved by knitting a
thread, pressing the piece and then unravelling
the knitting prior to sewing into position. Or
nué was used but often over cords instead of
gold. Knotted stitches and bullion knots were
also popular for foliage or areas of ground. In
addition, long and short stitch, satin stitch and
laidwork were used extensively. Small pieces of
canvaswork were applied worked in tent, brick,
rococo, velvet and Florentine stitches. All
applied embroidered pieces were pasted on the
reverse side before being cut out, to prevent
the edges fraying.

In addition to pictures, stumpwork was used
for caskets which would contain sets of
pincushions and accessories. Mirror frames
were also popular, being finished in a great
variety of shapes. The caskets or cabinets had
either a flat or a sloping lid, often with a mirror
inside. The top tray would sometimes contain a
three-dimensional garden. There would also be
drawers and compartments inside the cabinet,
to hold sewing tools, scent bottles, button
hooks, ear spoons, pounce boxes and love
letters.

A cabinet maker would make up the box
when the embroidery was finished. Some
cabinets have plainer back panels, often long
laid threads mounted on paper, which would
seem to be an addition by the cabinet maker,
where too few panels had been embroidered.

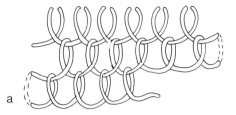

a

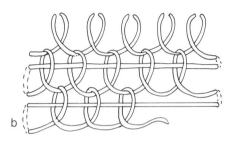

b

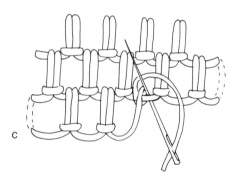

c

Figure 59
Diagrams of detached buttonhole-stitch fillings.
(*a*) The stitches are worked back and forth in both
      directions; the loops alternate in each row giving
      a textured effect.
(*b*) The stitches are worked in one direction only,
      the thread being brought back to the original side
      either as a transverse thread, as shown, or passed
      through and behind the fabric.
(*c*) A two-stage stitch called either up-and-down
      buttonhole or buttonhole filling stitch, giving a
      spaced knotted surface.

HANNAH SMITH

The earliest dated stumpwork figure is on a casket made by Hannah Smith, now in the Whitworth Art Gallery, Manchester. It is particularly interesting as a letter concerning the casket was found in one of the drawers. It reads as follows:

The yere of our Lord being 1657; if ever I have any thoughts about the time; when I went to Oxford, as it may be I may; when I have forgotten the time; to fortifi myself; I may loock in this paper and find it, I went to Oxford in the yere of 1654, my being there near 2 yers, for I went in 1654, and I stayed there 1655, and I cam away in 1656, and I was almost 12 yers of age when I went, and I mad an end of my cabbinete; at Oxford; and my [guenefteh] is my cabbinet, was mad up, in the yere of 1656 at London, I have ritten this, to fortiffi myself, and thos that shall inquir about it. Hannah Smith. [The word in brackets is indecipherable.]

The lid, showing Joseph raised from the pit, is worked in metal thread, coloured silks and seed pearls, in plush stitch, raised embroidery, long and short stitch and laidwork. The front doors show Deborah and Barak on one, and Joel and Sisera on the other. They are worked on fine canvas in tent and rococo stitches. The two side panels show Summer and Winter, on a linen ground in satin stitch and long and short stitch, in metal thread and coloured silks. The back of the cabinet is just long laid stitches, not worked on fabric, suggesting that this may be an addition by the cabinet maker.

Figure 60
Casket, embroidered by Hannah Smith, British. Coloured silks, chenilles, spangles and metal threads on a cream satin ground.
(Whitworth Art Gallery, Manchester)

MARTHA EDLIN

The Victoria and Albert Museum has all the known examples of Martha Edlin's childhood pieces. They consist of her coloured sampler, completed in 1668, her whitework sampler, completed in 1669, her cabinet, completed in 1671, and her beadwork jewel box, which she completed in 1673.

She was born in 1660.

Canvaswork

The seventeenth century brought a greater degree of comfort to the home, and the advent of upholstered furniture increased the use of canvaswork further. Being a hard-wearing technique, it lends itself to the purpose. Much of the work on the chairs was pictorial, worked in a combination of worsted wool and silk. The pictures on the back and seat of a chair would usually be set within a cartouche and worked in tent or cross stitch over one thread. Outside the cartouche the remaining design would often be worked over two threads. The upholstery could be in Turkey work (carpet tufting), using a Giordes knot. Florentine work was very popular, and is thought to have originated in Hungary, spreading across Europe, Britain and, eventually, to the United States of America. There has been a revival of this technique in the twentieth century; in America it is known as 'bargello'. In Florentine work all the stitches are the same length and the zig-zag patterns have given rise to the term 'flame stitch' (*Figure 61a*). Hungarian point is similar to Florentine work, but some of the rows have stitches shorter in length, giving a different look to the work (*Figure 61b*). An excellent example of Hungarian point hangings can be seen on the Great Bed and in an anteroom at Parham House, Sussex.

Canvaswork was also used for little pictures, similar in size, design and content to those worked in stumpwork, but embroidered in tent stitch on a very fine canvas. A feature of the canvaswork of the seventeenth century is a particular method of shading, where four or five shades are rigidly worked from light to dark within a shape. Used in this way it is known as 'Stuart shading' (*Plate 6*). In examples worked in America, this shading was less pronounced, giving a much 'flatter' look to the pictures.

Bookbindings were worked in canvaswork, in fine tent stitch, with pictorial subjects on prayer and devotional books. Embroidered bookbindings were probably more popular in

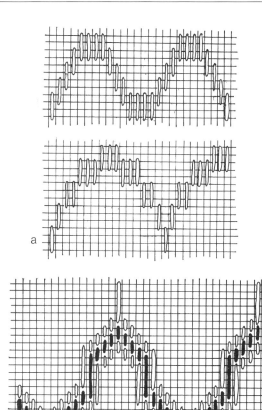

Figure 61
Florentine and Hungarian point.
(a) Florentine, with shaped rows of stitches all of the same length.
(b) Hungarian point, with shaped rows of stitches of two lengths.

the seventeenth century than at any other time. Each book would have had an embroidered bag or wrapper to protect it, and would be placed on an embroidered cushion when in use. In addition to canvaswork, bookbindings were worked in silks and metal thread on silk.

HATTON GARDEN HANGINGS

Some large wall hangings were worked in canvaswork, often incorporating a variety of stitches. A surviving set now in the Victoria and Albert Museum was found behind panelling in a house in Hatton Garden, London. Dating from the second half of the seventeenth century, they are worked on linen canvas with wool in tent, rice, cross, brick and rococo stitches, with couching and French knots. There are six panels, each with two classical pillars entwined with plants bearing fruit and flowers, very typical of the baroque style. The flowers include the tulip, lily, peony, honeysuckle, rose and carnation. Exotic birds decorate the upper part of the hanging, with a range of animals in the lower area. Each panel measures approximately 236 × 122 cm (7 ft 9 in × 4 ft).

Figure 62
Hatton Garden hangings, English. Panel of linen canvas embroidered with coloured wools. One of six. 517 to 522–1896.
(Victoria and Albert Museum, London)

Crewelwork

The crewelwork designs of the seventeenth century show strongly the Indian influence, but to the European taste. Many designs are based on the Tree of Life form, with exotic foliage, flowers and fruit growing from little hills.

In 1600 Elizabeth I granted the East India Company a charter allowing them a monopoly of trade with India. The Mogul rulers allowed the East India Company to set up a trading post in the State of Gujarat in 1612 and, by 1658, it was the largest factory in the area, moving to Bombay in 1687. The early records of the East India Company show that English embroidery

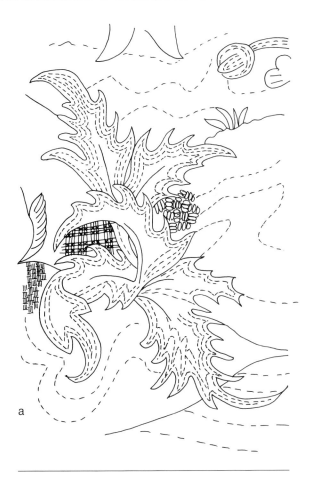

a

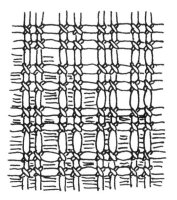

b

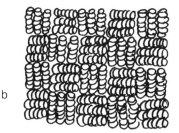

Figure 63
(*a*) Detail of crewelwork hanging shown in *Figure* 55.
(*b*) Three fillings.
  Laid threads with a double trellis secured with cross stitches.
  Blocks of four straight stitches forming a bricked pattern, gobelin filling.
  A chequerboard pattern of groups of three bullion knots, rose ground.
(Embroiderers' Guild, Hampton Court Palace)

was taken to India and prized by the Mogul princes. They sent lengths of fabric to England to be embroidered for coats. Later records show that as the Indians learned to do the work for themselves, the value of the English work fell.

In the early Indian work the embroidery virtually covered the ground fabric with little scenes and pictures. The first examples to arrive in England were in white on a coloured ground, and sales were disappointing. The process was then reversed to give colour on white, but with no increase in popularity, as people were accustomed to the chinoiserie designs. This resulted in patterns in the 'Chinese taste' being sent out to India to be copied, but these were interpreted with an Indian flavour, culminating in a strange mixture of the two.

Figure 64
Detail, crewelwork, seventeenth century, British.
Speckling and stem stitch in red wool on a cotton
and linen twill ground. Note the drawing where the
embroidery has worn away. EG1981.
(Embroiderers' Guild, Hampton Court Palace)

The crewelwork of the seventeenth century was worked on a twill fabric woven from cotton and linen, this being stronger than linen alone (*Figure 64*). The embroidery was worked in crewel wool and worsteds – very hard-wearing, highly twisted yarns. The dyes were not all fast and in many surviving pieces the yellow has faded, making the greens look more blue than they would have done originally. Many stitches were used; chain, detached chain and stem stitches, long and short stitch, and many forms of knotted stitches. Some of these were used as fillings together with laidwork and speckling (*Figure 63*).

TWO BEDS AT COTEHELE

Cotehele was built in Cornwall between 1485 and 1627 and contains much original furniture and embroidery. Among its contents are two beds complete with their hangings. They make ideal subjects for comparison, both in style and also to illustrate the difference between restoration and conservation.

Restoration is the act of making something old or damaged look as it did when new. You may see tapestries with areas that are much more brightly coloured than the untouched original. This has the effect of destroying the balance between old and renewed, as the new work will dominate. Often restoration involves destroying part of the original item, which is undesirable in the long term.

Conservation is the act of making something old or damaged safe, holding the damage at the present level. You should not be able to see where the old and the new meet. Conservation techniques consist only of reversible and non-damaging methods. If, at a later date, a better method is found, the previous work can be removed and replaced without any damage to the item.

One of the Cotehele beds is embroidered in coloured worsted wools, originally on a linen twill in the manner of the over-sized Tree of Life form. This bed has been restored. The damaged background fabric has been cut away close to the embroidery, which was then re-applied onto a new ground fabric. In some places the edges of the embroidery have been turned under and, in others, the appliqué has been secured with a buttonhole stitch. Not only has this process changed the look of the embroidery, by making it appear far more raised than the original, but as a result of the woollen stitches being stretched they have fractured and become detached.

The second bed is very light, open crewelwork relating to the scrolling stem design (*Figure 54*). The embroidery is worked in a red worsted wool on a fine linen twill. This bed was conserved in a professional workshop. The original damaged background fabric and embroidery were mounted onto a matching linen ground, the whole laying flat and merging into one. It is interesting to see how the greatest damage was concentrated on the corner of the bed that caught the light from the window. The hangings on the other side are in comparatively good condition.

THE ABIGAIL PETT BED

A set of bed curtains and valances worked by Abigail Pett during the second half of the seventeenth century can be seen in the Victoria and Albert Museum, London. They are a very good example of amateur work, with an amusing mixture of animals, birds and foliage. There is a delightful camel which looks as if it has been drawn from a description. The motifs are repeated, but each one is worked slightly differently. Most of the foliage is in heavy long and short stitch with laidwork fillings. In addition to wool, chenille is used on some of the animals. The bed is signed *Abigail Pett*, but the Pett family included several Abigails, and it is not possible to identify exactly which one worked the embroidery. The top valance has a good example of a knotted fringe.

Figure 65
Detail from the Abigail Pett bed, late seventeenth century, English. A dragon in encroaching satin stitch and stem stitch filling in shades of yellow and green, with a bright red tongue. Standing on a hillock of three shades of brown, with a flower of red, green and yellow. Worsted wools on linen. (Victoria and Albert Museum, London)

Many domestic and costume items were embroidered in crewelwork, including workbags, pockets and petticoats. The workbags were often signed and dated. Crewelwork continued into the eighteenth century, although it changes in style and emerges again as art needlework in the nineteenth century. In the twentieth century there was a revival of crewelwork in wools, in the style of the seventeenth century. This is known as 'Jacobean work'.

Etching or Printwork

Small pictures, sometimes memorials, were worked in black or brown silk copying the etchings that were popular at the time. Portraits were popular, Charles I being a fashionable subject. In many, watercolour washes were used for the sky or background. Some examples were worked in human hair. This technique continued into the eighteenth and the nineteenth centuries, although the style and subjects changed.

7

NEEDLEMADE LACES

Real lace does not date back any earlier than the second half of the sixteenth century, although crochet and network are referred to in the reign of Edward III (1312–77). Netting has also been found in Egyptian tombs, but these techniques are not true laces. References in the fifteenth century record laces being used to fasten together costume items and shoes, and the use of braids. However, as we have seen when looking at the technique of needlebinding in chapter 1, the basic stitch used for needlemade laces was known at a much earlier time, although serving a different purpose.

Filet or Lacis

Filet (French) or lacis (Italian) dates from early times and is made by weaving a design with a needle into a hand-knotted net background (*Figure* 66). The net is made with a form of shuttle and the size of the mesh is controlled by gauges. A square of net is commenced at one corner and worked to form a diamond shape. When complete the net is mounted, by lacing, into a rectangular frame before the decorative work is begun. Buratto is basically the same, except that the background is woven for the purpose.

Handmade Lace

There are two methods of making handmade lace:

1   With a needle using various forms and patterns of buttonhole stitch and laid threads.
2   With bobbins giving a woven or plaited structure.

The two methods sometimes combined to give a mixed lace. True lace is always made on a firm backing which is then pinned to a pillow. These come in many shapes depending on the type of lace being made.

For needlelace, the cordonnet, or outline, is usually heavier than the thread used for the lace and is couched to the backing. The term 'gimp' is used when referring to English laces. The lace stitches are then built on this framework without penetrating the backing. When completed, the stitches holding the cordonnet in place can be removed from the reverse side, allowing the lace to be lifted from the backing.

The bobbin-made and the needlemade lace industries operated in parallel with one another, the popularity of one over the other depending on the fashions of the time. During the sixteenth and early seventeenth centuries,

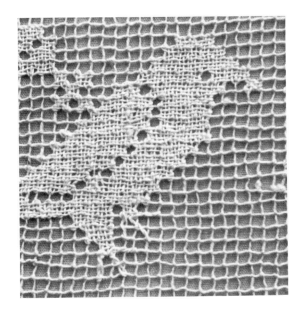

Figure 66
Filet, or lacis. Insertion, late nineteenth century.
Cotton thread. Note the knot at each corner of the
mesh, which is made first, the design being woven
into the stretched mesh afterwards.
(Author's collection)

a stiff lace was required for the ruffs and cuffs of
the time. Needlemade lace tends to be stiffer
than bobbin-made lace; hence the
predominance of the former at this time. Later
in the seventeenth century, when both ladies
and gentlemen wore their hair longer, the
fashion changed to falling collars, and the
demand for bobbin-made lace was greater. Its
popularity continued throughout the
eighteenth century, although the needlemade
laces of the time were also light and soft. The
advent of machine-made imitations of all types
of lace in the early nineteenth century severely
hit the production of handmade lace.

The revival of needlelaces and imitation
laces in the nineteenth century is dealt with in
chapter 11. Those wishing to study all forms of
lace in detail should refer to *Lace, A History* by
Santina Levey, published by Maney and the
Victoria and Albert Museum.

Techniques

The term 'needlepoint' should refer only to
laces made with a needle. Its usage in
connection with canvaswork is a modern
innovation introduced from America.

The lace of the sixteenth century was
preceded by cut and pulled work, which
developed from the desire to decorate
handspun, handwoven linen.

CUTWORK

In early cutwork – punto tagliato – small areas
of the linen were cut away and the edges
overcast. The open cut areas were decorated
with needlemade fillings. The remaining areas
of fabric were then opened up with pulled work
– punto tirato – or with counted satin stitch
and, finally, decorated with raised bars and
bullions (*Figure 67*).

RETICELLA

This form of lace always has a strong geometric
design as it is based on woven fabric. Threads
are withdrawn from the fabric in two directions
leaving a rectangular framework of pairs or
groups of threads. This framework is then
mounted on a backing onto which the design
has been drawn. The remaining threads are
needlewoven or overcast together and
additional diagonal threads are added, on
which the final decorative buttonhole stitch
patterns are built (*Figure 68*).

An early pattern book for this type of work
by Federico Vinciolo was published in 1587
called *Singuliers et Nouveaux Pourtraicts*. It was
the forerunner of many similar publications,
containing patterns for both needlepoint lace
and lacis. Designs from this book are shown in
Figures 69 and 70.

Figure 67
Cutwork, early seventeenth century, British. White linen thread on linen. Cut and pulled ground, decorated with detached buttonhole stitch and bullion knots.
(Embroiderers' Guild, Hampton Court Palace)

Figure 68
Reticella, in the style of 1600, late nineteenth-century reproduction, British. Linen. Buttonhole stitches built on a framework of withdrawn threads.
(Embroiderers' Guild, Hampton Court Palace)

Figure 69
Patterns for reticella and punto in aria.
Four patterns by Federico Vinciolo, from *Singuliers et Nouveaux Pourtraicts*, published in 1587.
(Reproduced from *Renaissance Patterns for Lace, Embroidery and Needlepoint*, Dover Pictorial Archive Series 1971)

PUNTO IN ARIA

Literally meaning 'stitches in air', punto in aria is somewhat similar to reticella, except that instead of withdrawing threads from fabric, the initial structure is formed with couched threads laid down onto a backing. This was obviously better than removing threads from a fabric which had previously been carefully handwoven.

The early examples are very similar in appearance to reticella as often the same designs were used. The difference can be seen at the junctions of the original threads; in reticella one sees the threads weaving over and under one another, while in punto in aria one set of threads crosses over the other. The designers and workers soon became aware that they could curve the shapes, and punto in aria developed into a much more flowing design (*Figure 71*). The use of both reticella and punto in aria extended well into the seventeenth century.

Figure 70
Patterns for filet or lacis.
Three patterns by Federico Vinciolo, from *Singuliers et Nouveaux Pourtraicts*, published in 1587. (Reproduced from *Renaissance Patterns for Lace, Embroidery and Needlepoint*, Dover Pictorial Archive Series 1971)

VENETIAN POINT

The Venetian laces of the seventeenth century were mainly for ecclesiastical use; only the most wealthy could afford to use them for their cravats and cuffs. The designs were very sculptural and fitted in well with the baroque style, having highly raised decorated edges. These laces were also more manageable for the workshops to produce. Reticella and punto in aria were worked in one piece to the size of the

finished article, whereas with Venetian lace the individual motifs could be made by separate workers and then assembled at the final stage.

Venetian point is generally a straight lace with, at most, a scalloped edge. It remained popular until the middle of the eighteenth century. Any pieces with a deep Van Dyke edging or made to a curved shape are nineteenth century and have been remade or are revival pieces.

The patterned fillings were worked first within a cordonnet, built up from straight rows of buttonhole stitch with geometric designs formed by spaces (*Figure 72*). The second stage involved the building up of the padding supported by a ladder-like base. Lastly, the padding was buttonholed over very closely, incorporating decorative picots. The motifs

Figure 71
Punto in aria, cuff, 1630s, English. Worked on a framework of linen threads and decorated with detached buttonhole stitches. EG L166.
(Embroiderers' Guild, Hampton Court Palace)

Figure 72
Gros Venetian point, detail of Figure 73, seventeenth century. Patterned fillings of solid and spaced buttonhole stitch, with raised cordonnets decorated with picots. The motifs are original, but the bars are a nineteenth-century reconstruction.
(Author's collection)

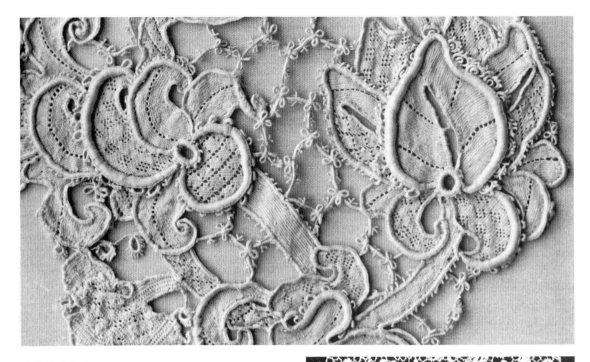

Figure 73
Fragment, gros Venetian point, seventeenth
century. Large-scale motifs re-assembled during the
nineteenth century. The bars and picots are less
structured than those that would have been worked
originally. The thread used for the bars does not
match that of the original motifs.
(Author's collection)

could then be assembled on a backing to the
final design and joined by decorated brides or
bars.

There were three main types of raised
Venetian point:

1 Gros point, at its peak in 1665, with very
   large motifs and cordonnets highly padded
   with wool or horsehair. The motifs are
   filled with geometric patterns worked in
   straight rows and are joined with bars
   decorated with picots (*Figure 73*).

2 Rose point, 1665–95, has motifs about
   2.5–4 cm (1–1¹/₂ in) across and a slightly

Figure 74
Fragment, Venetian rose point, seventeenth
century. Linen thread. Probably an ecclesiastical
piece.
(Embroiderers' Guild, Hampton Court Palace)

less raised cordonnet. The flower-like motifs sometimes have two or three layers of petals and the bars are more highly decorated with multiple picots (*Figure 74*).

3 Point de neige has very tiny flower-like motifs with many layers of petals and delicately decorated bars.

There are also flat Venetian needlepoints called point plat, coralline and reseau Venise.

These variations do not have any raised cordonnets.

Burano is a later development of Italian needlepoint lace with a net-like ground instead of only bars or brides (see below). Spanish needlepoints are very similar to the Venetian needlelaces and only the use of certain motifs distinguishes them.

HOLLIEPOINT

The use of holliepoint has been recorded from the seventeenth century, through the eighteenth and into the nineteenth century. Holliepoint is a flat lace with patterns worked in straight rows, but not forming motifs. It is worked in a knotted buttonhole stitch with spaces left to create the design, the whole forming a piece of lace often used as an insertion. Originally used for church linen, the name may come from 'Holy Point'.

Figure 75
Burano, Italian needlepoint, late eighteenth to early nineteenth centuries. Cotton. The reseau is formed by buttonhole loops which are then laced with a second thread, giving a linear appearance. The cordonnet is loosely stitched.
(Embroiderers' Guild, Hampton Court Palace)

Figure 76
Sampler, 1727, British. Holliepoint, reticella fillings and counted satin stitch. Linen thread on linen. Note the signature and date at the top centre. EG24–1987.
(Embroiderers' Guild, Hampton Court Palace)

The use of holliepoint reached its peak in the second half of the eighteenth century and was used mainly for babies' caps and the shoulder seams of their gowns. Sometimes the nannies' cuffs would also be trimmed with holliepoint. This is an interesting lace as many pieces are dated and have initials within the design (see above).

FRENCH NEEDLEPOINT

Point de France, or French needlepoint, c. 1660, was very popular at the Court of Louis XIV (1643–1715) and its production severely damaged the Venetian industry. The motifs were relatively small, with elegant designs usually of flowers, urns, fleurs-de-lys and figures. The use of bars forming hexagons distinguishes this lace from others. There were several developments of French needlepoint:

1   Alençon, c. 1717, had a background of basic buttonhole stitch which was then

twisted with an extra thread giving a linear rectangular appearance (*Figure 77*).

2 Argentella, a later development, had an elaborate background of honeycomb shapes.

3 Argenton had a basic buttonhole ground which was closely worked over with additional buttonhole stitch to give a strong, decorative hexagonal effect.

4 Point de Colbert, a very crisp lace, was made in the Bayeux area in the mid-nineteenth century. With distinct stylized floral designs, the pieces feel very hard to the touch owing to the use of machine-spun thread.

FLEMISH NEEDLEPOINTS

The Flemish needlepoints of the eighteenth century are rarely found. They resemble flat Venetian point, but have a slightly raised cordonnet.

Probably the best-known needlelace is Brussels needlepoint, point de gaze, dating from the 1850s. This was the only needlemade lace to survive the advent of machine-made lace throughout the nineteenth century, remaining popular until the First World War. It is a delicate flower-like lace with extra layers of petals and a simple buttonhole background (*Figure 78*).

Figure 77
French needlepoint, Alençon. Late eighteenth to early nineteenth centuries. Reseau of buttonhole loops which are laced with a second thread. The heading is bobbin-made lace.
(Embroiderers' Guild, Hampton Court Palace)

Figure 78
Point de gaze, nineteenth century. Reseau of simple buttonhole loops. The cordonnet is closely buttonholed, featuring a distinctive treatment of the flowers with a second layer of petals. (Embroiderers' Guild, Hampton Court Palace)

IRISH NEEDLEPOINT

The Irish needlemade lace industry began in the 1840s and was introduced as a result of the hardship brought on by potato famine. Most of the laces were copies of Venetian raised and flat points, but they are easily identified by the inferior quality of the thread. Old, presumably damaged, pieces of Venetian point were reassembled to contemporary fashions. However, the difference in the thread of the original motifs and the thread used for the reconstructed bars can easily be seen.

A later type, imitating point de gaze, was a flower-like style known as youghal (pronounced 'yawl'). It is distinguished by the regular shading of alternate petals, achieved by the closeness of the spacing of the stitches.

Much coarse needlepoint lace has been, and is still being, made in this century in Ireland, Belgium, Cyprus and, in vast quantities, in China and the Far East. Items from China and the Far East are sold throughout the world in centres renowned for their lace, as local work.

THE MIGRATION OF EUROPEAN EMBROIDERY TO NORTH AMERICA

The colonization of North America took place gradually, from the early years of the seventeenth century, the first families landing in 1620. They arrived with their possessions, including needlework and embroidery, which were greatly treasured. The migration to Canada was later and slower than that to the United States.

The struggle for survival was paramount; although the land was rich in raw materials, the development of the means to use them was slow. There was also the threat of attack from the Indians to cope with.

In the cold climate, the priority was warm clothing and bed coverings. These were constantly patched and mended, and eventually the surviving scraps were patched together to make the early patchwork, which was purely utilitarian. The quality of life had to improve considerably before there was the time or the means for decorative work. Unfortunately none of these early seventeenth-century bed covers have survived.

It is likely that the earliest attempts at decoration would have been crewelwork on pockets, petticoats and small costume items. The women spun and dyed their own wool and linen yarn. By the latter half of the eighteenth century life was easier and both the time and the materials were available for women to begin to consider the decorative possibilities of needlework. However, they were still conscious of the need to avoid waste, as many of the fabrics were imported and therefore expensive.

Quilting, patchwork and candlewicking were popular; quilting and patchwork, often used together, reached a high point in the second quarter of the nineteenth century. Quilting 'bees', or parties, were occasions when women came together to make a quilt, perhaps at harvest time. Album quilts, made by several people, were popular, each piece with a personal favourite pattern or motif. Appliqué quilts were also made, sometimes with printed designs cut from fabric and then applied. Many of these quilts were for special occasions, such as a wedding. Crazy patchwork was popular by the late nineteenth century and was often decorated with embroidery, for example feather stitching over the joins in the fabric. The patches might also have embroidered motifs. These were sometimes intended for the parlour and called 'slumber throws'. The 1930s Depression brought a return to utilitarian practices, but there has been a great revival in recent years throughout North America.

One early technique taken out from England was Turkeywork, a knotted pile used for chairs, table carpets and bed covers, but not at that time for the floor. Later, rugs of all kinds and sizes were made in a variety of techniques. Needlework rugs were very popular, as were hooked rugs worked in a frame, using wool or strips of fabric.

Samplers served the same function in America as in Europe. Early samplers were reference pieces, and later examples were made for display.

During the 1740s Moravian work was introduced. The Sisters of Bethlehem founded schools in Pennsylvania, spreading later into the Southern States. They taught, and were renowned for, fine silk needlework, whitework and other techniques. The silk work mainly featured memorial pictures, maps, religious and military subjects. The whitework embroidery followed the fashions of Europe (see chapter 11).

A great number of examples of all types of needlework survive from the eighteenth century and are similar in style to those of Britain and Europe. It was, by then, possible to buy a wide range of fabrics and threads imported from London. Inventories show many items of canvaswork and crewelwork, including chair coverings, bed hangings and furnishings, firescreens, pocket books and costume items. The abundance of crewelwork done in Britain during the seventeenth and eighteenth centuries had its counterpart in America. However, the design and embroidery never quite reached the excessive heaviness and extreme ornamentation that it did in Britain. Fewer elaborate stitches were used. The designs were much lighter and more open than those of seventeenth-century Britain. Some examples were executed in blue and white thread, a technique that was revived later by the Deerfield Society.

During the nineteenth century, ladies' magazines and periodicals were very popular with the amateur needlewoman. They promoted the latest fads and crazes with charts, designs and patterns together with the necessary working instructions. Berlin wool work (see chapter 10) was probably the most popular and widespread technique used, being easily worked even by the most inexperienced hand. The wools were known as 'zephyrs' in the United States. The term 'needlepoint' is used in North America to denote canvaswork, but its correct usage is in connection with needlemade laces. Most of the popular ladies' crafts (netting, crochet, knitting, etc.) were followed in America, and were promoted widely by the magazines.

From the 1870s 'art needlework' was very popular in Britain. This fine silk embroidery in long and short stitch, depicting naturalistic subjects, was possibly a reaction to the excesses of Berlin wool work. A centennial fair was held in Philadelphia in 1876 and the Royal School of Art Needlework staged what became the most popular exhibit. Ladies flocked to see the 'Kensington embroidery' as they called it. Some came to England to the Royal School to learn the technique, and eventually similar establishments were set up throughout the United States, the first being founded by the Boston Museum of Fine Arts. Along with the technique came the fashion for the designs of William Morris, one of the Royal School's designers. The American, James McNeill Whistler (1834–1903), introduced an interest in the Japanese style which also lent itself to the technique. Examples were executed in pale greys and lavender shades. The Society of Decorative Arts was founded by Louis C. Tiffany (1848–1933), Samuel Coleman (1832–1920) and Robert W. de Forrest (1848–1931). Candice Wheeler directed the embroidery of large wall hangings by the Associated Artists, and her work was influenced by William Morris's designs and by the Japanese style.

In 1896 the Blue and White Society was formed in Old Deerfield, Massachusetts by Margaret C. Whiting and Ellen Miller. They were both skilled needlewomen, painters and trained teachers. The designs were the traditional floral motifs associated with crewelwork. In addition to blue and white threads, light browns and fawns were used. The embroideries were protected by a trade mark, a 'D' in the centre of a spinning wheel (*Figure 79*). This group of needlewomen also

Figure 79
Trade mark of the Blue and White Society within a crewel work motif.

set up their own spinning and dyeing industry producing silk and wool in beige and three shades of blue. The Society came to a close in 1925.

Needlework continued to flourish throughout the twentieth century in North America; quilting and patchwork abounded. In the 1970s and '80s the experimental use of fibres, soft sculpture and 'pop art', together with the combining of textile methods, extended the boundaries of embroidery and needlework.

Quilting, Patchwork and Appliqué

There are three main types of quilt, using quilting and patchwork:

1 The quilted counterpane, often one colour interlined with wool or old blankets, or cotton in the Southern States. It is made from three layers: top fabric, interlining and lining.

2 The pieced, or patchwork, quilt with the design formed from repeating patterns joined to make a whole.

3 The pieced, or patchwork, quilt made from small elements to give one overall large design.

The last two can be a combination of quilting and patchwork, patchwork alone, applied motifs alone, or any combination of the three.

The quilted counterpane was of two main types:

(i) The all-white counterpane in trapunto or corded quilting, two layers of fabric with only selected areas padded. The designs were usually floral scrolls, fruit, or feather waves (*Figure 80*).

(ii) The linsey-woolsey counterpane, most often made of wool, although silk and cotton examples are known. The woollen fabric was 'glazed' with egg white and water and then polished when it was dry. This was to imitate the imported glazed cottons that were so popular. Designs were very large scale, featuring scrolling stems with flowers or fruit, the wavy feather border being particularly popular.

Many of the patterns on the pieced or patchwork quilts have evolved and developed from local origins and have special names. Some patterns are based on early symbols or are associated with certain events. Many spreads are made up from lap-sized pieces that were

Figure 80
Feather-wave pattern used for quilting.

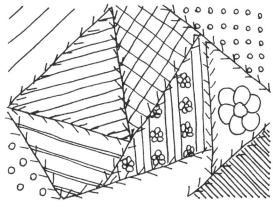

Figure 82
Crazy or kaleidoscope patchwork. Irregular overlapped shapes with additional decorative stitchery.

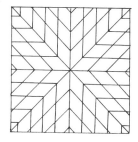

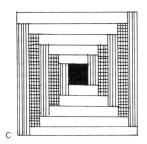
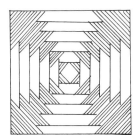

Figure 81
Patchwork blocks and patterns.
(a) Motifs that are repeated or combined to give an all-over effect.
(b) One small template creating a single all-over pattern.
(c) Log Cabin and Pineapple motifs.

very convenient to work as lap quilting. The repeated blocks were joined to give an overall design (*Figure 81a*). Others were made from small shapes that when joined make one large design. The Star of Bethlehem is a good example (*Figure 81b*). Another popular method used strips of fabric for Log Cabin or Pineapple patchwork (*Figure 81c*). There are many books on patchwork and quiltmaking which give details of the numerous patterns.

Crazy patchwork was a late nineteenth-century fashion which was used for housecoats and covers as well as for quilts. Its main use was as a slumber throw, kept in the parlour to throw over the settle or the piano. The technique of crazy patchwork is in some respects similar to appliqué, as it consists of the haphazard piecing together of scraps on a backing, with the joins and sometimes the pieces embroidered (*Figure 82*).

Appliqué quilts were made by cutting designs from either printed or plain fabric which were then applied to the ground fabric, the edges being turned under and hemmed. Some of the early examples were cut from

Figure 83 (*right*)
Hawaiian appliqué motif, constructed by folding
paper and cutting. The cut fabric shape is applied to
the ground fabric, the edge being rolled under and
hemmed. The design is then quilted with contour
lines following the motif, creating linear patterns.

Figure 84
American crewelwork chair seat, eighteenth
century, in the Museum of Fine Arts, Boston.
54.113. Coloured wools on linen.
(Reproduced from *Historic Floral and Animal Designs
for Embroiderers and Craftsmen*, Dover Pictorial
Archive Series)

chintzes and imported printed fabrics. The fine details were added with embroidery. Album quilts were popular, each square containing a favourite motif or picture. These quilts were often made by a group of women as a gift, and appropriate motifs would be chosen to suit the occasion.

Hawaiian quilts are a very attractive form of appliqué which developed in the early nineteenth century and were often only in two colours. These intricate designs resembled folded cut paperwork with the design accentuated by contour quilting, rows of running stitches following the outlines of the appliqué to create new patterns (*Figure* 83). Designs are based on local folklore and traditional motifs, all with their own names.

Candlewicking

This technique produces a textured design formed of loops which can either be cut or left uncut. In earlier pieces the loops were not cut. These spreads are made in two ways:

1   As a woven cloth on a loom, the loops forming part of the weaving process.

Figure 85
Detail, crewelwork, late seventeenth to early eighteenth centuries, Indian, in the Museum of Fine Arts, Boston. 53.2202.
(Reproduced from *Historic Floral and Animal Designs for Embroiderers and Craftsmen*, Dover Pictorial Archive Series)

2 With the design embroidered using a thick cotton or roving (a thick twisted cotton thread), worked in running stitch leaving loops. There was a great assortment of designs composed from flowers, fruit, animals, etc.

Crewelwork

Embroidered spreads were worked in crewelwork on homespun linen, using long and short stitch, satin and stem stitches, and French knots, thus reflecting the stitches used in seventeenth- and eighteenth-century crewelwork in Europe. Many subjects were popular but floral motifs (*Figure 84*), birds and animals (*Figure 85*), were the most common. These motifs were either scattered all over the spread or took the form of the Tree of Life. There was often a floral border to the sides and foot of the spread. Most spreads were worked in many colours, but some were all in white using a great variety of stitches. The designs were generally lighter and more open than those in Britain. Another method, usually all in white, was the couching down of a hand-knotted thread.

Bed Rugs

Bed rugs were heavy bed covers and were very textured. The designs were on a very large scale with stylized flowers or foliage. The design filled the whole spread, which had a coarse homespun base. There was a variety of ways of working these bed rugs:

1 Several strands of thread were used together in either a looped running stitch or in rows of chain or stem stitch, the embroidery covering the whole ground.
2 The threads were hooked through the ground fabric to form loops. In some

examples strips of fabric have been used for this method.

3 Rags were stitched to the ground fabric in one of two ways. The first method involved cutting circles of fabric, folding them into quarters and stitching them by the centre to the backing fabric (*Figure 86*). The second method used strips of fabric folded in half lengthwise and gathered with a thread before being stitched to the ground fabric (*Figure 87*). These rugs were made for the bed and for the floor.

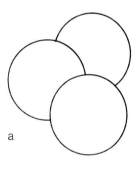

a

b

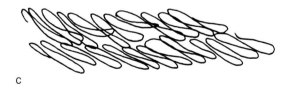

c

Figure 86
A method of making rag rugs and covers.
(*a*) Cut circles of fabric.
(*b*) Fasten a thread to the centre of each circle and stitch to the backing fabric in rows, as in (*c*).

Printed and Woven Spreads

Other types of spread were decorated with stencils on inexpensive cotton fabric. Stencils were also used on the walls and furniture. Spreads were also printed with floral 'chintz' or Tree of Life designs.

There were woven covers using three different methods:

1   Overshot designs – the weft skips over the warp to give a longer thread on the surface, forming geometric patterns.
2   Double weave – rather like two layers of fabric but as the design changes the warp and weft of one layer passes through the other, and the two layers change places. The reverse side is a counterchange image of the right side.

Figure 87
An alternative method for rag rugs and covers. Strips of folded fabric are gathered and sewn to a background.

3   Jacquard weave – the pattern is created by a series of punched cards which determine which of the warp threads are to be raised. Very intricate patterns and even detailed pictures can be woven.

Embroidery of the Eighteenth Century

The widespread interest in science and learning that began in the seventeenth century continued to grow and flourish in the eighteenth century. This was the age of Sir Christopher Wren (1632–1723), who prepared a plan for the re-building of the City of London after the Great Fire – his plan was not used, but his greatest achievement is St Paul's Cathedral; of Vanbrugh (1664–1726), who designed Blenheim Palace; of the four Adam brothers, one of whom, Robert, designed an area of London between Charing Cross and the Thames; and of Grinling Gibbons (1648–1721), probably the best-known woodcarver of his age, who worked with Wren on the choir of St Paul's Cathedral. Sir Joshua Reynolds (1723–92) became the first director of the Royal Academy of Art, the first art school, which set the pattern for many others.

A fashion for collecting developed, bringing people together to discuss their findings and the results of the study of their particular subject. George III was a keen botanist and like many amateurs collected stones, plants, eggs, etc. This interest in the natural sciences had a great influence on the naturalistic style of design of the eighteenth century.

Social gatherings were important because they provided the opportunity to display one's costume, to exchange news and gossip, to see others and to be seen. The popularity of the theatre, particularly the opera, encouraged

further use of textiles. The audience did not sit in the dark and politely watch the players on the stage. They ate, drank and generally joined in, the costume of the audience being as important as that on stage.

The eighteenth century was very much one of social 'one-upmanship': the need to be seen to display the very latest in fashion and manners. Spa towns developed as a result of the interest in the nature cure, encouraging travelling and adding to the social whirl. Whole households migrated to 'take the waters'.

Information and new ideas spread faster than ever before. The printing of magazines brought design sources and instruction to a very large section of the population. Ladies of the upper class learned to paint and draw, receiving tuition from the best artists of the time. They used flowers in particular in their embroidery designs, which accounts for the closeness to the originals.

After the ornate baroque style, the eighteenth century brought the rococo period which began in the Court of Louis XV (1710–74) in France and spread throughout Europe. The heavy baroque gave way to the use of pastel colours, with mirrors and lighter gilding. The continuing fashion for the display of sculpture within the home was supplemented with delicate porcelain figures. Thomas Chippendale (1718–79), introduced

exotic designs in furniture, hangings and curtains, mixing the influences of Chinese, Louis XV and Gothic. His book *The Gentleman and Cabinet Maker's Directory* (1754) was regarded as a landmark in furniture design.

With the arrival of the second half of the century the neo-classical style became the fashion – pure and simple compared with rococo. This style was partly influenced by the excavations at Herculanium and Pompeii, stimulating an interest in antiquity. Designs began to feature urns, classical figures, and festoons and swags of flowers. During the 1790s the Empire style came in, once again reflecting the taste of the French Court.

The Neo-Classical Period

A set of fourteen hangings was made for Newliston, West Lothian, Scotland, possibly when the house was redecorated in 1789. The hangings were designed by Robert Adam and were of painted felt applied to a cream woollen background with embroidery in silk threads. The design is of urns set on a table, with baskets of flowers suspended by chains, linked by trailing stems and ornamented medallions (*Figure 88*). A bed from the same house can be seen in the Georgian House in Edinburgh. The embroidery was worked in 1773 by Lady Mary Hog (née Maitland). It is somewhat unusual in that the dainty floral swags on a curving stem are applied felt, but many of the petals are anchored only at the centre of the flower, allowing them to be free of the pale yellow ground fabric. The rosebuds are stitched with short straight stitches to represent the hairy spikes, a very popular feature of the period. The work has a very light, naive feel and the edges of the spread and valances are bound with fabric. The present bedspread has been assembled from two surviving matching curtains.

Classical embroidered pictures were popular, mainly copied from engravings. Many were

Figure 88
Neo-Classical design from a hanging, late eighteenth century, English, designed by Robert Adam. Applied painted felt on a cream woollen background, with embroidery in coloured silks. (Newliston, West Lothian)

allusions to mourning, young women in classical dress gesturing towards a tomb (*Figure 89*). Alternatively the subject would be a pastoral scene set in the countryside as in so many of the paintings of the eighteenth century. Country houses were also depicted, as were portraits of royalty or contemporary personalities. Among the artists most frequently copied by the embroiderers were Nicholas Poussin (1594–1665), Francesco Zuccurelli (1702–88), Angelica Kauffmann (1741–1807), Francesco Bartolozzi (1727–1815) and Frances Wheatley (1747–1801).

Figure 89
Picture, classical scene, *Fame strewing flowers on Shakespeare's tomb*, late eighteenth century. English. Silk embroidery in coloured silks in long and short stitch, split stitch and stem stitches with speckling. Details painted in watercolour. 35 × 30 cm (14 × 12 in). 39–1874. (Victoria and Albert Museum, London)

Some of these pictures continued to be worked, as in the previous century, in black silk and were called printwork; a few were worked in human hair. A favourite subject was a ruined abbey or castle, or a portrait. When figures were included, the face and hands would be rendered in watercolour, as would the sky in a scene. Many pictures continued to be worked in coloured silks and chenilles in long and short stitch, split, stem and satin stitches and, as above, with the faces, hands and the sky painted with watercolour. However, raised stitchery was rarely used as in the seventeenth century. A great number of these small pictures were rendered on canvas in tent stitch in a similar style to the pictures of the seventeenth century. Cross stitch was used for larger items and upholstery. Geometric and abstract patterns were popular later in the century, particularly for use on furnishings such as settees and chairs.

The copying of oil paintings, known as needlepainting, was very common. The most well-known exponents were Miss Mary Knowles and Miss Mary Linwood, although one of the earliest was Miss Anne Morritt whose large collection of work can be seen at Rokeby Park, County Durham.

Much of the amateur embroidery was adapted, at later dates, for bed hangings, screens and covers. We know of them from letters, inventories and wills, but few examples survive compared with the quantity of needlework produced. Much was destroyed owing to the change in fashion for plain painted walls, or the later use of wallpapers. Wallpapers were handpainted for many of the larger houses. Orders were sent to China and exotic designs of flowers, trees, birds and animals were painted to fit the room, allowing for doors and windows.

MRS DELANY (1700–88)

Mrs Delany (née Granville) travelled throughout the country and had connections with the Court through her aunt, Lady Stanley, Maid of Honour to Queen Mary. She worked in many areas of crafts, embroidery and shellwork, and is most noted for her cut paper pictures. Mary Delany's greatest gift to us is the abundance of letters she wrote giving detailed information about every aspect of her life and times, as well as her craftwork. Her forthright comments on her contemporaries bear witness to the often ridiculous excesses of court life during the eighteenth century.

The letters were published in six volumes by Richard Bentley in 1861, in *The Life and Correspondence of Mary Granville, Mrs Delany*, edited by Lady Llanover. Her contemporaries called her a living library of knowledge, as she met most of the great men and women of her time and had first-hand experience of many historical events.

Mrs Delany was a friend of the Duchess of Portland, who was famous for her garden at Bulstrode. There she met many horticulturists, botanists and botanical artists of the time. She had drawing lessons from Hogarth, and her paper 'mosaicks', as she called them, won the praise of Sir Joshua Reynolds. These were cut paper renderings of botanically correct flowers and plants, so detailed that it is difficult to realize that each colour change is a different piece of paper; nothing has been painted in. Each picture is made up of hundreds of pieces of cut paper, and there are many, many pictures, now in the British Museum. These 'mosaicks' were much admired by King George III and Queen Charlotte, who formed an intimate friendship with her. In her later years, the King gave Mrs Delany a house at Windsor and a pension of £300 a year, which was delivered to her personally by the Queen, to avoid paying tax.

Mrs Delany obviously had a strong personality, often defying convention, and during her early life she experienced many changes of circumstance. The death of Queen Anne in 1714 had a great effect on the position of her family, who were Jacobite supporters. Her father, Colonel Granville, was arrested in 1715, but Mary and her sister Anne were saved from imprisonment by Lady Stanley. On Colonel Granville's release, late that year, the family moved to Buckland in Gloucestershire and lived quietly.

In 1717 Mary went to live at Longleat, the home of Lord Lansdowne, and was subsequently married against her will to Alexander Pendarves, MP, a man of sixty. Her family, and Lord Lansdowne, hoped to regain favour at Court through this marriage. Mary wrote: 'I was married with great pomp. Never was woe drest out in gayer colours, and when I was led to the altar, I wished from my soul I had been led, as Iphigenia, to be sacrificed'. She was taken to a bleak house, which had not been occupied for many years, in Cornwall. Her husband drank and gambled away his money, and had willed his estate to his family, excluding Mary. Towards the end of his life his health failed owing to his excesses and Mary nursed him. He realized how badly he had treated her and finally relented, saying he would alter his will but, adding insult to injury, died that night, in 1724.

Mary went to live with Lady Stanley and steadfastly refused many wealthy and titled suitors before finally marrying, against the wishes of her family, Dr Delany, an Irish clergyman and friend of Dean Swift. She lived happily with him at Delville, near Dublin, where she had the opportunity to cultivate her interest in gardening and craftwork. Dr Delany died in 1768 and Mary went to live with the Duchess of Portland at Bulstrode, where she decorated a shell grotto.

Mrs Delany first met King George III and Queen Charlotte in 1776. The first references to her paper 'mosaicks' also date from this year.

Her letters tell us that she had to give up making them in 1782, at the age of 82, owing to failing eyesight. She died in 1788.

Two additional accounts of her life have been written: *Mrs Delany*, by R. Brimley Johnson (Stanley Paul 1925), and a fully illustrated publication, *Mrs Delany, her Life and her Flowers* by Ruth Hayden, Collonade (British Museum Publications Ltd 1980).

Costume of the Eighteenth Century

Eighteenth-century costume, like the social life, was elaborate and exotic, with much decoration of all kinds, including embroidery in coloured silks and metal thread. The large areas of fabric presented by the extremely wide petticoats and skirts of the dresses lent themselves to exaggerated designs. Dresses were worn over extremely wide frames extending to each side, rather like a walking sideboard! We may consider them ridiculous, but they were just another display of wealth: one had to be able to afford two servants to open two doors to allow one through. In 1740 Mrs Delany describes a petticoat worn at Court as being 'of a design of brown hills with all sorts of weeds and twining flowers, and with an old tree stump running up to the waist'. She refers to another design as being 'much properer for the stucco staircase than the apparel for a lady'. Readers of her published letters will find endless humorous references such as these.

Much lace was worn, mostly bobbin-made, at the cuff and neck and as lappets hanging from the hair. The eighteenth century saw the peak of excellence for bobbin-made lace. Its fineness and beauty is breathtaking, and its manufacture took a long time. Lace was, therefore, extremely expensive. Smuggling was rife and highwaymen would demand lace as well as money and jewels.

Woven silks were dominant in the late seventeenth century and throughout the eighteenth century, but many of the accessories were embroidered. Ladies who could not afford the costly woven silks embroidered, or even hand-painted, their own copies. Examples exist of embroidered and hand-painted pieces which closely relate to the floral designs used for Spitalfields silk.

Men's coats and waistcoats were lavishly decorated. Some of the patterns on the silks were embroidered to shape and many examples exist that have never been made up. These examples show the fronts, pocket flaps and buttons embroidered to the shape of the garment. These prepared lengths could be purchased and taken to the tailor to be made up. Gentlemen wore coats and waistcoats of rich fabrics, sometimes with the design woven to the shape of the coat and often incorporating metal threads. Even the embroidered examples could be on a richly woven brocade ground or a cut velvet. The embroidered designs were mainly floral, worked in brightly coloured silks and metal threads (*Plate 7*). Some examples include satin stitch over little card shapes, giving a raised sharp edge. Waistcoats were made for use on special occasions; for example, a design of brightly coloured cockerels would be worn to a cock fight. Other examples were worked entirely in metal thread embroidery, with extensive use of plate and purls. Spangles – small metal discs of gold or silver – were used with metal thread and silk embroidery.

Early in the eighteenth century gentlemen's coats and waistcoats were long, with buttons and buttonholes down to the hem, even though they did not fasten. Gradually the coat was cut away at the front and the waistcoat became shorter until, by the 1790s, the coat front was cut right away and the waistcoat was waist-length and worn with a cummerbund.

Figure 90
Apron, early eighteenth century, English. Silk embroidered with coloured silks and metal thread. Edged with metal bobbin-made lace. T19–1940. (Victoria and Albert Museum, London)

As the century progressed, mechanized spinning and weaving brought woven patterned fabrics to a wider section of society and reduced the demand for professional embroidery. James Hargreaves, a weaver, invented a carding machine in 1760 and the spinning jenny in 1764, enabling several threads to be spun simultaneously by one person. In 1733, John Kay patented the flying shuttle, which speeded up the weaving process. The spinning jenny was improved in 1779, by Samuel Crompton, when he produced his spinning mule.

Aprons remained popular, being mostly of fine embroidered muslin and longer in length during the earlier part of the century, later giving way to shorter silk aprons embroidered richly with coloured silks and metal thread (*Figure 90*). The apron was part of the costume and equally rich in decoration. It formed part of the ritual when the lady of the house poured tea for her guests, tea still being a luxury.

By the eighteenth century, sleeves were set in, sewn from the inside on the lower half of the armhole and from the outside on the upper half; this gave the impression of narrow shoulders. The join was covered with decorative robings. The placing of the cuff was important, being at a different height with various trends, but always with a generous showing of lace undersleeves.

The sack-back dress took many forms during the century. Seven yards of fabric was used in the back pleating, allowing for constant re-modelling with the regular changes in fashion. The sack-back was essentially formal wear; a simpler princess style was used for normal wear. In the 1730s the gown was worn over a round

hoop, followed by an oblong hoop during the 1740s, and with sleeves above the elbow, finished with wide cuffs. Fan-shaped hoops came in during the 1750s. The 1760s brought an excess of decoration even on the rich fabrics. Gowns were embellished with a great variety of applied trimmings, gathered frayed edges, knotted edgings and fringes, metal laces, silk flowers, flounces and puffs. By the 1770s the mantua was formal court dress, worn with three frills above the elbow. The trimmings became even more important than the gown. After the 1770s fashion favoured the polonaise drape, held in place on the inside of the gown with tapes and adjusted to various lengths. This was often used to make upper-class ladies appear pastoral – the shepherdess or milkmaid look. Marie Antoinette actually had a dairy in the grounds at Fontainebleu, where she and her friends played at being milkmaids.

At the same time, painted silks which imitated the fashion for costly brocades became popular. Painted silk was imported, mostly from India, but enterprising ladies could paint their own.

Chiné silk was used, mostly floral motifs with the look of ikat, often set within stripes. In the technique of ikat the warp or the weft is tie-dyed before weaving. Chiné silk is produced by printing the pattern on the warp threads before the fabric is woven, giving the distinctive 'feathered' outline.

By the end of the century the Empire line was fashionable, with clinging see-through muslin dresses in tiny, delicate floral patterns leading to the production of sprigged muslin. Dresses at this time generally had detachable sleeves. During the morning the arm would be completely covered and the neckline filled with a chemise. For afternoon tea, the lower sleeve could be removed. Evening wear would allow the removal of the chemise to reveal a very low neckline. Some young ladies were known to dampen the muslin to make the dresses cling. The production of embroidered muslin is described in chapter 11.

English Silk Design

The Spitalfields workshops in London were the most notable in Britain. The designs were light and airy, mostly naturalistic floral designs, and were called Lutestring Silks. The workers were paid by piecework. The cheapest fabrics were the damasks (float weft) with the brocades (extra weft used only where the coloured design comes) being more expensive. These cost an extra 3d a yard if metal thread was included. Real gold or silver wire doubled the cost of the fabric.

A back-shoot brocade is where the coloured weft passes across the whole width of the fabric, a much less prestigious fabric than the eighteenth-century Spitalfields brocade. Many of the large patterns only allowed one repeat in the width of the fabric, but after 1742 patterns were lighter. The brocades included a damask background. On the design sheets the brocade area is shown in colour and the damask as a grey shape.

Probably the most well-known designer was Anna Maria Garthwaith, who was much influenced by the botanical artist Ehret. Her designs often included the magnolia and the auricula, and she also featured the aloe after a book of illustrations was published in 1739.

There were four main features of rococo design:

1   The asymmetrical botanical naturalism popular after 1743, following closely the illustrations of the time.
2   Hogarth's 'line of beauty', a serpentine line shown in the swathes of the brocades and damasks, echoed in the decorative robings on the gowns. It features as a vermicular line on embroidered quilts, called the Stormont pattern.
3   The use of rocai and shells as part of the structure of the design, echoed in costume, furnishings and architectural features (*Figure 91*).
4   The asymmetrical cartouche, referred to as the 'fire-shovel design', seen mostly in the large-scale weaving designs.

By the late 1740s and into the 1750s, block-printed fabrics were beginning to compete with weaves and embroidery, and the serpentine line became more angular, almost a zig-zag. Carnations, roses and rosebuds dominated. During the second half of the century damasks were popular, in very bright colours in Europe and pale colours in North America.

Calico printing was beginning to take over from woven patterns. They were imported from India and then copied in all the other major centres of production. Eventually France regained the monopoly of weaving prestigious fabrics.

Samplers

During the early years of the eighteenth century the fashion for embroidered cabinets, boxes and mirrors declined and there was a

trend toward more practical items. Embroidery became part of the school syllabus and samplers were more rectangular than the previous long, narrow shape. They were worked mostly on a woollen canvas with rows of letters, figures and formal motifs with verses, usually in cross or eyelet stitch. Houses and gardens became a feature. Some examples have a floral border in stem stitch and long and short stitch, or contain panels of florentine or rococo stitch.

Samplers became objects for display, and towards the end of the century map and almanac samplers were very popular, emphasizing the educational side of the exercise.

Canvaswork

In addition to the small pictures mentioned earlier in this chapter, canvaswork was used for chair seats and backs, wall hangings, carpets and fire screens. Hunting or pastoral scenes, classical, biblical or theatrical subjects were favoured for upholstery. Whereas during the seventeenth century figures would have appeared in contemporary dress, in the eighteenth century attempts were made to present them with more historical accuracy.

Figure 91
Detail, embroidered dress, *c.* 1740, English. Cream silk ground embroidered with coloured silks in long and short stitch, stem and satin stitches, with gold and silver metal thread laid and couched work over padding. T260–1969.
(Victoria and Albert Museum, London)

The upholstery was executed in cross or tent stitch in coloured wools and silks on a linen ground, often over a single thread in the pictorial area and over two threads outside the cartouche. Geometric designs were worked in a large cross stitch in combinations of wool alone or wool and silk together. Many varied designs were used for the tops of card tables, the most common depicting hands of cards laid out, or a game in progress with dice and counters.

Flowers played a prominent part in eighteenth-century designs. When used for canvaswork they retained the feel of the Chinese and Indian influences, but were not necessarily any longer in the form of a Tree of Life. Gradually the little hills disappeared. The flowers were placed in vases, bunches, garlands and festoons, or in cornucopias; the vases or bowls were often distinctly Chinese, in blue and white. Later the bowls or vases were placed on a black-and-white tiled floor, bringing in a Dutch influence. In addition to the flowers, areas of the design were divided by strapwork decorated with rococo shells. Embroidered carpets returned to fashion, with elaborate designs of large flowers and leaves.

Posing as a husband whose wife and daughters embroidered, Doctor Johnson wrote the following in an essay in 1758:

'We have twice as many fire-screens as chimneys, and three flourished quilts for every bed. Half the rooms are adorned with a kind of futile pictures, which imitate tapestry . . . boxes filled with garters and braided shoes . . . twenty covers for side-saddles embroidered with silver flowers . . . curtains wrought with gold in various figures.'

THE STOKE EDITH HANGINGS

Large embroidered hangings featured in many large houses. The Stoke Edith Hangings are now on display in Montacute House in Somerset. The three large hangings were originally made for Stoke Edith in Hertfordshire, where they hung until the house was destroyed by fire. They were eventually accepted by the Treasury in lieu of death duties in 1961. The hangings date from the early eighteenth century and are thought to be among the finest examples to have survived from the period. They have undergone conservation work by the Victoria and Albert Museum workshop.

One of the three hangings shows a design from Cleyn's illustration for Virgil's *Aeneid*, published by Ogilby in 1658. It depicts Aeneas and Achates confronted by Venus dressed as a huntress before Carthage. The hanging is worked in tent stitch.

The other two hangings accurately portray a formal garden scene, possibly in springtime, as the drawing has sharply defined shadows which are worked as solid dark areas. One hanging has a group of figures seated at a table wearing the costume of the first few years of the century. The artist has displayed a sense of humour, as the footman carrying the tray to the table has tripped over one of the many little dogs and is seen falling down the steps. Exotic birds and monkeys complete the scene. The second hanging has fewer figures, who appear towards the back of the scene. The hangings are worked in tent stitch but have additional surface stitching. The plants in the large Chinese-style pots in the foreground and the little dogs are worked in stem stitch used as a filling. The larger pots on each hanging are applied embroidered fabric with oriental designs. The hangings have at some time been mutilated – one can see where a slit has been cut to accommodate a door.

The three panels were at one time credited to the five successive wives of the second

Thomas Foley. He inherited the estate in 1737 and married his last wife in 1744. However, the panels are not mentioned in his very detailed household accounts, and one hanging shows the heraldic arms of the wife of the previous Thomas Foley (d.1737). The house was visited by Celia Fiennes on at least three occasions, but the hangings are not mentioned by her in any of the copious and detailed letters that she wrote. It is now thought that they were produced by a professional workshop in St Paul's churchyard between 1700 and 1737.

ANNE GRANT

A hanging at Monymusk in Aberdeenshire is signed *Anne Grant 1750*. It is worked in fine tent stitch in wools and silks, and measures 240 × 203 cm (7 ft 10½ in × 6 ft 8 in). This hanging is a very good example of the complete mixture of influences of the eighteenth century. Under three arches supported by columns wreathed in flowers are vases of flowers and a potted tree (Indian-style flowers in Chinese-style pots) standing on a black-and-white tiled floor (Dutch) against a yellow background.

LADY JULIA CALVERLEY
(1686–1736)

Lady Julia was the wife of Sir Walter Calverley of Esholt Hall, Yorkshire. She worked ten hangings, each of which measures 290 × 89 cm (9 ft 6 in × 35 in). As she completed them in only three-and-a-half years, one can assume she had access to some helping hands. The hangings are in tent stitch in wool and silk, with a cross stitch ground worked in thick white cotton (*Figure 92*). One hanging is inscribed *1717 Julia Calverley*. The designs, which vary slightly, are typical Tree of Life forms as used in the crewelwork hangings of the seventeenth century and they appear to be professionally drawn. The panels are mounted within rococo frames into the walls at Wallington Hall, Northumberland.

Lady Julia also worked a six-fold screen in tent stitch in silk and wool, showing scenes of country life, some of which are taken from Virgil's *Eclogues and Georgics*, illustrated by Francis Cleyn and published in 1654. The screen is signed *Julia Claverley 1727*. The style and use of rigid shading is reminiscent of seventeenth-century canvaswork.

Figure 92 (*opposite*)
Three canvaswork panels set into cartouches in the Needlework Room at Wallington Hall, c.1717, worked by Lady Julia Calverley. Wools on canvas in tent stitch. The design reflects the heavy Tree of Life style, used mostly for crewelwork in the late seventeenth century.
(By courtesy of Wallington Hall, National Trust)

Crewelwork

The heavy crewelwork of the seventeenth century gave way, in the eighteenth century, to more open, lighter designs (*Figure 93*). At first the Tree of Life form prevailed, but later designs had lighter leaves and fillings and far more space between.

Figure 93
Detail, fragment of crewelwork valance, eighteenth century. Possibly Indian for the European market.

Coloured worsted wool worked in chain stitch on a cotton and linen twill ground.
(Author's collection)

MARY HOLTE (1684–1759)

Mary was the daughter of Sir Charles Holte of Aston Hall near Birmingham and she is, by tradition, associated with six surviving pieces. Two canvaswork pieces form a pair, *c.* 1740, and are worked in tent stitch over one thread, and cross stitch over two threads, in fine wools on a white linen ground. The two hangings depict Aston Hall and Brereton Hall set within a central cartouche, surrounded by flowers, figures and foliage. Small scenes appear within ovals around the border, with two heraldic devices (*Figure 94*). These two hangings are the only pieces directly attributed to Mary Holte.

Three unfinished crewelwork hangings (1720–40) are in a similar, but lighter, style to those of the previous century, but the motifs are more isolated, containing some Chinese figures and houses. The embroidery was worked on a background of 45 cm (18 in) strips of linen joined together, two hangings of five strips and one of two, probably intended as bed hangings. There is no documentary evidence to suggest that these pieces are the work of Mary Holte.

A needlework carpet in canvaswork (1750–70), approx. 457.5 × 289.5 cm (15 ft × 9 ft 6 in) was also traditionally linked with Mary Holte but is now thought to be professional work. The central motif is of the

arms of the Holte family, surrounded by a floral border.

All six pieces are in Aston Hall, now in the care of the Birmingham City Council Museums and Art Gallery.

In 1775 Mary's great-niece married and, as the last of the Holtes, moved furniture, pictures, needlework hangings and a needlework carpet to Atherstone Hall in Warwickshire. In 1954 the hangings were at Morley Rectory. They were found to be extremely dirty and were washed in Lux – not the treatment one would consider nowadays!

Figure 94
Canvaswork panel, eighteenth century, English. Worked by Mary Holte. Cross stitch on linen. The central panel showing Aston Hall and the small oval panels around the border are worked over one thread. The remaining areas are worked over two threads.
(With the kind permission of Aston Hall, Birmingham City Council Museums and Art Gallery)

The crewelwork of the eighteenth century gradually became very naturalistic. Embroiderers were able to use the accurate botanical illustrations that were readily available for their design source. Much of the crewelwork on costume and small panels was worked in fine floss silks, the colours closely following the originals. Crewelwork was frequently combined with other techniques, as in the small pictures, often with chenille or with metal thread work on costume, aprons and bed covers. It featured on some of the splendid examples of flat quilted bed covers.

Needlepainting

A very popular form of crewelwork was needlepainting, the copying of oil paintings in worsted wools using the stitches to represent the brush strokes.

ANNE ELIZA MORRITT (1726–97)

Anne Morritt was one of the first of the needlepainters; forty-seven pieces, including forty-three needlepaintings, have survived and may be the complete collection of her work. There are, in addition to the needlepaintings, two etching pictures, a silk crewelwork spray and a colifichet. The collection can be seen at Rokeby Park, near Barnard Castle, County Durham.

On display is an oil painting of Anne Morritt working one of the pieces now hanging in the hall, *St Roneuld's Dream* (undated). The original painting is reputed to be in the Vatican in Rome. A needlework copy of Anne taken from this painting hangs on the first landing, set within an oval mount, measuring 66 × 57 cm (26 × 22½ in). The needlework frame at which Anne is working is still in the possession of the family. Many of the pieces are very large copies of complete paintings, but some are selected areas from larger paintings (*Figure 95*). There are numerous romantic landscapes that were popular at the time. Most have small groups of figures or shepherds and sheep against a wild background with ruined buildings. Among the artists that Anne copied are Zuccarelli, Poussin, Rubens and Salvator Rosa. One small piece is a portrait of her younger brother Bacon, from an original painting in the collection. However, the painting shows the young man with three curls in his hair, but the embroidery, measuring 24 × 19 cm (9½ × 7½ in) only has two.

The silk crewelwork spray of honeysuckle, moss roses and a poppy on a patterned woven silk background is thought to have been worked when Anne was twelve years old. The two etchings are of ruined buildings, *Dryberg Abbey* and *Window in Dunfermline Abbey*, and were also probably worked when she was a young girl. The former has watercolour details. The colifichet spray of rosebuds is worked in fine silks on paper or parchment and was one of the fashionable exercises of a young girl. More

details of this technique can be found at the end of this chapter.

In the boudoir at Rokeby there is a group of needlepaintings, each of which is a detail from an oil painting hanging in the same room. The painting is by Craddock and shows cocks, hens, ducks, pheasants and robins, as do two other paintings in the house by the same artist. One of the needlepaintings in this series shows a pheasant, another a mallard drake with ducklings. A third is of cocks, chickens and

Figure 95
Needlepainting, *The Head of Bacchus*, eighteenth century, worked by Anne Eliza Morritt. Coloured worsted wools on a twill ground.
(With the kind permission of Sir Andrew Morritt of Rokeby Park)

chicks, and a fourth is a tiny picture of two robins. All are dated 1756.

When listing the dated pictures in order, it would seem that Anne Morritt began by copying the pictures that were in the house, progressing later to copying more famous paintings and portraits. Many artists made reproductions of their paintings in the form of coloured engravings or etchings, which were widely available. The style of the needlework resembles that of Mary Knowles (see below), with large-scale stitches making it obvious that the picture is embroidered. The pieces are worked in worsted wools on a twill fabric.

Anne Morritt's needlework pictures are mentioned in articles written by various travellers. Arthur Young, in *A Six Month's Tour through the North of England* (1771) refers to her works as 'curious things . . . by a lady of most surprising genius'. *A Tour in Teesdale including Rokeby and its Environs*, a guide book of 1813, states 'The needlework, imitating paintings, rival in excellence with the celebrated productions of Miss Linwood . . .'. In fact, the style and scale do not compare with the pictures by Mary Linwood (see below), which are in fine wools and very small stitches.

Anne Morritt was the eldest child of Bacon Morritt and resided at one time in the Little House, part of the Treasurer's House in York. Her brother, J.S. Morritt, purchased Rokeby in 1769. After her father's death in 1775, Anne Morritt returned, with her unmarried sisters, to live at the Little House in York. A leaflet listing and describing all the embroideries in the collection is available from Rokeby Park, Barnard Castle, County Durham.

MARY KNOWLES (1733–1807)

Mary Knowles was one of the two most famous needlepainters of her time and is contemporary with Anne Morritt. However, many ladies are known to have done this kind of work. The work of Mary Knowles is very coarse, in worsted crewelwool, using large stitches which can be seen to be embroidery from some distance.

She was commissioned by Queen Charlotte to copy a portrait of George III by Zoffany, painted in 1771. This embroidered picture can be seen in the Victoria and Albert Museum. Mary then, in 1779, worked a portrait of herself embroidering the George III portrait by Zoffany; this piece is in the collection of Her Majesty Queen Elizabeth II.

MARY LINWOOD (1755–1845)

Mary Linwood was the most renowned of all the needlepainters. She had her very fine crewel wools especially dyed for her and she worked on a coarse linen ground that was specifically woven for her. In contrast to the work of Mary Knowles and Anne Morritt, that of Mary Linwood is fine and the stitches are very small. Even close to the work one can easily mistake it for a painting. There is a portrait of Napoleon I in the Victoria and Albert Museum. Some of her work is to be found in the City of Leicester Museum and Art Gallery, in particular, *Woodman in a Storm*, after Thomas Gainsborough. As the original painting was destroyed by fire, Mary's is the only accurate copy.

From 1809 to 1845 she had a permanent 'one-man' exhibition which opened in Savile House, London, and later moved to Leicester Square. There were sixty-four pictures and each was hung in its own elaborate setting. The exhibition was considered to be one of the

sights of London and Mary introduced gas lighting into the gallery so that it could remain open on winter afternoons.

Mary Linwood was well known and had royal patronage; Catherine of Russia offered to buy all the pictures in the exhibition, and Napoleon gave Mary the freedom of Paris. She considered her greatest masterpiece to be a copy of *Salvator Mundi* by Dolci and was offered, and refused, three thousand guineas for it. It was bequeathed to Queen Victoria. Other works included copies of the *Madonna della Sedia* by Raphael and the *Head of King Lear* by Reynolds.

Throughout her years of popularity Mary tried to get her work into the Royal Academy but was refused. However, she was awarded a medal by the Society for the Encouragement of Arts for her 'imitations of pictures in needlework'.

After her death the value of her work dropped dramatically. The fashion for needlepainting waned; people preferred actual paintings. The entire collection was offered to the British Museum, but they refused it.

In Samuel Boswell's *Life of Johnson*, Mary Knowles is referred to as 'the quaker, that works the sutile pictures', and A. F. Kendrick, writing in 1904 in his *English Embroidery*, says: 'Copies of oil paintings in woolwork, such as were produced by Miss Mary Linwood and Miss Knowles, . . . represent the climax of this mistaken art.' Throughout history people seem to decry the style or works of their immediate predecessors.

Quilting

Quilting has been used throughout the ages for warmth and protection but reached a zenith during the eighteenth century. It was a technique used by both amateur and professional needlewomen on the beautiful fine fabrics that were available. Records show that Grisel Bailey, bought 'quilting by the yard for her childrens clothing' and that she 'kept her early rising milkmaids working until nine at night quilting'. Quilting was popular on all items of clothing – bed covers, caps, petticoats, etc. During the eighteenth century there were four main types of quilting:

1 *Wadded quilting*, also known as English, miners' and Durham quilting. This form has two layers of fabric, the top fabric and the backing, with a layer of padding evenly dispersed between them. The design is stitched through all three layers using back or running stitch.
2 *Flat quilting* was worked mainly in the eighteenth century and had two layers of fabric without any padding. The most sumptuous examples are in silk satin backed with linen and quilted with metal thread with areas of coloured silk work in long and short stitch, split and satin stitches. Many of these examples are sets of bed covers, bolsters and pillows that would have been given as prestigious wedding gifts. These were usually professionally worked. There is, however, in the Victoria and Albert Museum, an example of amateur work by a lady who accompanied her Jacobite husband into the Tower of London and worked a set during his term of imprisonment. In some examples it is possible to see that the flat quilting was done first, as it clearly passes under the coloured embroidery. However, in others one can see that the quilting only reaches the edges of the coloured motifs. Many other examples exist – pillow covers and costume items, worked on two layers of linen. Although some are stitched in a white thread, many are sewn in a yellow silk thread, possibly in imitation of the metal thread. One of the most popular patterns for the background quilting was

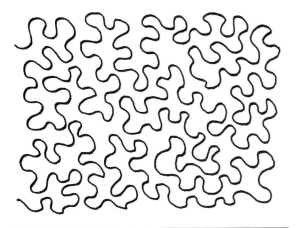

Figure 96
The vermicular line or Stormont pattern, popular for the ground of flat quilting in the eighteenth century. Also used extensively by Harriet Wyatt on her four nineteenth-century frontals.

the vermicular line or Stormont pattern (*Figure 96*).

3 *Corded, or Italian, quilting* has two layers of fabric which are stitched with patterns formed by parallel lines. Cord was threaded between as a padding. Some examples from the eighteenth century are incredibly fine.

4 *Stuffed quilting, or trapunto*, also has two layers of fabric which are stitched, but only selected areas are stuffed. Stuffed quilting was also combined with corded quilting.

During the eighteenth century both corded and stuffed quilting was used with pulled thread work. In addition to the items already mentioned, many fine examples of men's waistcoats have survived (*Figure 97*). Two layers of fabric, the top one of evenweave, are first stitched around the areas to be quilted and either corded or stuffed. Then the back layer of fabric is carefully cut away from the areas which are to be worked in pulled thread technique. This combination gives a beautifully rich surface with the contrast of the

raised areas and the openwork. Some larger items were made by lap quilting; that is, working on small lap-sized pieces which were then joined together.

Marcella, or Marseilles, quilting consists initially of two layers which are first corded or stuffed, then the whole is placed over a further layer of padding, and wadded, or English, quilted.

Knotting

Knotting began in the late seventeenth century and was known as 'frivolite', the forerunner of tatting. It was, however, at its most popular during the eighteenth century. A length of thread is tied with overhand knots along its length, close together or evenly spaced. By doing this with threads of various weights in string, linen, silk or wool, a lady could create her own 'novelty' threads. These were then couched onto a background to form a design,

Figure 97
Detail, pocket area of a man's waistcoat, eighteenth century, English. Corded quilting with pulled thread work in linen on a linen ground. EG M309. (Embroiderers' Guild, Hampton Court Palace)

or the threads were made into fringes. The knotting was worked with a shuttle, about twice the size of a tatting shuttle, often made of decorated ivory or gold and kept in an embroidered bag.

During the eighteenth century a lady could not be seen to do any work, but it was thought shameful to be seen to be idle. Knotting, embroidery and various forms of craftwork were considered acceptable. Knotting also gave a lady the opportunity to display the beauty of her hands.

In Cotehele House, near Plymouth, there is a set of chairs that are covered solidly in coloured knotting to a floral design. The threads have been knotted without any spaces between the knots. This set of chairs is referred to as being of Queen Anne tatting, presumably because the name 'frivolite' was also used for the craft of tatting.

Mrs Delany worked a coverlet in knotted thread. In one of her letters she writes, 'I am sorry I have no knotting of the sort you want done, I cannot promise too much for you till I have finished a plain fringe I am knotting to trim a blue and white linen bed I have just put up . . . send me the sized knotting you want.'

Parfilage or Drizzling

These are names given to a practice that began in early times, was prevalent in the Tudor era, and continued until the nineteenth century. Parfilage, or drizzling, was the unravelling and unpicking of gold and silver threads to be re-used or melted down for the value of the metal. Evidence of this practice can be found in many household bills and accounts.

During the eighteenth century drizzling became a popular pastime. Sets of ornamental tools, scissors, tweezers and a stiletto were carried at all times in decorated boxes or bags. The craze began in France at the Court of Louis XVI and came to England with the refugees after the French Revolution. At the height of its excess ladies would endeavour to strip as much 'bounty' as they could from the uniform or costume of their gentlemen dancing partners and, presumably, had great delight in comparing the spoils.

Colifichets

Colifichets are decorative embroideries worked on paper or parchment in fine floss silks in reversible satin stitch and long and short stitch. The designs are mostly vases or sprays of naturalistic flowers and romantic motifs. The technique became popular as a result of the custom of sending young ladies to France to finish their education. This form of embroidery was taught in finishing schools and particularly in convents. The examples were often framed between glass so that both sides can be seen, or they were used as bookmarks. Traquair House in Scotland contains three excellent examples of colifichets worked by early members of the family: two floral panels and a purse, which is rather unusual.

NINETEENTH-CENTURY EMBROIDERY TECHNIQUES

The embroidery techniques of Britain, Europe and North America progressed along very similar lines, differing mainly in the local variations of the designs used and the precise dates when they occurred. Styles and techniques were slightly later in reaching North America.

The nineteenth century brought the Industrial Revolution. In the 1880s steam and electricity allowed the mechanization of many processes. Ways were developed of manufacturing goods more quickly and cheaply, bringing them within the reach of a greater section of society.

It was also the age of class distinction. Whereas in earlier times rank was generally a matter of birth, the trading of the seventeenth and eighteenth centuries gave rise to a new merchant class that had bloomed into a wealthy upper middle class by the nineteenth century. This was a class of employers, both commercially and domestically, whose womenfolk were expected to spend their time in craftwork or charitable works. The poor continued to move from the country to try to find work in the towns, living in great poverty. Disease was rife and infant mortality was such

that losing a child was commonplace. Victorian families were, therefore, large. The social conditions and values of the time are reflected in the novels of Charles Dickens, and those of the middle class are represented in the works of Jane Austen and the Brontës.

It was a mark of affluence that a middle- or upper-class lady should be seen to have nothing to do; charity work and embroidery were among the few acceptable pastimes. Embroidery was produced in vast quantities, and used on every conceivable item.

There was much church restoration at this time, originally carried out by architects with no regard for the past, and many new churches were built. All this activity gave an impetus to a new generation of church embroidery.

The neo-classical influence of the eighteenth century continued into the early part of the nineteenth century, followed by a movement towards a Gothic revival during the 1840s. Designers and craftsmen looked back to medieval times as an example of excellence. The Society of Arts, which had been set up in 1754, established a system of examinations and public exhibitions with the aim of raising standards.

AUGUSTUS PUGIN (1812–52)

One of the prime personalities of the Gothic revival was Augustus Welby Northmore Pugin, the son of a French father and an English mother. He trained as an architect and between 1837 and 1843 assisted Sir Charles Barry with the interior designs for the Houses of Parliament. His designs were highly decorative, and he was responsible for training many of the masons and carvers. Pugin did much work for the Roman Catholic Church, a religion to which he converted in 1835, becoming a fervent follower. He married three times, fathering eight children, and had two broken engagements. His first two wives died young. He was a fanatical workaholic, producing an enormous amount during his short lifetime, which ended at the age of forty with insanity and religious mania.

In 1844 Pugin published his *Glossary of Ecclesiastical Ornament and Costume*. He designed many vestments, some of which were embroidered by a Mrs Powell of Hardman and Company in Birmingham. Examples can be found at St Mary's College, Oscott, Birmingham; St Chad's Cathedral, Birmingham; Westminster Cathedral, London; and St Peter's Church, Marlow, in Buckinghamshire. Pugin designed as a total concept – everything from the actual building to all its contents. His designs for the Houses of Parliament included most of the decorative features, even the coat hooks and letter racks. He also designed stained glass; six excellent examples are to be found in the windows of Bolton Abbey in Yorkshire. Sometimes his designs were altered during the building work; the Cathedral of St George, Southwark, and the church in Fern Street, Berkeley Square, in London, are examples. His work also includes St Chad's Cathedral in Birmingham, where his second wife is buried; Mount St Bernard, one of only a few new monasteries to be built; part of Alton Castle; and St Giles Cathedral, Cheadle, Cheshire. He also designed his own house, and St Augustine's Church, where he is buried, in Ramsgate in Kent.

Pugin's most acclaimed work was the Medieval Court at the Great Exhibition of 1851, which included pieces of furniture also of his design. A bookcase from this display is now in the Victoria and Albert Museum in London.

HARRIET WYATT (1832–1906)

The personalities and societies of the Arts and Crafts Movement are covered in chapter 12. Some talented amateur embroiderers were influenced by the Movement and also by the new wave of ideas coming from the Oxford Movement. One such lady was Harriet Wyatt.

The wife of a clergyman in the parish of Hawley in Sussex, Harriet was skilled at watercolour sketching, portrait painting and stone carving. Examples of her carving can be seen in the parish church at Hawley, on the font and capitals of the pillars. The deeply cut carvings depict wild flowers and foliage.

Harriet designed and worked four large embroidered altar frontals. She also worked a set of embroidered panels which were set into the altar at Hawley, but unfortunately these have disappeared. The designs for the frontals are all influenced by the paintings of Fra Angelico and by Italian mosaic patterns. All the frontals are worked in metal thread and coloured floss and twisted silks in laid and couched work, couching, long and short stitch and split stitch on a linen ground. The embroidery covers the entire area of each

Figure 98

(a) Frontal, embroidered by Harriet Wyatt, 1887, English. Laid and couched work in coloured silks and metal thread, with long and short stitch and split stitch.

(b) Detail of the superfrontal worked in the above techniques.

(c) Detail of the mosaic pattern covering the background.

(d) Border of stylized lilies.

frontal with no background fabric showing. All the main scenes are on padded areas and each superfrontal was made to extend forwards over a wooden bar to protect the raised areas. The superfrontals are all of deep red velvet, with applied embroidered diamond and circular medallions of laid work.

The first frontal was presented to Winchester Cathedral in 1887, having been begun in 1880. The main panel shows the

Transfiguration of Christ. This frontal has the most intricate of all the designs, the stitchery being rather finer than that on the later frontals (*Figure* 98). The main figures appear within a central quatrefoil, which is surrounded by eight circles containing the heads of James, John and Peter, four angels and, at the top, the Crown of Thorns. On either side are two quatrefoils with kneeling angels. Extending to either side of these are three circles, each one containing an angel playing a musical instrument. The remainder of the background is formed by a series of mosaic-like patterns.

The remaining three frontals are of a much simpler design. The second frontal was completed and presented to Chichester Cathedral in 1893. The central scene depicts the Resurrection, the figures appearing in a trefoil within a circle. The two outer panels show a multitude of angels within a cinquefoil. Between the three panels are vertical bands, each with a canopied panel containing an angel playing a musical instrument. During the 1930s the altar at Chichester was lengthened and two additional panels were added to the frontal. The frontal is no longer used, but can be seen on display in the Treasury.

The third frontal shows the Ascension of Christ in the main panel and was completed in 1897 for Christ Church, Oxford. The design is very similar to that of the Chichester frontal except that the outer panels of angels are enclosed in a quatrefoil.

The fourth frontal was presented to

Westminster Abbey in 1905 and is a second version of the Transfiguration of Christ. The main scene appears within a circle of seven arcs, being an almost faithful copy of Fra Angellico's *Transfiguration* in the San Marco in Florence. However, Harriet has substituted full-length figures for Elijah and Moses (*Plate 8*), whereas in the original only their heads appear, as in her interpretation on the Winchester frontal. The two outer scenes once again show a multitude of angels, and within the vertical bands are angels playing musical instruments. This frontal will soon be on display in a glass case within the Abbey.

Some of the frontals are being repaired and re-mounted, under the direction of the author, by one of the groups of workers in the Guild of St Faith's. The Guild of St Faith's consists of four groups of volunteer workers who maintain, restore and conserve the textiles of Westminster Abbey. One group undertakes work for other cathedrals. As Westminster Abbey, like many cathedrals, wishes to continue to use its textiles for many years, the methods used are different to those of museum conservation. Museums make safe and protect, knowing that the textile is to be managed and stored or displayed under controlled conditions. When a vestment or church furnishing is to continue to be used, steps have to be taken not only to protect and make safe, but to strengthen as well. Measures have to be introduced to ensure that future storage and handling are appropriate.

Design Sources

The nineteenth century saw the publication of numerous magazines and needlework books for amateurs, encouraging the vast amount of work that was done in a full range of techniques. Among the most popular magazines were the following:

The Englishwoman's Domestic Magazine, 1852–79.
The Young Ladies' Journal, 1864.
The Studio, Arts and Crafts, The Hobby Horse and *Weldons' Practical Needlework*, all 1893.
The Girl's Own Paper, 1880–1901.

Books included:

The Art of Needlework, from the Earliest Ages, the Countess of Wilton, 1844; the earliest history of embroidery to be written.

The Dictionary of Needlework, by Caulfield and Saward, 1882, now available as a reprint from Dover Publications, re-titled *Encyclopedia of Victorian Needlework*.

Needlework as Art, Lady Marion Alford, 1886, another early book on the history of embroidery.

A Book of Art Needlework, Ellen Masters, and *A Housewife's Treasury of Domestic Information*, Mrs Beeton, both published in the 1880s.

The Gentlewoman's Book of Art Needlework, Ellen Masters, 1892.

Decorative Needlework, May Morris, 1893.

Nature and Ornament, Lewis F. Day, 1896.

Embroidery or the Craft of the Needle, W. Paulson Townsend, 1899.

The illustrations of Kate Greenaway were also popular as a design source during the 1880s.

Many handicrafts were practised: knitting, crochet, tatting, knotting and netting. Magazines and periodicals contained a wide selection of patterns and instructions.

Berlin Wool Work

This form of canvaswork embroidery was so popular that some books published during the nineteenth century refer to it as 'embroidery', as if no other technique was worked. The concluding paragraph of A.F. Kendrick's *English Embroidery*, published in 1904, reads, 'Of the nineteenth century we must say very little. Taste during the earlier part of the century was not good.'

The following extract from a poem in *A History of Needlemaking* by M.T. Morrall (1852) reflects the thoughts of the long-suffering male who was on the receiving end of this mountain of embroidery:

I hate the name of German wool, in all its colours bright:
Of chairs and stools and fancywork, I hate the very sight:
The shawls and slippers that I've seen, the ottomans and bags
Sooner than wear a stitch on me, I'd walk the street in rags.

Ah! The misery of a working wife, with fancywork run wild,
And hands that never do aught else for husband or for child;
Our clothes are rent and minus strings, my house is in disorder,
And all because my lady wife has taken to embroider.

(For the full-length poem, see Appendix 1.)

This reaction to Berlin wool work is not surprising, as the Victorians used it on almost everything: carpets, sofas, cushions, pole screens, hand screens, bell pulls, waistcoats, slippers, braces, garters, bags, watch pockets, furnishings, mats and covers of all kinds. A pair of curtains in the Bowes Museum, Barnard Castle, County Durham, features a multitude of large plushwork flowers. Some very unsuitable designs were also used for church work.

Berlin wool work originated in Europe at the beginning of the nineteenth century, taking its name from Berlin where the first hand-coloured charts were produced by a printseller named Philipson. In 1810 a Madame Wittich, the wife of a Berlin printseller, persuaded her husband to produce them and he became the leading publisher. The early charts were exported to the whole of Europe, Britain and North America.

In 1831, a Mr Wilks opened a warehouse in Regent Street, London, and imported all the requirements for Berlin wool work. The charts were very expensive and after use could be returned to Mr Wilks and part-exchanged for new ones. By 1840 some 14,000 had been published. The charts were first printed in

black and white with symbols denoting the various colours. They were then delivered to outworkers who carefully hand-coloured each chart. The earlier examples show the use of many finely graded colours (*Figure* 99).

By the middle of the nineteenth century many countries were producing designs – England, France, Russia, Sweden, Denmark, the Netherlands, the United States of America, Australia and New Zealand. The quality of the designs gradually declined once the magazines were printing them in great number. Printed canvases were produced in the second half of the nineteenth century; an example was shown at the Great Exhibition of 1851.

The wool was a very soft merino wool, originally from Saxony sheep. It had a high bulk and only a little twist, being available in various weights. Eventually the wool was also produced in all the countries that produced designs. Shaded wools were available called 'partridge' or 'rainbow' wools. The early wools were dyed with natural dyes until, in 1856, William Perkin discovered and patented aniline chemical dyes. (The name comes from the Hindustan word *anil*, which means 'indigo'.) These bright colours became popularly known as 'gaslight' colours. The first colour was a purple known as 'Perkin's mauve', followed in 1860 by magenta. The ladies of the time used these new vivid colours with great enthusiasm, but not always with a great deal of taste. During the 1870s soft, faded colours returned to favour, in imitation of antique work.

There were two main types of design: pictorial subjects and floral sprays. Pictures were popular throughout the whole century and were often worked in both wool and silk, some examples including beads, metal thread and braid. Many subjects were religious or mythological, particularly during the first half of the century. The drawing was competent. Many examples of the early work are signed and dated. Other subjects reflected the popular

Figure 99
Hand-coloured Berlin wool work chart, early nineteenth century, German. Chart no. 2518 published by A. Todt of Berlin.
(Author's collection)

paintings of the period, romantic subjects which were given the name *style troubadour*. Scenes from the novels of Sir Walter Scott were often depicted, as were well-known artists like Landseer, whose *Chevy Chase* and *Bolton Abbey in the Olden Time* were much copied. Sometimes the chart-makers took liberties with the artist's work and would 'brighten it up' with colourful skies and vivid green foliage. Many animal studies were worked – dogs and cats on cushions, often royal pets. Even the Prince of Wales as a baby did not escape, and was shown playing on a tartan rug.

Floral subjects were worked throughout the period, though with decreasing taste as the century progressed. The early patterns tended to be on a small scale and delicately drawn. The examples that appeared in the magazines were less well designed and had limited colours, eventually developing into the

Figure 100
Tea-pot stand, Berlin wool work, after 1850s, English. Deep red cross stitch background in Berlin wool with design in grisaille work with silver, grey and white beads. Edged with French knitting. (Author's collection)

tasteless designs and subjects of the later work. Illustrations of birds were also used as a source of design, Audubon's *Birds of America* being a favourite. These were often considered an appropriate area for plushwork.

After 1850 charts were also designed for work in silk or glass beads, usually within a plain-coloured wool background of red or blue. Black backgrounds came in around the middle of the century. The beadwork was often worked in shades of silver, greys, white and black, known as grisaille work (*Figure 100*).

Figure 101
Canvas lace work. A modern example copied from a Berlin wool work sampler of the mid-nineteenth century, English, in the collection of the Victoria and Albert Museum.
(Author's collection)

The finest beads came from France. The larger beads, known as 'OP' beads, were first imported in 1853–54. The smaller beads were called 'pound beads' because they were sold by weight. Cruder, more inferior beads were made in Britain during the second half of the century.

During the 1840s there was a fashion for canvas lace work, imitating black lace. This was worked in two weights of thread in cross stitch over two threads of the canvas. A hole in the canvas falls between each cross giving the lace-like effect (*Figure 101*). Canvas lace work was used around the edge of small bags and on cushions, with patterned areas of coloured wool or silk.

By the 1860s–'70s, geometric patterns were used a great deal, especially on furnishing items. Patterns and motifs tessellated together to give an all-over pattern. Stripes formed of patterned bands and check or plaid designs were very popular for chair seats.

The needlewoman could purchase various types of canvas and, for small items, punched cards. Berlin or silk canvas came in black, white or pearl white and was very fine. The background did not have to be worked. German cotton canvas was the cheapest but its mesh is slightly rectangular, which can distort

the pattern. Every tenth thread is coloured yellow for ease of counting. French canvas has a very even square mesh. Penelope canvas has a double thread – it takes its name from the legend of Penelope who unravelled her work each night for three years to avoid choosing a suitor. 'Penelope' became a trade name in 1886. Embroidery was also worked on punched cards, popular in the 1870s. They can often be seen as mottoes hanging over a mantelpiece or bed, bearing the words 'Home Sweet Home' or 'Abide With Me'.

The stitches that predominated were tent stitch and cross stitch. Raised work was done in plush or velvet stitch, or in Victorian tufting (*Plate 9*). There are various accounts of how the tufting was done. One method, from *The Englishwoman's Domestic Magazine*, describes a stick with a reel of brass wire at either end, which is anchored to a weight. The end of the wool is then tied to the two ends of wire and held in the right hand and a round wooden gauge is used in the left. The wool is passed alternately under the right and left wire whilst rotating the gauge. This makes a fringe around the gauge which is combed after being cut free. This was then either sewn onto the canvas or used for three-dimensional wool flowers which would be displayed under a glass dome. The skill was to grade the colours required as the fringe was made. The second method was worked over a card or metal template. Layers of herringbone stitch in wool were worked over the templates and, on completion, cut through the centre, allowing the compressed layers of wool to open out. The template not only guided the worker with the shape of the motif, but prevented the canvas being cut when the stitching was complete. Velvet stitch was a third method. The finished piece of work with its flowers or birds was then taken back to the shop to be cut to shape professionally.

Berlin wool work began to decline in the 1870s and was almost totally overtaken in the 1880s by art needlework. Other types of cross stitch work became popular.

Cross Stitch and Counted Thread Techniques

Broderie russe or Russian embroidery is a cross-stitch technique with designs based on Russian patterns. The design is printed, rather like a transfer, on to a linen fabric in red, blue or yellow. The lines and dots show where to place the crosses and the colour to be used, so that there is no need to count threads.

French canvas embroidery is worked on a single thread canvas or evenweave fabric and embroidered in a thick white, ecru or red cotton in geometric blocks of counted satin stitch.

Another innovation was William Briggs's 'New Machine Perforated Batswing Cloth', a fabric perforated with various designs to be worked in cross stitch. The holes were only punched where the design appeared, unlike the punched cards which were a substitute for canvas.

Art Needlework and the Royal School of Art Needlework

Art needlework developed as a revival of the earlier crewelwork and also showed the influence of the Arts and Crafts Movement. It was worked in crewel wools and silks in soft colours. The designs were very naturalistic and unlike those of Berlin wool work which preceded it.

The technique was promoted and taught at the Royal School of Art Needlework, which was founded in 1872. The original aim of the school was to provide work for distressed gentlefolk. Work could be commissioned to be completed or just prepared. Embroiderers were not expected to design their own work. When the Royal School moved to new premises in 1875, Lady Marion Alford made a speech, which included the following statement: 'All embroidery should be as natural as possible, nothing should be left to the imagination of

the stitcher, each must copy the design which should be always placed in front of her.'

Many of the best designers of the time designed for the school – William Morris, Edward Burne-Jones and Lord Leighton among them. In 1875 a Higher School of Art was formed within the Royal School to train embroiderers, and G.F. Bodley taught drawing there. In 1906, sixteen students formed the Society of Certificated Embroideresses, which became the Embroiderers' Guild in 1920 with Louise Pesel as the first President. In 1876 the Royal School exhibited at the Centennial Exhibition in Philadelphia in the United States, and art needlework became the current fashion. Many ladies travelled to London to learn the technique, but branches and schools were soon founded all over the United States and Britain. In America art needlework was known as 'Kensington embroidery' and the use of rows of stem stitch as a filling was called 'Kensington stitch'.

By the end of the nineteenth century art needlework completely dominated embroidery. Other societies were formed with the same aims as the Royal School: the Ladies' Work Society (1875), the Decorative Needlework Society, the Wemyss Castle School (Scotland), the Donegal Industrial Fund (Ireland). The Ladies' Work Society embroidered the coronation robe for Queen Alexandra in 1902 and also that of Queen Mary in 1911.

The Leek Embroidery Society

The society was formed in 1879 by Elizabeth Wardle, the wife of Thomas Wardle, a silk printer and dyer in Leek, Staffordshire. It produced both domestic and church needlework. The main characteristic of Leek embroidery is that it was carried out on silk that had been specially printed for the purpose. The embroidery was worked in coloured silks

and often outlined in couched Japanese gold (*Figure 102*). The society produced church embroidery on damask fabrics and had many imitators.

Thirty-five ladies of the Leek Embroidery Society made a copy of the Bayeux tapestry in 1885–86. It then went on tour and was purchased by the Reading Museum and Art Gallery.

Leek embroidery was very popular but the printed silk grounds were expensive. Cheap printed cotton squares were substituted, some imported from India, which often featured the pine cone (*buta*) design. These were then used as a base for cotton or silk embroidery following the printed design. This substitute for Leek embroidery became known as 'Anglo-Indian embroidery'.

Transfers

Victorian ladies were also able to obtain designs in the form of commercially produced transfers. In 1874 letters patents were granted to John Briggs, Richard Hudson and Henry Grimshaw for the invention of the hot-iron transfer. These were marketed by William Briggs and Co. Ltd.

Chromo Embroidery

This was developed to allow those who were less able with a needle to achieve the technique of art needlework. The design was printed on paper with every stitch and colour indicated. The paper was tacked onto the background fabric and embroidered over, closely following the drawing. The paper remained under the worked embroidery and the surplus paper was removed from the edges. In the *Dictionary of Needlework*, first published in 1881, the editors, Caulfield and Saward, write:

Figure 102
Border, Leek embroidery, late nineteenth century, English. Embroidery in long and short stitch, stem and satin stitches with outlines of couched metal thread, on a ground of printed silk by Thomas Wardle. This design was also used by Wardle for a woven fabric. EG 5424.
(Embroiderers' Guild, Hampton Court Palace)

Chromo embroidery is especially useful to workers who are diffident about their powers of shading flowers and leaves naturally; the design being so close to the eye, they cannot fail to match the colours printed upon it, and by following it out, line by line, need be under no apprehension about the result.

Silk Spray Embroidery

Floral sprays, worked on fine muslin in highly glossy silks, were, on completion, glued on the reverse side to prevent fraying. They were then cut out and applied to items of costume.

Ribbons

Applied decoration to costume was very fashionable. It was possible to purchase all kinds of braids and ribbons from the haberdasher. Ribbons were woven using the Jacquard loom, with highly decorative floral patterns, known as Coventry ribbons. It was also the practice to embroider ribbons with silk, ribbonwork or chenille work. The ribbons could then be transferred from one dress to another.

Braids

Braids of many types and sizes could be purchased and couched down on costume items and accessories. They were also used to decorate curtains and furnishings. On some examples the braid is applied by machine, but amateur workers would stitch them on by hand. The designs were usually scrolls or scallops built into a pattern. The tapes used to make tape lace were also called braids. Their use is described in chapter 11.

Nineteenth-century Samplers

During the nineteenth century the sampler reverted to being a schoolroom exercise. Many survive showing motifs, verses and alphabets worked in a limited number of stitches. The verses were often concerned with mortality; death was a common occurrence in most families. One example from the sampler of a seven-year-old reads:

> And now my soul another year
> Of thy short life is past
> I cannot long continue here
> And this may be my last.

Some were in the form of a memorial, dedicating sad verses to lost parents. However, the Berlin wool work samplers fulfilled the original purpose as reference pieces for patterns and stitches. Worked on long narrow strips of canvas, woven for the use, they contain motifs, patterns and geometric designs. The sampler would have been rolled up and kept in the needlework box. Some examples are several feet long.

Three-dimensional Displays

In addition to the plush flowers and birds already mentioned, beads were threaded onto wire and manipulated into flower shapes and displayed under glass domes. Padded fruit and flowers made from velvet and linen were displayed in baskets, or around the base of potted plants. Green wool was knitted, pressed and then unravelled and arranged around the display to simulate grass.

Etching Embroidery

Originally called printwork, etching embroidery had been worked since the seventeenth century. The designs and pictures follow exactly the contemporary engravings of the time and were worked in straight stitches and seeding in black silk on a white silk ground which was sometimes tinted. Trees were often worked in French knots. Some examples exist that are worked in human hair. Nineteenth-century examples were also worked in muted colours on a fine cream wool.

Camera and Oleograph Work

Both these techniques featured a central pictorial area, usually a landscape or figures, surrounded by an embroidered garland of flowers. In camera work the picture was a specially prepared photograph with holes punched out around the edge, which were used to stitch it to the background fabric. This fabric would have a garland of flowers traced onto it, which the embroiderer would work in silks.

Oleograph work was similar, except that the picture was printed, in colour, directly on to the fabric, with the traced garland around the edge. In both cases only the garland was embroidered.

China Ribbon Embroidery

Continuing from the late eighteenth century, the China ribbon embroidery of the early

Figure 103
Nightdress case, *c.* 1840s, English. China ribbon work with details in coloured silks on a cream satin background.
(Author's collection)

nineteenth century was very delicate. Floral sprays were worked using narrow silk ribbons which, by the 1840s, were shaded from one side to the other. These ribbons were very soft and could be used in a needle in the same way as thread. Usually additional stitchery was worked in silk thread, perhaps for a stem. Sometimes slightly wider ribbons would be shaped into garlands or bows and applied to the surface (*Figure 103*). The work was mostly carried out on satin backed with muslin, and used for decorative items such as nightdress cases, pouches, blotters and writing cases. Watered silk was another favourite fabric.

The technique was revived in the 1880s in a slightly coarser form and was called 'rococo work', often with plain ribbons. The technique continued to be popular into the early years of the twentieth century. 'China ribbon work' is the term used when narrow silk ribbons are threaded through drawn thread borders.

Arrasene Embroidery

More commonly known as chenille work, this technique goes back to the seventeenth and eighteenth centuries. In the nineteenth century chenille was extensively used for ostentatious trimmings and tassels. However, by using a large needle it was possible either to stitch with it without stripping the pile, or to couch it down. The designs were mostly flowers and butterflies using stem and satin stitches, or couching (*Figure 104*).

The term 'arrasene' came into use in the nineteenth century. Some contemporary publications, including Caulfield and Saward's *Dictionary of Needlework*, make a distinction between arrasene and chenille work: arrasene is stitched, chenille work is couched. Other authors of the time do not make this distinction.

Feather and Jewel Work

Costume decoration was extremely popular with Victorian ladies. Jewelled and feathered decorations would be made on either net or buckram to be stitched to many items including hats, coats, dresses, picture frames and firescreens. The feathers were either white duck, which were dyed various colours, or pheasant, ostrich, pigeon, Guinea fowl and parrot. There was an enormous trade in exotic and rare feathers during the nineteenth century, causing the decline of many species.

Straw and Quill Work

Straw work was mostly carried out on net, the straw being used slightly damp to make it more pliable. The straw would be taken through a

hole in the net, bent back on itself and brought back through at the desired point. Sometimes whole net overdresses were worked in this way; the Hermitage Museum in Leningrad has some excellent examples. Used on a firmer fabric, the straw work technique is basically the same as using metal plate.

When quills were used instead of straw, the work was referred to as Canadian embroidery. Both quills and straws were also opened out flat, and intricate, decorative shapes were punched out, to be used as one would a sequin or bead. These could be purchased ready for use from haberdashers.

Breton Work

Breton work derived from the chain stitch decoration on the costume of Brittany in France. Worked in glossy silk, the chain stitch is used as a filling within a shape, spiralling around to exploit the shine of the silk. The technique was used extensively on costume during the 1870s–'80s. This was sometimes tamboured.

Figure 104
Collar, nineteenth century, Britain. Chenille embroidery on a dark blue satin.
(Embroiderers' Guild, Hampton Court Palace)

Fishscale Embroidery

The scales of perch, carp and goldfish were gathered, cleaned and sometimes tinted. Whilst still damp, a hole was made to one side to allow them to be stitched into place and the edges were cut to decorative patterns. The scales were then used to form petals for floral motifs, with details embroidered in silk threads. Flowers were built up by stitching the fish scales forming the outer layer of petals first, then gradually adding rows towards the centre, which could then be filled with French knots.

Patchwork, Quilting and Broderie Perse

The patchwork of the early nineteenth century was mostly traditional in design and technique. Later, rich velvets and embroidered silks were used, as were Coventry ribbons.

In the late 1870s pictures were worked in patchwork and appliqué. Crazy patchwork, also called appliqué, kaleidoscope and puzzle patchwork, was popular in the 1880s. Irregular pieces were joined and overlaid, often with embroidery covering the joins. The Log Cabin design was referred to as Canadian patchwork. Quilting, in all its forms, was worked throughout the century.

Broderie perse is the use of printed floral sprays cut out from cretonne or chintz, which are then appliquéd on to bedspreads and curtains. The edges are secured with either feather or open buttonhole stitch. Additional details are added with surface stitchery.

Smocking

Smocking is a technique designed to control the fullness of fabric. It was originally used for working clothes, especially the traditional smock. Dating from the middle of the eighteenth century, these garments were used by workers on the land, and there were many

regional patterns. The smocking was supplemented with feather and chain stitches.

Smocking was given an impetus during the nineteenth century by the introduction of sporting dress for ladies. This was the first time, except for riding, that ladies had less restricting clothes for the sports they were being allowed to take part in. Tennis was popular and smocking was used to control the extra fabric required. The Aesthetic Movement resulted in smocking being used on dresses, as the young women demanded freer, looser clothes.

The traditional smock was favoured by land girls during the First World War. Smocking was used extensively on children's clothes, often combined with feather and chain stitches and remaining popular until after the Second World War.

Ticking Work

This was bold embroidery worked on striped pillow ticking using surface stitches such as feather and herringbone, in very bright colours. Ribbons and braids were also applied. The technique was used to decorate garden chairs, bags and cushions. For small items, striped ribbons were used as a ground.

Machine Embroidery

The first attempt to patent a machine for embroidery was made in 1755 by C.F. Weisenthal. Many people were experimenting along similar lines and eventually the machine was perfected. Heilmann of Switzerland is generally recognized as the inventor of the first machine to execute embroidery. His patent was registered in London in 1829. The Metier à bras, Metier Swiss, or Handmachine, reproduced embroidery that imitated exactly work done by hand. The machine could also repeat motifs simultaneously throughout a length of fabric. It was operated by one worker

and was based on a pantograph. Throughout the length of the vertical frame, attached to the machine, were banks of needles. Each needle had a point at both ends and a hole in the centre, through which the thread passed. As the operator pointed to each position on the master design, the needles moved into position and pincers on either side of the fabric and frame passed the needles through the fabric.

When only one motif of the embroidery is examined, it is impossible to determine whether it has been worked by hand or machine. However, when more than one motif can be seen, the threads that pass across the reverse from one element to another are always positioned identically in machine work. A handworker would naturally vary the cross-over points of each motif. The machine was eventually developed to have 300 needles.

The House of Houldsworth imported twenty Heilmann Handmachines into England and had a monopoly on machine embroidery until 1875. By 1855, Houldsworth had developed the machine to produce a scalloped edge.

Designing for the machine became a skilled art, the object being to avoid wasting thread. The Government School of Design in Birmingham published a journal in 1859, listing the amount of thread required for certain moves on the machine.

Towards the end of the 1880s the Schiffli machine, also a Swiss invention (1863), began to be popular. It was used rather more for machine-embroidered lace than for embroidery. The Schiffli machine had a lock stitch with two threads, rather as our machines do today. This machine was mainly involved with the production of chemical lace (machine embroidery on a dissolvable background). The method used for manufacturing this lace is described in chapter 11.

The Cornely machine (1870s) was developed to imitate tambour work and produced a chain stitch. The pantograph was superseded by Jacquard punched cards around 1895. Modern commercial machine embroidery is produced by the multi-head machine, which is rather like several machines joined together.

WHITEWORK AND IMITATION LACES
OF THE EIGHTEENTH
AND NINETEENTH CENTURIES

Fine embroidery on muslin was an important feature of the eighteenth and nineteenth centuries. During the eighteenth century, it provided a substitute for the beautiful fine bobbin laces, which were at their height. They were also extremely expensive and available only to the very wealthy. The fashions of this period brought a demand for light sprigged muslin, which gave rise to an enormous industry to provide it.

Dresden or Tonder Work

During the second quarter of the eighteenth century there was a desire to make muslin look like lace, using embroidery. The main manufacture was in Denmark and Saxony. The finished items – fichus, collars, undersleeves and lappets – were distributed through dealers in Dresden.

The technique uses pulled thread fillings, sometimes combined with drawn thread, with surface stitchery or shadow work forming the 'solid' areas of the design. The finest examples closely resemble lace (*Figure 105*).

Efforts were made to promote the industry in Britain. The Anti-Gallican Society of England, the Dublin Society and the Select Society of Edinburgh offered prizes for the best imitations of Dresden work. Patterns also appeared in magazines to allow amateur ladies to copy the technique. In 1737 Mrs Delany, in one of her many letters, wrote thanking her sister for the 'handsomest and finest apron in England'.

In 1782 an Italian, Luigi Ruffini, came to Edinburgh to set up a school to teach Dresden work to children, bringing many examples of the work with him. The spinning and weaving of linen was carried out in Scotland, but eventually gave way to cotton, which produced even finer muslins. Muslin was imported in large quantities from India and North America to satisfy the enormous demand.

In addition to hand embroidery, the motifs were also tamboured. This is achieved with the use of a very fine, sharp hook which draws the thread through the muslin to form a chain stitch. The Dresden work and tamboured motifs of the sprigged muslin eventually gave way to Ayrshire work.

Ayrshire Work

The school set up by Luigi Ruffini was in constant financial difficulty. He initially had twenty apprentices aged between six and ten years, but as he took in more boarders conditions became insanitary and he was given a grant to move to larger premises. The

children produced sprigged muslin, the very young ones working spots and the older ones the sprays. They would sit twelve children to a frame.

The main industry thrived around Glasgow and Paisley, close to the centres of linen manufacture. Large 'warehouses' or workshops were set up for workers. However, Ruffini remained in Edinburgh, refusing to move, and eventually his enterprise failed completely. He was a very poor businessman. From 1825 the industry spread to other areas of Scotland, and five years later the north of Ireland was a serious competitor for trade.

The bulk of the work was carried out in the homes of outworkers at first. The 'webs', lengths of muslin and thread, were delivered and collected by travelling agents. Eventually, as the trade developed, some workers went to the warehouses to work, in addition to the multitude of outworkers. At the height of its popularity there were between twenty and thirty thousand workers producing Ayrshire work. Individual workers began

Figure 105
Fichu, eighteenth century, Saxony. Dresden work with pulled thread fillings and shadow work on fine muslin.
(Embroiderers' Guild, Hampton Court Palace)

to specialize in particular types of work – raised satin stitch, particular needlemade fillings, or openwork. A piece of work would then be passed from one worker to another to be completed.

In the early Ayrshire work, pulled and drawn fillings were used until, in 1814, Mrs Jamieson, an agent, saw a French christening robe with needlemade fillings. It took a little while for these new fillings to be accepted, but gradually they became dominant. On the very best examples of Ayrshire embroidery the

needlemade fillings are very varied; used with drawn, pulled and cut openwork (*Figure 106*). The quality of design was important and art schools in both Glasgow and Edinburgh set competitions and ran courses to raise standards.

Pay was very low and the work affected the eyesight, as workers had to sew from early morning until late evening. There are reports of them bathing their eyes in whisky to quicken the sight. Medical records of the time make frequent reference to the plight of the 'poor needlewomen'.

The workers were given printed patterns to follow, together with the materials. The early motifs of the 1820s were quite large and, until 1837, the patterns were printed with wood blocks. After that date they were lithographed. Amateur ladies could buy lengths of muslin, ready traced, from their haberdasher.

The demand for Ayrshire work was so great that a large quantity was worked in India for

Figure 106
Baby's gown, early nineteenth century, Scotland. Ayrshire work with needlemade and pulled thread fillings, eyelets, beading (tiny eyelets in rows) and padded satin stitch on a white cotton ground. (Embroiderers' Guild, Hampton Court Palace)

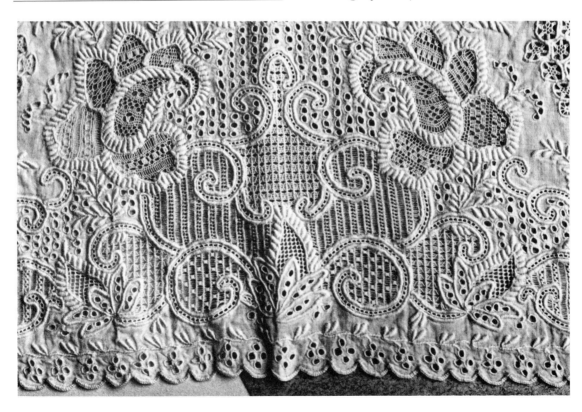

Figure 108
Broderie anglaise. Eyelets and overcast cut shapes with a buttonhole-stitched scalloped edge.

Figure 107
Double collar, 1840s–50s, Indian. Whitework on a fine muslin in imitation of Ayrshire work. One simple pulled thread filling and padded satin stitch. Compare with the variety of fillings on Figure 106. (Author's collection)

Civil War in North America cut off the supply of cotton, which severely affected the already declining production. Finally, a change in fashions in the 1870s, which demanded far less whitework, was the final nail in the coffin, and the industry faded rapidly.

import to Europe. The Indian substitute is very easy to identify as only one type of filling is used, at most in two sizes (*Figure 107*).

Ayrshire work was used for babies' robes, bonnets, ladies' collars and undersleeves. The trade began to wane around the middle of the nineteenth century. The Swiss embroidery machine, the Handmachine, was able to produce excellent imitations of Ayrshire work, and broderie anglaise was taking over from the hand work. Without the fillings it was quicker and cheaper to produce. The advent of the

Madeira Work

One form of Ayrshire work was taken to Madeira in the middle of the century. A Mrs Phelps went there to teach the women to enable them to earn a living after their usual income was lost owing to a vine fungus. The embroidery was done mainly in ecru and blue with very few, if any, fillings and it resembled broderie anglaise and cutwork rather than Ayrshire work.

Broderie Anglaise

The early examples of broderie anglaise in the mid-nineteenth century were finely worked and the designs were composed entirely of

oversewn holes. Gradually satin stitch and trailing was introduced as part of the design (*Figure 108*). As the century progressed some work became large and clumsy, partly due to the production of lengths of cotton fabric already punched with holes and ready to work. By the time the embroidery was carried out the holes were very large and misshapen.

Broderie anglaise was used for petticoat flounces, collars, undersleeves, nightwear and babies' clothes. It continued to be popular well into the twentieth century, as were the various forms of cutwork.

Fisherton-de-la-Mere

The Fisherton-de-la-Mere industry was established in Wiltshire by Mrs Arthur Newall. Her husband had a collection of Italian examples of double-sided cross stitch which stimulated her interest, together with some examples of Italian whitework that she saw. She went on to collect samplers and books on embroidery, and to study English examples of sixteenth- and seventeenth-century whitework. In 1890, Mrs Newall began teaching all forms of whitework, including both pulled and drawn thread work, the latter a revival of reticella, adapting the older designs to her own style. The finished pieces, mostly household linen, were sold.

In 1902 Mrs Newall moved to Fisherton-de-la-Mere and took the name for her industry. She worked in conjunction with the Wiltshire Arts and Crafts Society and, in 1907, joined with the Home Arts and Industries Association. The work of her students won many prizes and was regarded as exceptional.

Mrs Newall preferred to use hand-spun and hand-woven linen, the machine-made fabric being too regular for her liking. She used fabric of English manufacture when possible, but had to resort to Russian and Chinese sources to supplement the supply.

Greek Lace or Ruskin Work

This technique was a revival of reticella, but worked in cut squares rather than in its original form (see chapter 7). Threads were cut from the linen, leaving a structure of pairs or groups of threads within the square. These remaining threads were then whipped or needlewoven together, giving a framework on which patterns could be built up with blocks of buttonhole stitch (*Figure 109*).

The revival began in Langdale in the Lake District around the time that the Home Arts and Industries Association was being set up. Mrs Pepper, a follower of John Ruskin, was a weaver of linen, which she then embroidered. Her designs were based on Italian and Greek island sources, hence the name 'Greek lace'. Mrs Pepper taught the technique to local people, working closely with Albert Flemming, a friend of Ruskin. The technique was widely used, not only by other industries and workshops, but also by amateur ladies. Many

Figure 109
Greek lace or Ruskin work, nineteenth century, English. A revival based on reticella. Cut and drawn square worked in buttonhole stitch with an edging of bobbin-made lace. Typical of the patterns given in periodicals for amateur needlewomen. (Author's collection)

Figure 110
Detail from a bonnet veil, 1830s, Ireland.
Carrickmacross embroidery, lawn on a hexagonal
net with a couched outline and needlerun fillings.
(Author's collection)

manuals and magazines carried instructions for
various household items.

Machine-made Net

The invention of a machine that could make
net led to many forms of imitation lace being
developed. The first machine for making net
was developed in 1795, but it was John
Heathcoat's bobbin net machine, patented in
1808–9, that was the first great leap. It had two
advantages; it could be adapted to be power
driven, and it could use cotton thread.

The ability to produce net cheaply and in
quantity led to the development of
Carrickmacross, Limerick and Coggeshall
laces, all of which were shown at the Great
Exhibition of 1851. It also facilitated many
forms of appliqué on net, applied laces,
needlerun nets and machine-embroidered
laces.

Carrickmacross

Carrickmacross is a form of appliqué on a
hexagonal net ground. A layer of muslin or
lawn, on which the design is traced, is
mounted on top of a layer of net. The design
outlines are then couched closely with a thread
through both layers. The outline is always
couched in Carrickmacross technique. Any
other form, such as buttonhole stitch or a
tamboured outline, is simply appliqué on net.
When the couching is complete, the top layer
of lawn is carefully cut away revealing the net

underneath. The areas of net can then be
decorated with needlerun patterns (*Figure
110*). On some examples the net is also cut
away and bars or brides are worked, as in
cutwork. The original form of Carrickmacross
was a guipure, a single layer of lawn without
the net. After couching the outlines of the
design, the cut areas are connected with bars or
brides.

The technique was introduced to
Carrickmacross, in Ireland, in 1820 by Mrs
Grey Porter, and pre-dates Limerick lace.
However, the commercial production of the
lace dates from the potato famine in 1846.
Many items were made – collars,
handkerchiefs, stoles, undersleeves, bonnet
veils, and small decorative household items.

By the 1860s the standard of design and
workmanship was declining. This trend was
then followed by an improvement in design
due to the intervention of the Bath and Shirley

Estate School, only to finally decline again in the 1890s.

Limerick

Limerick lace was originally worked on a net with a diamond-shaped mesh. The embroidered design was formed by a needlerun outline with needlerun patterned fillings (*Figure 111*). The outline was usually worked in a slightly heavier thread, but many surviving examples have a tamboured outline.

The Limerick industry was set up in 1829 by an Englishman, Charles Walker, who married the daughter of a manufacturer of machine-made net from Essex. Twenty-four English workers taught the local women and in 1851 the Ladies Industrial Society showed their work at the Great Exhibition. Items made included collars, handkerchiefs, stoles, undersleeves and bonnet veils.

There was a decline in the 1860s, but designs improved during the 1880s and 1890s. The secular industry was taken over in the late 1880s by Mrs Vera O'Brien.

Coggeshall

This type of embroidery on net developed around Coggeshall in Essex, and was brought to the area by a Frenchman and his two daughters between 1810 and 1823.

Children were taught to do the work. They were paid very little – threepence rising to three shillings and sixpence after five years. The industry reached its peak by the middle of the nineteenth century, followed by a gradual decline due to changing fashions. The industry continued, in spite of the decline, into the 1930s, coming to an end finally with the Second World War.

Coggeshall lace is worked on an hexagonal net with a tamboured outline and decorative needlerun fillings. The designs are mostly wildflower sprays and sprigs. Some large pieces were made for overdresses.

Tape Lace

To imitate the meandering bobbin laces that had been popular, ladies could purchase woven decorative tapes. Various patterns and magazines printed patterns for this 'point lace' and ready-traced items on a coloured glazed cotton could be purchased. The tapes were tacked on to the backing fabric following the

Figure 111
Detail from a stole, early 1830s, Ireland. Limerick embroidery, needlerun outlines and fillings on a diamond-shaped net.
(Author's collection)

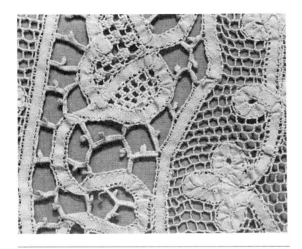

Figure 112
Detail, tape lace table runner, second half of the nineteenth century, English or Italian. Machine-woven tape laid with needlemade fillings. Note how the tape has been gathered to shape. A bobbin-made tape would be worked to shape on the pillow. (Author's collection)

traced design. The tapes were then connected, without stitching through the backing, by bars or with needlemade fillings, as indicated by the pattern. When the tapes were released by cutting the tacking stitches from the reverse side of the backing, the lace could be lifted (*Figure 112*). Collars, undersleeves, handkerchiefs, tablemats and runners were among the range of items made.

Chemical Lace

This is a form of machine embroidery that is worked on a dissolvable background. Chemical lace was usually made on a Schiffli machine with a loop stitch using two threads. It is very easy to identify because the stitches are somewhat rough. The first experiments were with a paper backing, but the paper was too difficult to remove. The main method was to use a backing of animal fibres, silk or wool.

After the machine embroidery was completed the backing was dissolved with caustic soda or potash. Care was taken to use a thread of vegetable fibre (cotton), which was not affected by the chemicals. Alternatively, if the backing was of a vegetable fibre, it had to be steamed or burned away. The thread used for the embroidery would have to be treated in advance to prevent it from disappearing too.

Crochet, Tatting and Knitting

Both crochet and knitting are formed by making loops, the former with a hook and the latter with knitting needles. Crochet came to prominence in the nineteenth century as a lace substitute. Many magazines produced patterns for the amateur craftswoman. Very theatrical heavy laces were produced to display on the wide-sleeved dresses. The copying and re-assembling of Venetian needlemade laces, already described in chapter 7, were also reproduced in crochet. Irish crochet was extremely popular. Raised motifs and layers of petals were assembled as part of the process.

Tatting was worked from the eighteenth century, and is a form of knotting. It was possible to produce motifs consisting of rings and bars, usually decorated with picots. A small shuttle is used to contain the working thread, together with a second thread from the spool or ball.

Knitting took over from needlebinding in the sixteenth century, and the invention of the warp hosiery frame in 1589 speeded up production. By the late seventeenth century these frames were being used to produce lacy fabrics. During the eighteenth and nineteenth centuries beautiful little bead bags were knitted. Beads were threaded onto the yarn using a chart as a guide. The yarn was then knitted in the round and, if the beads had been carefully counted, the pattern would emerge.

All three techniques have continued into the twentieth century.

THE INFLUENCE OF THE ARTS AND CRAFTS MOVEMENT

The roots of the Arts and Crafts Movement lay in the earlier work of the Gothic revivalist Pugin and in the reaction to the Great Exhibition of 1851. The exhibition was the first great international trade fair and, although Britain led the world in technology, the standard of design caused much concern. When compared with the European exhibitors – the French in particular – the British standard was found to be lacking.

The embroidery on display at the exhibition reflected the popular fashions of the time. The exhibits included a collar worked by an Irish peasant, three pieces of patchwork worked by men, a black silk rendering of Lincoln Cathedral, and a large amount of Berlin wool work. Machine embroidery by the firm of Henry Houldsworth was also shown.

The one area of excellence within the British exhibits was the Medieval Court designed by Pugin. His influence was felt in the work of later architects and designers, such as G.F. Bodley and Sir Ninian Comper. One of the pieces that Pugin designed for the exhibition was a bookcase, now on display in the Victoria and Albert Museum. The Gothic revival continued to thrive during the 1850s.

As a result of the realization that something needed to be done about the standard of design, a committee was set up which gave rise to the forerunner of the Victoria and Albert Museum. It was first based in Marlborough House, and then moved to the South Kensington Museum in 1857. The Society of Arts established a system of examinations and exhibitions in 1855 to help raise standards, as did many other societies later in the nineteenth century.

GEORGE EDWARD STREET
(1824–81)

George Edward Street was to the Church of England what Pugin was to the Roman Catholic Church. He, like Pugin, was an architect who looked back to medieval times and forms as an example of excellence. Like all the main architects of this era, he designed more than just the building. He also designed the interior decoration, furnishings, fittings and textiles – the whole project as a total concept.

George Street's sister and her friend, Miss Agnes Blencowe, embroidered the designs that he produced and, in 1854, they formed the Ladies Ecclesiastical Embroidery Society. The society's stated aim was to produce ecclesiastical embroidery based on ancient examples, under the supervision of an architect. The ladies involved gave their time freely and customers paid only for the materials used. In 1863 the Ladies Ecclesiastical Embroidery Society combined with the Wantage Church Needlework Association, formed by the religious Sisters and friends of St Mary's House, Wantage.

GEORGE FREDERICK BODLEY
(1827–1907)

G.F. Bodley, an architect, worked with George Edward Street and knew both his sister and Miss Blencowe. Bodley designed embroidery and vestments for his own churches, for the Ladies Ecclesiastical Embroidery Society and for Morris, Marshall and Faulkner. His figures and floral forms were very naturalistic, based on medieval forms. In 1870 he formed the firm of Watts and Company, who are still church furnishers today. After his death, Cecil G. Hare became the chief designer. Bodley also taught drawing at the Royal School of Art Needlework.

Among the surviving pieces of his work are three frontals in Liverpool Anglican Cathedral. The embroidery was worked by the Cathedral Embroidery Association. The white

Figure 113
Panel from a frontal designed by G.F. Bodley, late nineteenth century, English. Padded couched metal thread work and spangles on a ground of deep red velvet.
(Chichester Cathedral)

festal frontal has a figure of Christ in the centre within a rectangle, with saints on either side supported by foliated branches. Beside these are two smaller rectangles containing figures. The rectangles are divided by vertical bands, each with three circles containing angels. The red frontal has three foliated roundels, the central one showing the Agnus Dei and those on either side containing figures with inscriptions.

Chichester Cathedral has a red frontal designed by Bodley, which is on display in the cathedral. There are seven panels, alternating velvet and damask, with rich padded metal thread embroidery with spangles, the design featuring fleurs-de-lys and pomegranates (*Figure 113*).

During the 1870s many firms of church furnishers and ladies' societies were formed, the latter often established to provide work for 'distressed gentlewomen'. It was not acceptable for a young lady from a good family, however penniless, to work in a position beneath her, but she could produce needlework anonymously within a philanthropic society. The Ladies' Work Society was linked with the Royal School of Art Needlework in 1875 and

carried out 'conservation', which, to them, meant re-making old embroideries into new items. Other societies included, in England, the Decorative Needlework Society (1880), which repaired old embroideries. In Scotland, the Wemymss Castle School was founded by Lady Lilian Wemymss in the East Fife area and, in Ireland, the Donegal Industrial Fund was established in 1883, its designs reflecting Celtic sources with much interlacing.

WILLIAM MORRIS
(1834–96)

William Morris is probably the best-known personality of the Arts and Crafts Movement. He originally intended to enter the Church. However, at Oxford he met Edward Burne-Jones and decided to work in the area of the arts instead. Morris worked in the architectural office of George Edward Street in Oxford. There he met Miss Street, Miss Blencowe and G.F. Bodley, as well as Philip Webb, an architect who later designed Morris's first home, the Red House in Bexleyheath. He became interested in embroidery, learning by looking at historical pieces and unpicking old examples.

Morris had a frame made, and worsted threads spun and dyed, and worked an embroidery which now hangs in Kelmscott Manor. The embroidery completely covers the

background, a characteristic of his work, possibly reflecting the influence of medieval tapestries. The design is a repeat pattern of stylized trees on a ground of yellow wool, with scrolls containing the inscription *If I Can* (*Figure 114*). This is the only piece known to have actually been worked by Morris. Many of his embroidered designs closely resemble the repeating pattern of woven fabrics.

William Morris designed for the Royal School of Art Needlework, as did Edward Burne-Jones, G.F. Bodley, Selwyn Image and Walter Crane. Catherine Holiday, wife of Henry George Alexander Holiday, interpreted many of his embroidery designs.

Morris married Jane Burden in 1859, and taught her and their two daughters to embroider. They embroidered the crewelwork

Figure 114
Motifs from embroideries by William Morris.
(a) *If I Can* hanging, c. 1857. Crewel wools on
   linen. The embroidery covers the whole
   background. Trees with raised fruit, birds and a
   motto form a repeating all-over pattern with a
   yellow ground.
(b) *Sunflower* hanging, c. 1860. Laid and couched
   cream and brown wools on a fawn woollen
   ground.
(c) *Daisy* hangings, c. 1860, from the Red House,
   Bexleyheath. The design is based on flowers from
   fifteenth-century tapestries. Laid and couched
   red, cream and beige wools on a blue serge
   woollen ground.
(Kelmscott Manor)

a

b

c

bed at Kelmscott. The curtains show a central
flowering tree against a trellis, with other
trailing foliage and birds. The valance contains
a verse punctuated with small foliated motifs.

Morris disliked all things made by machine,
believing in the simplicity and purity of
craftsmanship. He wanted everyone to have
handmade articles in their home, but this was,
of course, an unrealistic aim because of the
cost. He formed the company of Morris,
Marshall and Faulkner in 1861, producing
furniture, carving, paintings, metalwork,
tapestries and embroidery. The work was all
done by hand and, therefore, remained out of
the reach of most people. Morris was obsessed
with the work of the past and much of his
design has the feel of the medieval tapestries.

He set up his second firm, Morris and Co.,
in 1875, and later investigated natural dyes
with the help of Thomas Wardle, the silk
printer and dyer. In 1881 Morris acquired the
Merton Abbey Tapestry Works and began
printing fabrics. In 1885 his daughter May
became head of the embroidery workshops of
Morris, Marshall and Faulkner, and J.N.
Dearle became the chief designer. By 1885
Morris was on the committee of the Arts and
Crafts Exhibition Society, which was formed
because of the refusal of the Royal Academy to
allow the work of the Arts and Crafts artists to
be exhibited. Other members of the society
included Walter Crane and Lewis F. Day. The
Society was, eventually, allowed to exhibit at
the Royal Academy in 1916.

EDWARD BURNE-JONES
(1833–98)

Edward Burne-Jones designed many large hangings for the firm of Morris, Marshall and Faulkner and for Morris and Co. William Morris realized that his own drawing of figures was not good and Burne-Jones drew figures to Morris's direction. Burne-Jones also designed for the Royal School of Art Needlework.

One of his tapestries, *Angeli Laudantes* (1896) was taken from a design for a stained-glass window in Salisbury Cathedral. It shows two angels amid a background of many flowers, set within a border of flowers, fruit and leaves. This is a particularly good example of the reflection of the style of the early millefleur tapestries. This piece, and some early embroideries executed by his wife, are in the collection of the Victoria and Albert Museum.

LEWIS F. DAY
(1845–1910)

Lewis Day was a writer and lecturer on design, both at the Royal Society for Arts and the Royal College of Art. He also designed textiles, wallpapers, stained glass and embroidery. He was an acknowledged authority on the history of ornament. Day criticized the elaborate designs of Edward Burne-Jones and Walter Crane, preferring simple lines. He was a founder member of the Arts and Crafts Exhibition Society. His books include the following:

The Planning of Ornament, Batsford, 1887.
Art in Needlework, Batsford, 1901.
Pattern Design, Batsford, 1903 and 1979.
Alphabets Old and New, Batsford, 1910.
Nature and Ornament, volumes I and II, Batsford, 1908.

SELWYN IMAGE
(1849–1930)

Selwyn Image was an artist and designer who studied under John Ruskin at Oxford. He first became a priest but resigned in 1883. Image designed stained glass and was a founder member of the Century Guild. He designed embroidery for the Royal School of Art Needlework.

LIBERTY AND CO.

Founded in 1875 by Arthur Lasenby Liberty, the shop originally specialized in imported goods from the East, reflecting the popularity of the Japanese influence. When the fashion waned, Liberty's went on to produce a range of printed textiles known as 'Liberty Art Fabrics'.

They also sold a range of furniture, silver and jewellery.

The soft draping quality of the printed silk fabrics made them popular with the young ladies of the Aesthetic Movement. Thomas Wardle produced printed silks for Liberty in

rich, muted colours reflecting the taste of the time. In 1887, Arthur Silver created the original 'Peacock Feather' design. A branch of the store was opened in Paris in 1890. The

famous small floral prints originated in the 1930s, with the 1950s bringing a revival of Art Nouveau.

SIR NINIAN COMPER
(1864–1960)

Born in Aberdeen, the son of a clergyman who was closely involved with the Oxford Movement, Ninian Comper learned to draw at the Aberdeen School of Art and spent one term at the Ruskin School at Oxford. He completed his training at the South Kensington School of Art. He entered G.F. Bodley's office to train as an architect in 1883 and in 1888 joined in partnership with William Bucknall. In 1890 Comper married Bucknall's sister Grace.

Comper designed for embroidery, church furnishings and painted glass. He was influenced by the styles of Botticelli and Fra Angelico. He shared with Pugin the dubious honour of being plagiarized, particularly by the Warham Guild, which was founded by Canon Percy Dearmer. In addition to designing new buildings, Comper restored many churches. St Margaret's, Braemar, is considered to be his best restoration.

In 1905 the partnership came to an end and, a year later, Comper travelled in Europe. He had a special method of making painted glass which gave a blue tint to the windows. From 1909 until his death he worked on a series of windows with abbots and kings for the north aisle in Westminster Abbey.

One of Comper's patrons, a banker named Birkbeck, brought back to this country a vestment of Russian cloth of gold, used at the Coronation of the Czar. Comper made it into a cope which was worn by the Bishop of Norwich at the Coronation of Edward VII in 1902. The

hood included a scene of the Annunciation which was embroidered by the Sisters of Bethany, who worked many of Comper's designs.

Most of Comper's designs contain a circle and he also tried to include, where possible, one of the flowers contained in his wife's wedding bouquet. He also designed the background fabrics of brocade or damask and was very particular about the precise colour. There are many surviving banners designed by Comper. Southwark Cathedral (Anglican) has three banners which demonstrate a progression of methods. The earliest of his banners used or nué, worked in the same manner as in the fifteenth century, i.e. the gold laid in horizontal rows, with the drapery on the figures shown by the density of stitch. Slightly later banners show the drapery in gold thread laid directionally, with coloured stitches shading the drapery. The banners dating from after the Second World War show figures with garments of applied cloth of gold, the details worked in coloured silks in stem stitch and couching.

Westminster Abbey has several Comper banners of the first and last type. The Abbey has a white Festival nave frontal, commissioned by George VI and Queen Elizabeth for their Coronation in 1937. The fabric, designed by Comper, is a brocade with a weft of silver metal thread and white silk, and a warp of blue silk. The fabric exists elsewhere with warps of other colours, but this is the only known example to use blue.

MARY J. NEWILL
(1860–1947)

Mary Newill was a member of the Arts and Crafts Exhibition Society and of the Bromsgrove Guild of Handicrafts. A skilled embroiderer, she won a scholarship to study in Paris. Her work was influenced by Burne-Jones and included designs for stained glass and book illustrations. Mary trained and taught at the Birmingham School of Art from 1882 to 1919. She worked large figurative panels in appliqué with stitchery in wool.

PHOEBE ANNA TRAQUAIR
(1852–1936)

Phoebe Traquair trained at Dublin School of Art in mural-painting, enamelling, jewellery, illumination and embroidery. She married the Keeper of the Edinburgh Museum of Science and Art. Her work was exhibited with the Arts and Crafts Exhibition Society in 1903 and an example of her work, a four-fold embroidered screen (1895–1902) is in the National Gallery of Scotland. In 1904 she exhibited with the St Louis International Exhibition in the United States of America. Her pieces were usually large scale, with the stitches completely covering the ground.

MAY MORRIS
(1862–1938)

The younger daughter of William Morris, May took over the embroidery workshop of Morris, Marshall and Faulkner in 1885. Although her designs showed strongly her father's Gothic influence, they have a more open feel and a linear quality that leans towards Art Nouveau. The surviving pieces that were both designed and worked by May show her to be a very competent needlewoman (*Figure 115*). Whereas William Morris had completely covered the background of his embroideries

Figure 115
Bishop's gloves, worked by May Morris, designed by Charles Ricketts, c. 1899. Exhibited in the Arts and Crafts Exhibition in New York in 1910. Silk embroidery on linen.
(Victoria and Albert Museum, London)

with stitchery, May used the same double running filling stitch, but allowed the fabric to show through. Much of the embroidery is executed in fairly heavy twisted silks, especially on the larger pieces.

May Morris exhibited with the Arts and Crafts Exhibition Society showing jewellery, lettering design and embroidery. In 1888 she published 'Chain Stitch Embroidery' in *The Hobby Horse*, volume 3, and, in 1892, 'Embroidery' in *Plain Handicrafts* edited by A.H. Mackmurdo. She published the first embroidery book to promote drawing as a basis for design, *Decorative Needlework* (1893). She believed that embroidery should be very personal.

In 1897, May joined the staff at the Central School for Arts and Crafts, directing the embroidery classes from 1899 to 1904. She lectured throughout the country. In 1907 she founded the Women's Guild of Art. The Guild designed a room for the Arts and Crafts Exhibition at the Royal Academy in 1916.

THE CENTURY GUILD

Arthur Mackmurdo founded the Century Guild in 1882, with Selwyn Image and Arthur Heygate. Mackmurdo was an architect and designer of furniture and textiles. The Guild produced work for various firms including Morris and Co. The embroidery technique is very similar to that of the Leek Embroidery Society (described in chapter 10), but the designs are more flowing and are influenced by Art Nouveau.

THE ART WORKERS' GUILD

The Art Workers' Guild was formed in 1884 by students and assistants of Norman Shaw, with the aim of providing a meeting place for practising designers and artists.

THE SILVER STUDIO

The Silver Studio was founded by Arthur Silver in 1880, specifically for the production of repeating designs for wallpapers, fabrics and floor coverings. Harry Napper and J.I. Kay were the two main designers (*Figure 116*).

As a result of the influence of these movements, guilds and societies, various quality magazines appeared, for example, *The Studio, Arts and Crafts* and *The Hobby Horse*.

Art Nouveau

The movement towards Art Nouveau began
with the symbolism of William Blake. It
developed through the work and beliefs of the
Pre-Raphaelite Brotherhood and then the Arts
and Crafts Movement. By the end of the
nineteenth century the style had taken its
name from a shop in Paris, owned by Samuel
Bing, called 'L'Art Nouveau'.

From the late 1890s until the First World
War, the style of Art Nouveau spread
throughout Western Europe and North
America. The style accentuated the lines of
nature, creating elegant, sweeping designs that
pervaded all areas of art and craft. Each
country had its own characteristics. The main
development in Britain was centred in
Glasgow, particularly at the Glasgow School of
Art. The main exponents in England were
Walter Crane and Christopher Dresser.

a

Figure 116
Repeating designs for woven fabrics, reflecting the
Art Nouveau style for commercial use.
(*a*) Silk, wool and cotton double cloth, probably
    designed by Lindsay P. Butterfield, woven by
    Alexander Morton and Co., *c.* 1900. T91–1973.
(*b*) Silver Studio, probably Harry Napper.
    'Santiago', cotton fabric woven in northern
    France, *c.* 1905. 253–1966.
(Victoria and Albert Museum, London)

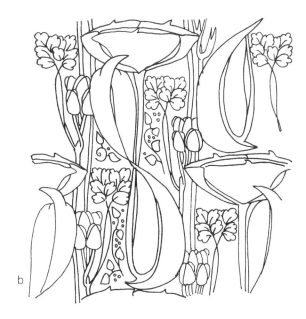

b

WALTER CRANE
(1845–1915)

An artist, book illustrator, painter and member of the Arts and Crafts Exhibition Society, Walter Crane also designed embroidery. His designs were used by the Royal School of Art Needlework, and William Morris used Crane's illustration for *The Goose Girl* as his first panel woven at Merton Abbey. Walter Crane also designed fabrics for Thomas Wardle. He became Master of the Art Workers' Guild and President of the Arts and Crafts Exhibition Society in 1888. Ten years later he became Principal of the Royal College of Art and wrote *The Bases of Design* (1898) and *Line and Form* (1900). He was very interested in the training of teachers.

CHRISTOPHER DRESSER
(1834–1904)

Originally a botanist, Christopher Dresser became a leading Aesthetic designer. He travelled to Japan and was much influenced by the Japanese style. Dresser designed for metalwork, woodwork, ceramics and wallpaper, as well as for textiles, some of which were sold in Paris by Samuel Bing. His designs for fabrics and wallpaper gave him an interest in repeating patterns.

THE OMEGA WORKSHOPS

The Omega Workshops were opened in London in 1913 by Roger Fry, artist, critic and writer. The aim was to encourage the revival of mural decoration and Fry painted large frescoes at his home, Durbins, in Guildford. The workshop was given a commission to decorate Henry Harris's house in Bedford Square, in London. The work was carried out by Duncan Grant and Vanessa Bell.

The First World War impeded the development of the workshops. They were financially insecure and finally closed in 1919.

GLASGOW SCHOOL OF ART

In 1894, Jessie Newbery, the wife of the Principal, opened an embroidery class. The Glasgow influence continued well into the 1920s. Charles Rennie Mackintosh and Ann Macbeth were both involved with the school.

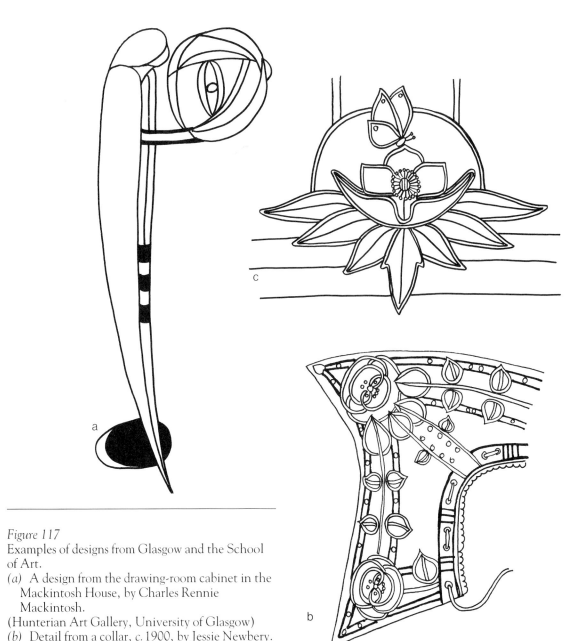

Figure 117
Examples of designs from Glasgow and the School of Art.
(a) A design from the drawing-room cabinet in the Mackintosh House, by Charles Rennie Mackintosh.
(Hunterian Art Gallery, University of Glasgow)
(b) Detail from a collar, *c.* 1900, by Jessie Newbery. Satin, with satin stitch, appliqué and couching in floss silks. T562.
(Victoria and Albert Museum, London)
(c) Detail, curtain, attributed to Ann Macbeth. Blue silk with appliqué edged with satin stitch in floss silk, with straight, running and stem stitches and couching.
(Glasgow School of Art)

CHARLES RENNIE MACKINTOSH
(1868–1928)

The Art Nouveau style in Scotland was developed by Charles Rennie Mackintosh. Originally trained as an architect, he designed the Glasgow School of Art and was closely associated with the school as a teacher.

Mackintosh designed furniture and interiors (*Figure 117a*), and was a painter. His work includes the Willow Tea Rooms in Glasgow. He married Margaret MacDonald in 1900.

Together with her sister, Frances, and Herbert McNair, they were known as the Glasgow Four.

Charles Rennie Mackintosh introduced horizontal and vertical straight lines into his form of Art Nouveau, which became known as the Glasgow Style. The colourings were often pearly greys, silver, pinks and lilac, reflecting the Japanese influence that was felt at the time. Stylized lettering was also a feature.

FRANCES MACDONALD
(1874–1921)

Frances MacDonald studied at the Glasgow School of Art from 1891 to 1894. She married Herbert McNair and was appointed as an assistant to the embroidery department in 1909. Her embroidery was in the style of Glasgow Art Nouveau. A watercolour design can be seen in the Hunterian Art Gallery, University of Glasgow.

MARGARET MACDONALD
(1865–1933)

Like her sister, Margaret studied at the Glasgow School of Art. She married Charles Rennie Mackintosh in 1900. Margaret MacDonald was an embroiderer and an artist and she designed the interiors of the Willow Tea Rooms. Examples of her embroidery can be seen in the collections of the Glasgow School of Art, the Glasgow Museum and Art Gallery, Kelvingrove, and the Hunterian Art Gallery, University of Glasgow.

JESSIE NEWBERY
(1864–1948)

Jessie (née Rowat) studied at the Glasgow School of Art and later became the wife of the Principal. She opened an embroidery class there and taught from 1894 to 1908. She was a friend of the two MacDonald sisters.

Her designs influenced and reflected the style of the school. She often incorporated lettering using both wools and silks and appliqué edged with satin stitch. Many of the examples of her work are dress accessories and household articles (*Figure 117b*).

Jessie Newbery exhibited throughout Great Britain, in the United States of America and in Europe. Examples of her work can be seen in the Glasgow Museum and Art Gallery, Kelvingrove, the Glasgow School of Art, the Victoria and Albert Museum, the Gallery of English Costume, Manchester, and the National Museum of Scotland, Edinburgh.

ANN MACBETH
(1875–1948)

Ann Macbeth was a student of Jessie Newbery and taught at the Glasgow School of Art after Mrs Newbery retired. She exhibited in Turin in 1902.

She was very interested in teaching embroidery to children and believed that the technique chosen should give rise to the design and stitchery. She thought that the copying of paintings was undesirable, a reaction against Berlin wool work and the earlier practice of needlepainting.

Margaret Swanson was Ann's deputy and together they produced the magazine *Educational Needlecraft*. Ann Macbeth published *The Playwork Book* (1918), *Schools and Fireside Crafts* with Mary Spence (1920), *Embroidered Lace and Leatherwork* (1924), *Needleweaving* (1926) and *The Countrywoman's Rug Book* (1929).

Ann Macbeth's work often featured appliqué edged with satin stitch (*Figure 117c*), or flowers in chain stitch. She worked two large religioius hangings, both set against the countryside around Patterdale. *The Nativity* (1940) is worked in silks and wool on a natural linen, using a wide range of stitches. The hanging has a crochet edge and is mounted on a blue linen ground. This piece forms part of the collection in the Glasgow Museum and Art Gallery, Kelvingrove. *The Good Shepherd* (1936) is worked in silks and wool on a natural linen and is mounted in the same way as *The Nativity*. It is to be found in Patterdale parish church.

Much of Ann Macbeth's work is in private collections, but examples can be seen in the collections of the Glasgow School of Art, the Victoria and Albert Museum, and the National Museum of Scotland, Edinburgh.

A Summary of the Embroidery
of the Early Twentieth Century

The embroidery of the twentieth century has been fully documented in recent publications. Therefore this chapter simply summarizes the main design trends, influences and techniques.

Details of most of the main personalities can be found in *Twentieth-Century Embroidery in Great Britain*, four volumes by Constance Howard, published by Batsford. Many of the embroiderers are featured individually in books, magazine articles and exhibition catalogues which are listed in 'Further Reading'.

The amateur embroidery of the early twentieth century was based firmly on the transfers and traced items available. The naturalistic floral style of art needlework dominated, with the designs greatly simplified to accommodate the less able needlewoman. Pictorial samplers were popular during the early part of the century. Cross stitch and counted thread work was used a great deal on household and decorative items, particularly during the 1950s and 1960s, reflecting the techniques and designs of Scandinavia. Many printed canvases based on popular paintings were available. Needlework shops would issue an illustrated catalogue of designs, and most of the women's magazines featured patterns and charts for embroidery.

Within the art schools, the main impetus of embroidery and design development came from Scotland until the early '20s, with the English schools leaning towards more traditional work. Competitions and exhibitions continued to be promoted, with the aim of raising standards. The Worshipful Company of Broderers played an important role to this end. The Women's Institute was founded in 1913, maintaining the technical standards of embroidery but working to traditional designs, particularly in the 1920s and 1930s. The institute held classes to teach a wide range of crafts, the emphasis being on technical excellence rather than original design.

The Art Nouveau style continued from the nineteenth century and into the early 1920s, developing along different lines throughout Europe. Many of the personalities of the late nineteenth century continued to work well into the twentieth century.

An impetus was given to ceremonial embroidery by the coronations of Edward VII (1902), George V (1911), George VI (1937) and Elizabeth II (1953), involving the Royal School of Needlework and the Ladies' Work Society. From the 1950s, the *haute couture* houses featured embroidery, particularly tambour beading.

The First World War encouraged projects to help wounded soldiers in hospital, and by the outbreak of the Second World War the value of this work as a healing process was apparent, leading to the recognition of occupational therapy. Both the wars were followed by a

revival of all types of crafts, especially local interests such as the Welsh quilters. Boards were set up to encourage and develop these as local industries, although rationing during and after the Second World War restricted the supply of materials.

Schools, Societies and Schemes

In 1919, the Bauhaus opened in Weimar. This was the first school of art to teach fine art and commercial practices side by side. Instruction in design for mechanized processes was included in the syllabus, and geometric shapes were a strong influence. The Bauhaus moved to Dessau until 1933 when it was closed.

The Embroiderers' Guild was founded in 1906 by ex-students of the Royal School of Needlework. Louisa Pesel (1870–1947) was the first president and changed the name from the Society of Certificated Embroiderers.

Louisa Pesel studied under Lewis F. Day and founded a school in Athens to give tuition and employment to children. She had a special interest in counted thread embroidery and looked at historical examples, particularly samplers. The Victoria and Albert Museum collection contains a set of stitch samplers worked by Louisa Pesel. In the 1930s she formed a group to work the hassocks for Winchester Cathedral.

In 1931 the first branch of the Embroiderers' Guild opened in the North-West. Louisa M. Chart (d.1963) was a founder member of the Embroiderers' Guild and was later involved with the Needlework Development Scheme. She also repaired embroideries in the Palace of Holyroodhouse, Edinburgh. In 1961 the Guild held an exhibition showing a lot of traditional and counted thread work. However, in the 1966 exhibition there was a predominance of panels and free embroidery. In 1971 the Guild had a historical exhibition which stimulated an interest not only in the embroidery of the past but also in the need for conservation. Karen

Finch, a leading authority on conservation, originally had a workroom in her home in Ealing, London, where she trained students. Eventually she was given an apartment in Hampton Court Palace to continue her work but left recently. The students at the Textile Conservation Centre undertake a four-year post-graduate course.

In 1934 the Needlework Development Scheme was set up by the firm of J.P. Coats, with the aim of encouraging embroidery in Scottish schools. A collection of traditional embroidery from all over Europe was circulated. The scheme extended to schools throughout the British Isles and other groups asked to be included, among them adult education institutes, the Women's Institute and the Townswomen's Guild. The collection was built up to include work by contemporary embroiderers, supplemented by books and leaflets. By 1962, J.P. Coats felt that they had achieved their aim and the scheme closed. The collection was divided between the Embroiderers' Guild and museums.

Trends and Techniques

The human figure featured in many designs during the early part of the century. Both Phoebe Traquair and Mrs Walter Crane exhibited pieces. The popularity of Bakst's designs for the Russian ballet in 1909 and Poiret's *haute couture* creations took Paris by storm and had an influence on English embroidery. In the early 1920s Lanvin showed Egyptian embroidery in his collection, influenced by the interest in the opening of Tutankhamun's tomb. Peasant styles were also very much in favour.

Appliqué with clear, simple shapes was used for both decorative and household items. Crewelwork in silks and wools, echoing Elizabethan floral motifs, was popular.

The 1930s brought the Art Deco style, influencing architecture, furnishings, dress and

embroidery. The designs were geometric and abstract in style, and techniques were used to form areas of flat pattern: darning on net or fabric, pulled thread work, appliqué and machine embroidery (*Figure 118*). *Embroidery* magazine was first published by the Embroiderers' Guild in 1932.

During the 1940s design and techniques were fairly rigid and stiff, although many techniques were used. Fabrics were limited. Many designs were figurative, as in the work of Dorothy Allsopp, Nancy Kimmins, Evelyn Woodcock and Christine Risley.

By the early 1950s new synthetic fabrics and threads were being used, but some were not durable. There was much rebuilding and refurbishment of churches. Many sets of kneelers were undertaken, for example the Embroiderers' Guild organized those designed and made for St Clement Danes. This impetus spread throughout the country. Embroidered panels and hangings were more evident, showing a move to less practical items. Figurative designs continued to be popular and during the 1950s the rigidity of the '40s began to pass. The slipped outline and the overlapping of shapes, which led to the abstraction of the '60s.

Design and technique became much freer during the 1960s and the general interest in embroidery increased. Plastic and 'found' objects were combined with mixed techniques and, eventually, the barriers between the textile crafts were removed. Three-dimensional work and 'pop art' portraits were popular. The 1960s continued the revival in church embroidery, bringing with it a renewed interest in metal thread work.

A Few Notable Personalities

Women's magazines gave advice on design, for example the *Woman's Magazine* and the *Girl's Own Paper*, edited by Flora Klickmann.

Mrs Archibald Christie (1872–1938) edited *Needle and Thread* (1914) and wrote *Samplers and Stitches* in 1920. The samplers that she worked for this book are in the Victoria and Albert Museum. She advocated a strong link between the design and the stitches. Mrs Christie also wrote the definitive work on Opus Anglicanum, *English Medieval Embroidery*, Clarendon Press, 1938, and *Embroidery and Tapestry Weaving*, John Hogg, 1906. She was the first embroidery teacher at the Royal College of Art, followed by Kathleen Harris in 1921.

Kathleen Harris (1880–1963) was one of the first embroiderers to work on patterned fabrics and pillow ticking. She later worked with the Needlework Development Scheme and edited *Embroidery* magazine from 1951 to 1960.

Mary Hogarth (1862–1935) published *Modern Embroidery* in 1933, a book covering work exhibited in 1932. She was originally a painter, her work imitating the work of modern painters. Mary advocated 'speed and economy, the work being of the present time'.

Rebecca Crompton (1895–1947) taught at Northampton and Croydon Schools of Art and at Bromley College of Art in the 1930s, later working with Dorothy Benson for the Singer Company. She was one of the first embroiderers to encourage the use of cut paper for designs and to overlap applied shapes underneath her embroidery stitches. In 1936 she wrote *Modern Design in Embroidery*, emphasizing a broad-minded use of colour and freedom of design.

Dorothy Benson (1902–77) worked for the Singer Sewing Machine Company and became well known as a machine embroidery teacher and examiner. She wrote *Your Machine Embroidery*, Sylvan Press (1952) and *Machine Embroidery, the Artistic Possibilities of the Domestic Sewing Machine*, Singer Sewing Machine Company.

Beryl Dean (1911–) studied under Rebecca Crompton at the Bromley College of Art. Her work is influenced by Byzantine design. Originally trained as a designer for the theatre, Beryl Dean is best known for her ecclesiastical

Figure 118
Panel, Art Deco, 1930s, English. Transparent fabrics layered with stitchery. EG3860. (Embroiderers' Guild, Hampton Court Palace)

embroidery. A set of five panels can be seen in St George's Chapel, Windsor.

Kathleen Whyte (1907–) was senior lecturer at Glasgow School of Art, and her work reflects the wild Scottish scenery. She has written *Design in Embroidery*, Batsford (1969) and many articles in *Embroidery* magazine.

Winsome Douglass wrote *Discovering Embroidery* in 1955. She believed in building patterns from stitches and often worked in white on coloured or patterned fabrics. Some of her work was used by the Needlework Development Scheme.

Constance Howard (1910–) was senior lecturer at Goldsmiths College of Art in

London, and she encouraged experimentation with a wide range of materials. She designed a large hanging, depicting the work of the Women's Institute, now at Denman College, worked by her students to celebrate the Festival of Britain in 1951. It contains much three-dimensional work, appliqué and padded work.

Recent Trends

The 1970s developed the soft sculpture of the late '60s with quilting and heavy padding used for panels and three-dimensional pieces. The use of mixed media continued. Machine embroidery predominated, especially in colleges and art schools. The landscape was popular as a design source, with an interest in using dyes and paints on fabrics as a background.

Fabric-covered mounts were much in evidence in the mid-1980s, frequently with embroidery spilling on to the mount. The late '80s brought the use of paper and felt, together with more inventive ways of hanging finished pieces. The development of artistic patchwork began during the late 1970s, followed by an enormous interest in the '80s. Ecclesiastical embroidery continued to thrive with groups associated with most of the large cathedrals.

At the present time there appears to be a watershed in the field of embroidery. Questions are being asked: What is embroidery today? Where is embroidery going? What is the next step? It would be interesting to be able to step into the future and look back to see what, of all the many aspects of this incredible craft, will be seen as representative of our time. Will it be the experimental work of the art schools? Or the wider influence of the growth of City and Guilds courses bringing together technique and design? Given that Opus Anglicanum is the first and Elizabethan the second, are we, indeed, experiencing the third great era of English embroidery?

APPENDIX 1

THE HUSBAND'S COMPLAINT

I hate the name of German wool, in all its colours bright;
Of chairs and stools in fancy work, I hate the very sight;
The shawls and slippers that I've seen, the ottomans and
    bags
Sooner than wear a stitch on me, I'd walk the streets in
    rags.

I've heard of wives too musical, – too talkative – too
    quiet,
Of scolding and of gaming wives and those too fond of
    riot;
But yet of all the errors known, which to the women fall;
For ever doing fancy work, I think exceeds them all.

The other day when I went home no dinner was for me,
I asked my wife the reason; she answered, 'One, two,
    three,'
I told her I was hungry and stamped upon the floor
She never even looked at me, but murmured 'One green
    more.'

Of course she made me angry, – but she didn't care for
    that,
And chatters while I talk to her 'A white and then a black
Seven greens and then a purple, – just hold your tongue
    my dear,
You really do annoy me so, I've made a wrong stitch
    here.'

And as for conversation with the eternal frame,
I speak to her of fifty things – she answers just the same!
'Tis 'Yes my love, five reds and then a black, I quite agree
    with you,
I've done this wrong, seven, eight, nine, ten, an orange
    then a blue.'

If any lady comes to tea, her bag is first surveyed,
And if the pattern pleases her, a copy there is made.
She stares too at the gentleman, and when I ask her why,
'Tis 'Oh my love, the pattern of his waistcoat struck my
    eye.'

And if to walk I am inclined ('Tis seldom I go out)
At every worsted shop she sees Oh how she stares about
And there 'tis 'Oh! I must go in that pattern is so rare,
That group of flowers is just the thing I wanted for my
    chair.'

Besides the things she makes are such touch-me-not
    affairs,
I dare not even use a screen – a stool – and as for chairs!
'Twas only yesterday I put my youngest boy on one
And until then I never knew my wife had such a tongue.

Alas for my dear little ones, they dare not move or speak:
'Tis, 'Tom be quiet, put down that bag, Harriet, where's
    your feet?
Maria standing on that stool – it was not made for use,
Be silent all – three green one red and then a puce.'

Ah! The misery of a working wife, with fancy work run
    wild,
And hands that never do aught else for husband or for
    child;
Our clothes are rent and minus strings, my house is in
    disorder,
And all because my lady wife has taken to embroider.

I'll put my children out to school, I'll go across the seas
My wife's so full of fancy work, I'm sure she won't miss
    me;
E'en while I write she still keeps on her one, two, three
    and four,
'Tis past all bearing, on my word, I'll not endure it more.

From *A History of Needlemaking* by M.T. Morrall, 1852

APPENDIX 2

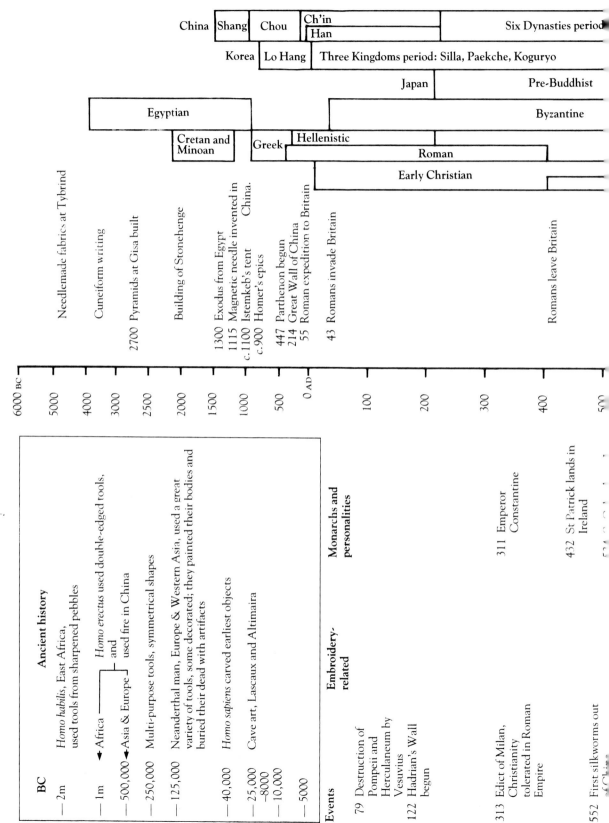

China | Shang | Chou | Ch'in / Han | Six Dynasties period

Korea | Lo Hang | Three Kingdoms period: Silla, Paekche, Koguryo

Japan | Pre-Buddhist

Egyptian | Byzantine

Cretan and Minoan | **Greek** | Hellenistic | Roman

Early Christian

BC — **Ancient history**

- 2m — Homo habilis, East Africa, used tools from sharpened pebbles
- 1m — Homo erectus used double-edged tools, and used fire in China
- 500,000 — Africa → Asia & Europe
- 250,000 — Multi-purpose tools, symmetrical shapes
- 125,000 — Neanderthal man, Europe & Western Asia, used a great variety of tools, some decorated; they painted their bodies and buried their dead with artifacts
- 40,000 — Homo sapiens carved earliest objects
- 25,000 – 8000 — Cave art, Lascaux and Altimaira
- 10,000
- 5000

Embroidery-related

- Needlemade fabrics at Tybrind
- Cuneiform writing
- 2700 Pyramids at Gisa built
- Building of Stonehenge
- 1300 Exodus from Egypt
- 1115 Magnetic needle invented in China.
- c.1100 Istemkeb's tent
- c.900 Homer's epics
- 447 Parthenon begun
- 214 Great Wall of China
- 55 Roman expedition to Britain
- 43 Romans invade Britain
- Romans leave Britain

Monarchs and personalities

- 311 Emperor Constantine
- 432 St Patrick lands in Ireland

Events

- 79 Destruction of Pompeii and Herculaneum by Vesuvius
- 122 Hadrian's Wall begun
- 313 Edict of Milan, Christianity tolerated in Roman Empire
- 552 First silkworms out of China

6000 BC | 5000 | 4000 | 3000 | 2500 | 2000 | 1500 | 1000 | 500 | 0 AD | 100 | 200 | 300 | 400 | 500

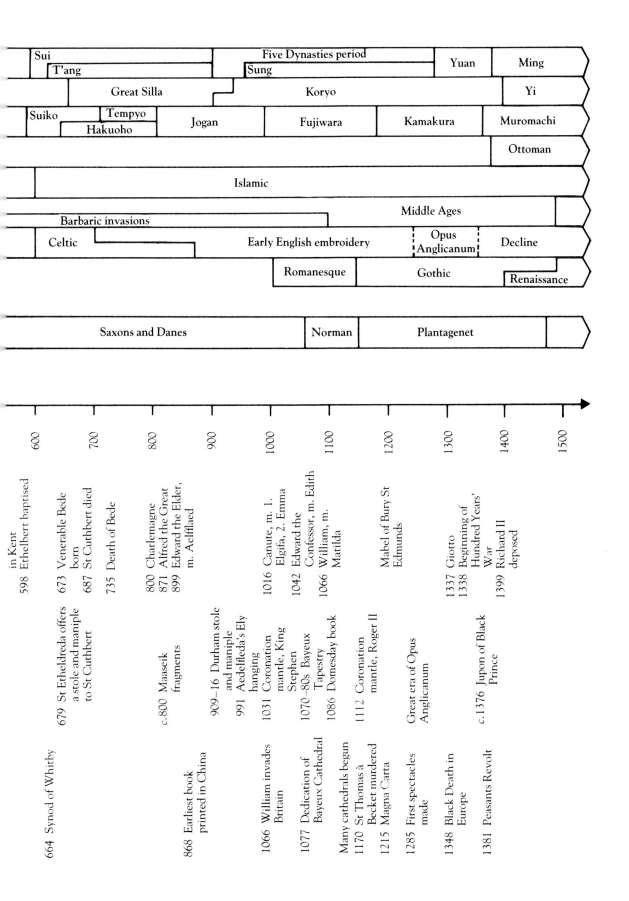

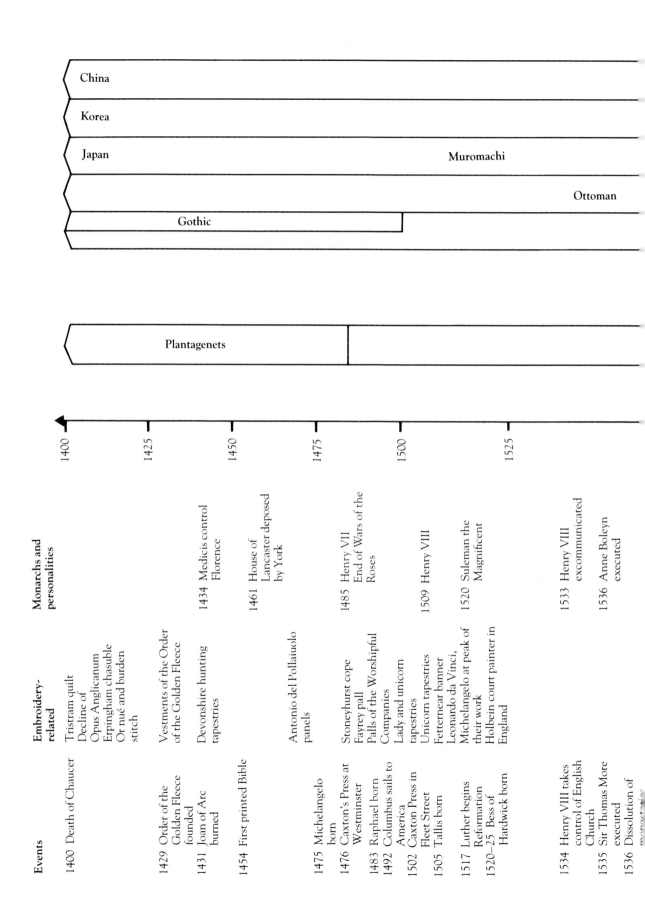

China

Korea

Japan   Muromachi

Ottoman

Gothic

Plantagenets

1400   1425   1450   1475   1500   1525

Monarchs and personalities

1434 Medicis control Florence

1461 House of Lancaster deposed by York

1485 Henry VII End of Wars of the Roses

1509 Henry VIII

1520 Suleman the Magnificent

1533 Henry VIII excommunicated

1536 Anne Boleyn executed

Embroidery-related

Tristram quilt
Decline of
Opus Anglicanum
Erpingham chasuble
Or nué and burden stitch

Vestments of the Order of the Golden Fleece

Devonshire hunting tapestries

Antonio del Pollaiuolo panels

Stoneyhurst cope
Fayrey pall
Palls of the Worshipful Companies
Lady and unicorn tapestries
Unicorn tapestries
Fetternear banner
Leonardo da Vinci, Michelangelo at peak of their work
Holbein court painter in England

Events

1400 Death of Chaucer

1429 Order of the Golden Fleece founded

1431 Joan of Arc burned

1454 First printed Bible

1475 Michelangelo born

1476 Caxton's Press at Westminster

1483 Raphael born
1492 Columbus sails to America

1502 Caxton Press in Fleet Street

1505 Tallis born

1517 Luther begins Reformation

1520–25 Bess of Hardwick born

1534 Henry VIII takes control of English Church

1535 Sir Thomas More executed

1536 Dissolution of monasteries

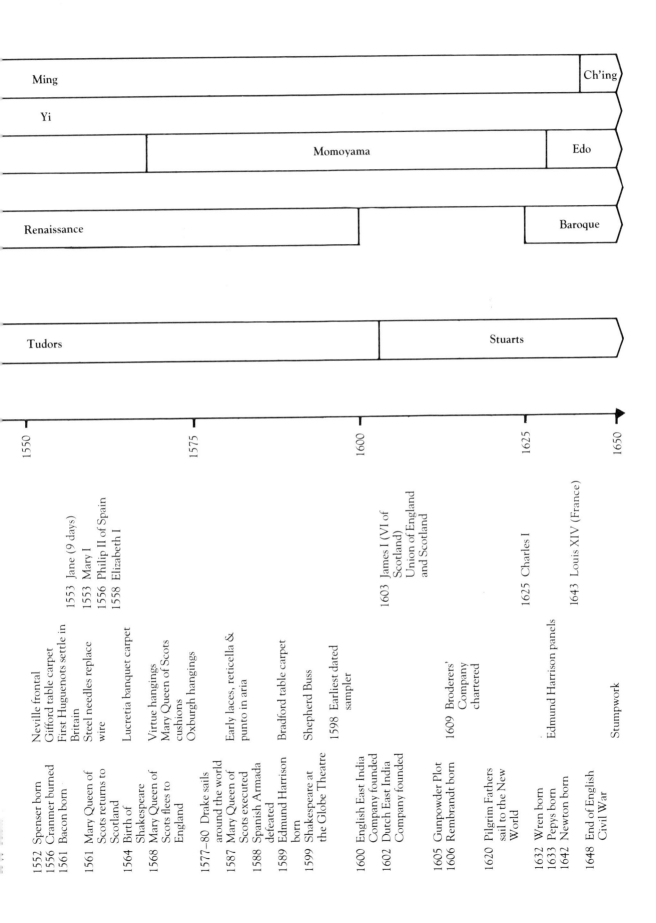

Ming | Ch'ing

Yi

Momoyama | Edo

Renaissance | Baroque

Tudors | Stuarts

1550 — 1575 — 1600 — 1625 — 1650

1553 Jane (9 days)
1553 Mary I
1556 Philip II of Spain
1558 Elizabeth I

1603 James I (VI of Scotland) Union of England and Scotland

1625 Charles I

1643 Louis XIV (France)

Neville frontal
Gifford table carpet
First Huguenots settle in Britain
Steel needles replace wire

Lucretia banquet carpet

Virtue hangings
Mary Queen of Scots cushions
Oxburgh hangings

Early laces, reticella & punto in aria

Bradford table carpet

Shepherd Buss

1598 Earliest dated sampler

1609 Broderers' Company chartered

Edmund Harrison panels

Stumpwork

1552 Spenser born
1556 Cranmer burned
1561 Bacon born

1561 Mary Queen of Scots returns to Scotland
1564 Birth of Shakespeare
1568 Mary Queen of Scots flees to England

1577–80 Drake sails around the world
1587 Mary Queen of Scots executed
1588 Spanish Armada defeated
1589 Edmund Harrison born

1599 Shakespeare at the Globe Theatre

1600 English East India Company founded
1602 Dutch East India Company founded

1605 Gunpowder Plot
1606 Rembrandt born

1620 Pilgrim Fathers sail to the New World

1632 Wren born
1633 Pepys born
1642 Newton born

1648 End of English Civil War

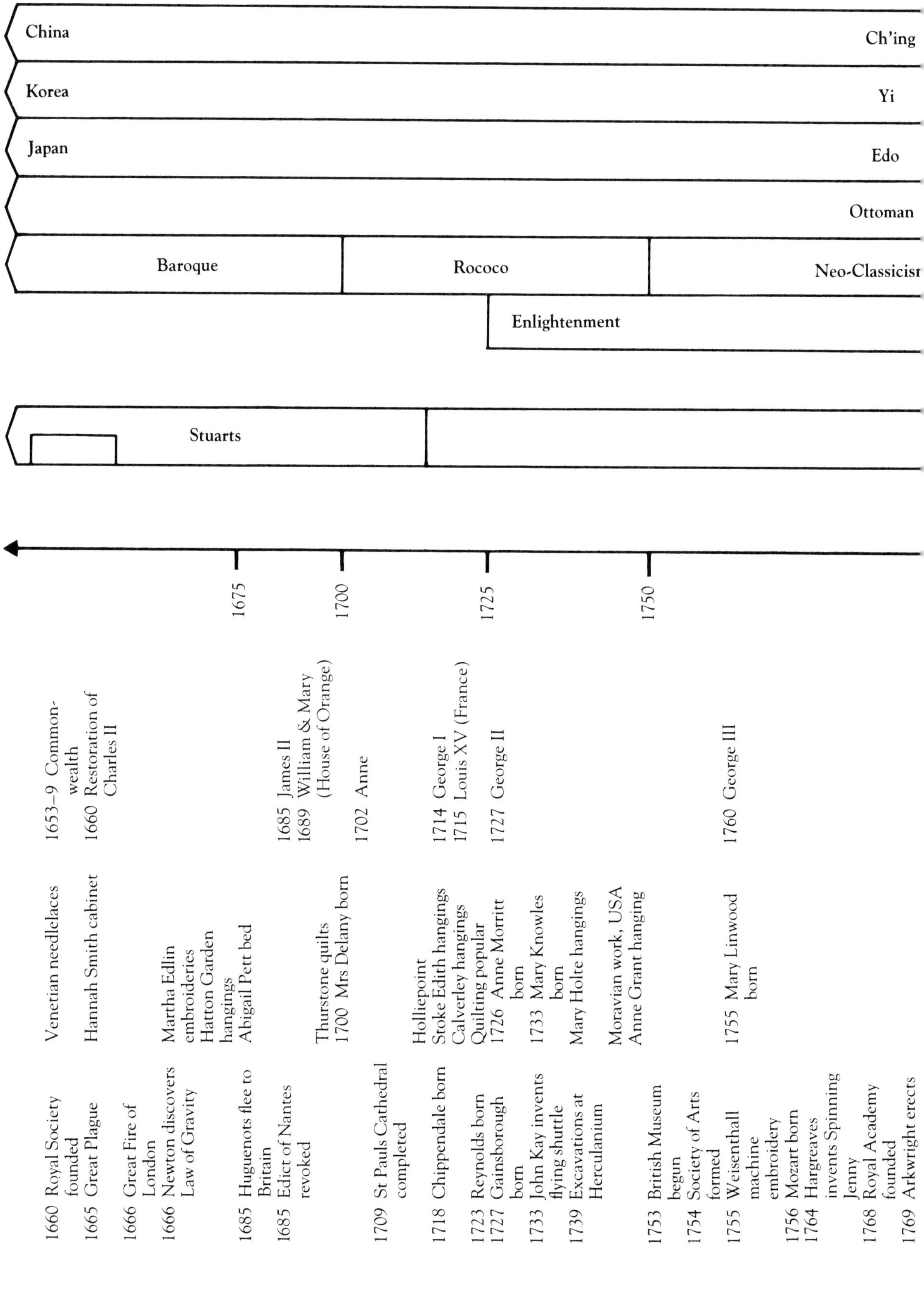
China
Ch'ing
Korea
Yi
Japan
Edo
Ottoman
Baroque
Rococo
Neo-Classicisr
Enlightenment
Stuarts
1675
1700
1725
1750
1653–9 Commonwealth
1660 Restoration of Charles II
1685 James II
1689 William & Mary (House of Orange)
1702 Anne
1714 George I
1715 Louis XV (France)
1727 George II
1760 George III
Venetian needlelaces
Hannah Smith cabinet
Martha Edlin embroideries
Hatton Garden hangings
Abigail Pett bed
Thurstone quilts
1700 Mrs Delany born
Holliepoint
Stoke Edith hangings
Calverley hangings
Quilting popular
1726 Anne Morritt born
1733 Mary Knowles born
Mary Holte hangings
Moravian work, USA
Anne Grant hanging
1755 Mary Linwood born
1660 Royal Society founded
1665 Great Plague
1666 Great Fire of London
1666 Newton discovers Law of Gravity
1685 Huguenots flee to Britain
1685 Edict of Nantes revoked
1709 St Pauls Cathedral completed
1718 Chippendale born
1723 Reynolds born
1727 Gainsborough born
1733 John Kay invents flying shuttle
1739 Excavations at Herculanium
1753 British Museum begun
1754 Society of Arts formed
1755 Weisenthall machine embroidery
1756 Mozart born
1764 Hargreaves invents Spinning Jenny
1768 Royal Academy founded
1769 Arkwright erects

Romanticism

Hanover

1775 1800 1825

1792 France becomes a republic
1804 Napoleon I (France)

1820 George IV

1830 William IV

1765 Painted silk imported from China

Quilting popular

1782 Luigi Ruffini to Edinburgh
1798 Mary Linwood's exhibition
       Ayrshire work (early)

       Berlin wool work
1809 Chinese interiors at Brighton Pavilion completed

1814 Needlemade fillings used in Ayrshire work.
       Carrickmacross

       Limerick
       Mountmellick work
1827 G.F. Bodley born
1831 Wilks' Emporium opens

1769 Machine for net patented
1770 Excavations at Pompeii
1775 Warp hosiery & lace machines patented
1776 American Declaration of Independence
1779 Crompton invents Spinning Mule
1785 Cartwright invents power loom

1789 French Revolution

1812 Pugin born

1824 Street born
1825 First railway opened
1827 University of London founded
1828 Heilmann developed embroidery machine

Timeline

Region/Theme	Period(s)
China	Ch'ing
Korea	Yi
Japan	Edo
	Ottoman
	Romanticism → Impressionism
	House of Hanover

Timeline axis marks: **1850**, **1875**

Chronological entries

- 1834 William Morris born
- 1837 Victoria
- 1838 National Gallery opened
- 1841 *Art of Needlework*, Countess Wilton
- 1844 *Glossary of Ecclesiastical Ornament*, Pugin
  Irish laces
  Broderie Anglaise
  Point de gaze
- 1845 Lewis F Day born
- 1847 British Museum opened
  Photography develops
- 1851 Great Exhibition
- 1851 First Singer trade machine
- 1856 First Singer domestic machine
- 1856 Perkin's chemical dyes
- 1859 Darwin's *Origin of the Species*
- 1861–65 American Civil War
- 1865 Antiseptic surgery, Lister
- 1869 Suez Canal opened
- 1870s Machine imitations of Ayrshire work
  Royal School of Art Needlework founded
  Decline of Berlin wool work
  Embroidery transfers
  Art Needlework
  Leek Embroidery Society
- 1876 Centennial Fair, Philadelphia
- 1880s Cross stitch techniques
  Smocking
  Ruskin work
  Greek lace
  Cutwork
- 1891 First sewing machine with swing needle
- 1895 Art Nouveau
- 1896 Blue and White

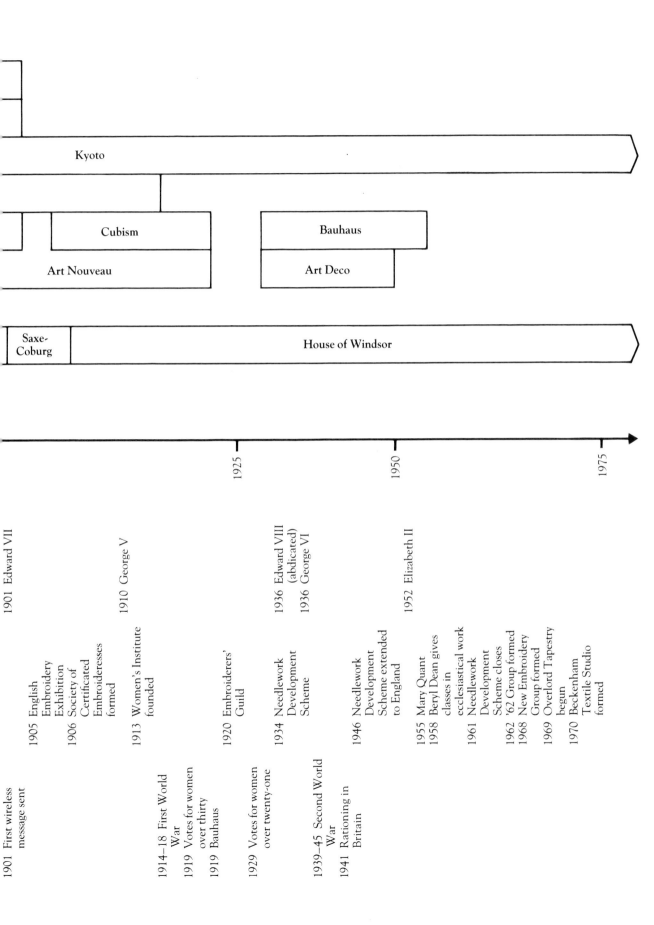

Kyoto

Cubism

Bauhaus

Art Nouveau

Art Deco

Saxe-Coburg

House of Windsor

1925

1950

1975

1901 Edward VII

1910 George V

1936 Edward VIII (abdicated)
1936 George VI

1952 Elizabeth II

1905 English Embroidery Exhibition
1906 Society of Certificated Embroideresses formed

1913 Women's Institute founded

1920 Embroiderers' Guild

1934 Needlework Development Scheme

1946 Needlework Development Scheme extended to England

1955 Mary Quant
1958 Beryl Dean gives classes in ecclesiastical work
1961 Needlework Development Scheme closes
1962 '62 Group formed
1968 New Embroidery Group formed
1969 Overlord Tapestry begun
1970 Beckenham Textile Studio formed

1901 First wireless message sent

1914–18 First World War
1919 Votes for women over thirty
1919 Bauhaus

1929 Votes for women over twenty-one

1939–45 Second World War
1941 Rationing in Britain

APPENDIX 3

SUMMARY BY TECHNIQUE

Date	Techniques	Examples	Sources
Crewelwork and surface stitching			
Early	Laid and couched work.	Bayeux Tapestry, Icelandic hangings.	Manuscript and stained-glass artists.
	Chain, split or stem stitch.	Gerona Creation.	↓
	Split stitch and laid work.	Opus Anglicanum.	
1500s	Long and short stitch, split stitch and satin stitch alone;	Covers.	Herbals, woodcut illustrations.
	with metal thread and spangles; with detached buttonhole stitch	Coifs, nightcaps, costume items.	Scrolling stem design
	continuing into ↓		developing into ↓
1600s	Long and short stitch, stem stitch, knotted stitches and laid work in wool.	Bed hangings (Pett), valances and costume items and workbags.	Tree of Life. Indian imports.
	Long and short stitch, split stitch, satin stich, in silk and chenille	Small pictures (also in canvas work, woven tapestry and stumpwork).	Etchings and engravings.
	continuing into ↓		
1700s	Lighter patterns.	Bed hangings, valances and costume items.	From Tree of Life to stems in pots.
	Used with flat quilting.	Bed covers, pillows, cushions and costume items.	Botanical illustrations, cartouches.
	Needlepaintings.	Pictures.	Etchings, engravings and paintings.
	Etching work.	Pictures.	

Date	Techniques	Examples	Sources
1800s	Art Needlework, Arts and Crafts Movement.	Household and costume items, pictures.	Transfers, magazines and traced items. Morris, Royal School of Art Needlework (RSAN).
	'Jacobean' revival.	Household items.	Transfers and traced items.
	continuing into		
1900s	Floral motifs, hangings and banners.	Household items and costume. Samplers. Pictures.	Transfers, magazines and traced items.

Canvaswork

Date	Techniques	Examples	Sources
Early	Tent stitch, cross stitch and long-armed cross stitch.	Ecclesiastical, orphreys and burses.	Heraldic devices and ecclesiastical symbols.
1500s	Tent stitch and cross stitch, sometimes with other stitches.	Cushions of all kinds. Slips. Table carpets and wall hangings. Bags.	Woodcut illustrations, herbals, etc.
1600s	Tent stitch and cross stitch.	Small pictures. Cushions and book-covers.	Woodcut illustrations, etchings and engravings.
1700s	Tent stitch and cross stitch, sometimes with others.	Wall hangings, Holte and Calverley.	Sometimes in the Tree of Life style of the previous century.
1800s	Tent stitch, cross stitch and plush stitch. Perforated cards.	Berlin wool work on almost everything! Pictures. Mottoes and bookmarks.	Hand-coloured charts; later magazines.
1900s	Tent stitch, cross stitch.	Pictures, cushions and household items.	Magazine charts, painted and printed canvas and kits.

Needlemade surfaces

Date	Techniques	Examples	Sources
Early	Needlebinding (Europe and Middle East).	Gloves, mittens, hats and trimming on garments. Whole garments.	
	Needlelooping (Tibet and Far East).	Badges of rank, religious and ceremonial hangings.	Ancient symbols.
1500s	Reticella leading to punto in aria	Costume and ecclesiastical items.	Pattern books.
	continuing into		

Date	Techniques	Examples	Sources
1600s	Venetian needlepoints.	Costume and ecclesiastical items.	Pattern books.
	Holliepoint.	Ecclesiastical items.	
	Stumpwork.	Caskets and pictures.	Etchings, engravings and woodcut illustrations.
1700s	Burano, point de France and Brussels needlepoint.	Costume.	Professionally made.
	Hollie point.	Babies' caps and gowns.	
1800s	Point de gaze and Youghal.	Costume.	Mostly professionally made.
	Tape laces.	Costume and household items.	Magazines and periodicals.
1900s	Revival of needlemade laces during the 1970s and '80s.	Costume, household items and art forms.	Lace guilds and publications. Creative and artistic uses.
	Far Eastern imitations.		

	Appliqué	*Quilting*	*Patchwork*
Early	Funeral tent of Queen Istemkeb.		Tibetan and Far Eastern combined with embroidery and needlelooping.
		Popular throughout history, for warmth.	
		Used for protection; Gipon of the Black Prince.	
1500s	Slips and canvaswork panels (cushions and hangings). Virtue Hangings.		Born from utilitarian re-use of fabrics.
1600s	Slips and made-up pieces on stumpwork.		
1700s	Applied and stitched ribbons.	Flat quilting. Padded or corded quilting combined with pulled thread work.	Decorative patterns; wider range of fabrics available.
1800s	Hawaiian appliqué.		Crazy patchwork.
	Broderie perse.		

Date	Techniques	Examples	Sources
1900s	Banners. Applied fabrics edged with satin stitch.	Revival in rural areas, 1940s. Revival in 1970s and '80s.	Revival in 1960s, developing into art hangings in the 1970s and '80s.

Metal thread embroidery

Date	Techniques	Examples	Sources
Early	Couched gold with coloured silks in split stitch and stem stitch.	Saxon, Maaseik and Durham Relics.	Ecclesiastical. Manuscript and stained-glass artists.
1200 to 1400	Underside and surface couching, silver-gilt with coloured silks in split and stem stitches and laidwork.	Opus Anglicanum. ↓	↓
1500s	Or nué (Low Countries). Raised and padded work (Europe).	Decline. Ecclesiastical.	
	Plaited braid and composite stitches with coloured silk embroidery.	Costume, covers, book-covers, etc.	Woodcut illustrations, herbals.
1600s	Or nué (England). Edmund Harrison.	Religious pictures.	
	Stumpwork.	Caskets, pictures, cushions and mirror frames.	Illustrations, engravings and etchings.
1700s	Low-relief padding with embroidery in coloured silks.	Costume, bed hangings and cushions.	Botanical illustrations, etchings and engravings.
	Used for flat quilting with embroidery in coloured silks.	Bed furnishings and costume.	Pots and urns, etc.
1800s	Leek embroidery, coloured silks and metal thread on printed fabrics.	Ecclesiastical, household and decorative textiles.	Printed fabrics. William Morris, Arts and Crafts Movement.
	Padded metal thread, basket stitch, etc.	Ecclesiastical (Bodley).	
	continuing into ↓		
1900s	Revival of or nué. Revival of metal thread with experimental work.	Panels. Panels and decorative textiles.	Original designs.

Date	Techniques	Examples	Sources
	Whitework		
Early	Cutwork with surface stitches.	Ecclesiastical and costume.	
	developing and continuing alongside		
1500s	Reticella and punto in aria.	Ecclesiastical and costume.	Pattern books.
1600s	Voided designs, Russian drawn ground.	Ecclesiastical and household.	←
	Cutwork squares alternating with filet, lacis.	Household.	←
1700s	Dresden work (N. Europe), brought to Britain.	Costume, lace substitute.	←
	developing into		
1800s	Ayrshire work, needlemade fillings.	Babies' clothes, costume items.	Professional, but traced items for the amateur.
	Broderie anglaise and Madeira work.	Costume and household.	Traced and ready-punched fabric.
	Fisherton-de-la-Mere and Greek, or Ruskin, lace.	Household.	Magazines and periodicals.
	Carrickmacross, Limerick and Coggeshall lace.	Lace substitutes.	
	continuing into 20th century		
1900s	Disruption of two World Wars.		
	Revival of all forms during the 1970s and '80s.		

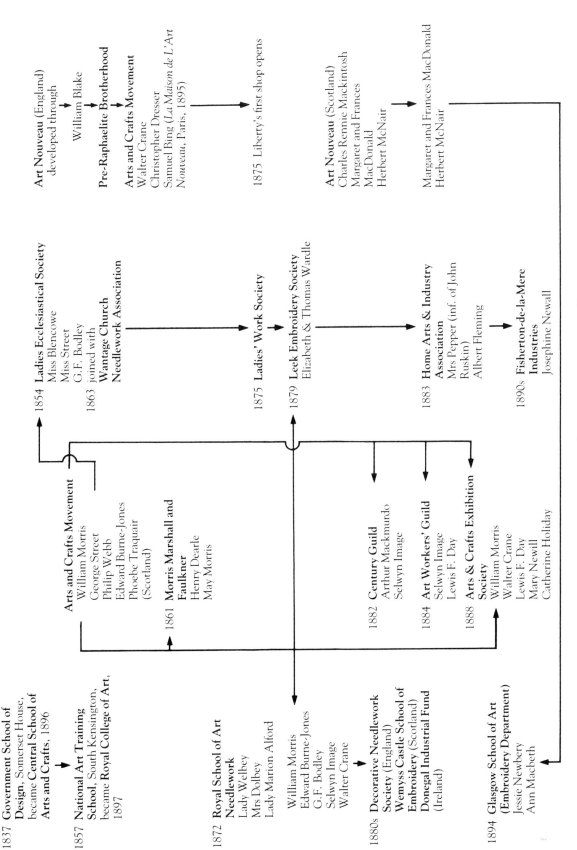

and examinations

Exhibition (Paris)

Pugin

Art Nouveau (England)
developed through

→ William Blake →

Pre-Raphaelite Brotherhood

Arts and Crafts Movement
Walter Crane
Christopher Dresser
Samuel Bing (*La Maison de L'Art Nouveau*, Paris, 1895)

1875 Liberty's first shop opens

Art Nouveau (Scotland)
Charles Rennie Mackintosh
Margaret and Frances MacDonald
Herbert McNair

Margaret and Frances MacDonald
Herbert McNair

1837 **Government School of Design**, Somerset House, became **Central School of Arts and Crafts**, 1896

1857 **National Art Training School**, South Kensington, became **Royal College of Art**, 1897

Arts and Crafts Movement
William Morris
George Street
Philip Webb
Edward Burne-Jones
Phoebe Traquair (Scotland)

1861 **Morris Marshall and Faulkner**
Henry Dearle
May Morris

1854 **Ladies Ecclesiastical Society**
Miss Blencowe
Miss Street
G.F. Bodley

1863 joined with **Wantage Church Needlework Association**

1875 **Ladies' Work Society**

1879 **Leek Embroidery Society**
Elizabeth & Thomas Wardle

1883 **Home Arts & Industry Association**
Mrs Pepper (inf. of John Ruskin)
Albert Fleming

1890s **Fisherton-de-la-Mere Industries**
Josephine Newall

1872 **Royal School of Art Needlework**
Lady Welbey
Mrs Dolbey
Lady Marion Alford

William Morris
Edward Burne-Jones
G.F. Bodley
Selwyn Image
Walter Crane

1880s **Decorative Needlework Society (England)**
Wemyss Castle School of Embroidery (Scotland)
Donegal Industrial Fund (Ireland)

1882 **Century Guild**
Arthur Mackmurdo
Selwyn Image

1884 **Art Workers' Guild**
Selwyn Image
Lewis F. Day

1888 **Arts & Crafts Exhibition Society**
William Morris
Walter Crane
Lewis F. Day
Mary Newill
Catherine Holiday

1894 **Glasgow School of Art (Embroidery Department)**
Jessie Newbery
Ann Macbeth

APPENDIX 4 NINETEENTH-CENTURY CONNECTIONS

MUSEUMS, COLLECTIONS AND ECCLESIASTICAL VESTMENTS

Always enquire in advance if you wish to visit a collection to see a specific item.

United Kingdom and Ireland

England

ABINGDON, Milton Manor, Oxfordshire.

AYLESBURY, Waddesdon Manor, Waddesdon, HP18 0JH (costume).

BAKEWELL, Chatsworth House, Derbyshire DE4 1PN.

BARNARD CASTLE, Rokeby Park, County Durham, DL12 8NP.

BATH, The American Museum in Britain, Claverton Manor, BA2 7BD.
   The Museum of Costume, Assembly Rooms, Bennett Street, BA1 2QH.

BEDFORD, The Cecil Higgins Museum and Art Gallery, Castle Close, MK40 3NY.

BIRMINGHAM, Aston Hall, Trinity Road, Aston, West Midlands, B6 6JD.

BLACKBURN, Lewis Textile Museum, Exchange Street, BB1 7AJ.
   Stoneyhurst College, Whalley, Nr Blackburn, Lancashire.

BOLTON, Museum and Art Gallery, Civic Centre, BL1 1SE.

BRISTOL, Museum and Art Gallery, BS8 1RL.

BURY ST EDMUNDS, Moyse's Hall Museum, Cornhill, Suffolk, IP33 1DX.

CAMBRIDGE, Fitzwilliam Museum, Trumpington Street, CB2 1RB.
   University Museum of Archaeology and Ethnology, Downing Street, CB2 3DZ.

CANTERBURY, Canterbury Cathedral, Kent.

CHICHESTER, Chichester Cathedral.

COGGESHALL, Paycocke's, West Street, Colchester, CO6 1NS.

DOE LEA, Nr Chesterfield, Hardwick Hall, Derbyshire, S44 5QJ.

DURHAM, Gulbenkian Museum of Oriental Art, University of Durham, Elvet Hill, DH1 3TH.
   The Cathedral Treasury.

EAST GRINSTEAD, Standen, West Sussex, RH19 4NE.

EXETER, Killerton, Broadclyst, EX5 3LE.
   Rougemont House Museum.

GUILDFORD, Clandon Park, West Clandon, GU4 7RQ.

HALIFAX, Bankfield Museum, Boothtown Road, HX3 6HG.

HATFIELD, Hatfield House, Hertfordshire, AL9 5NQ.

HEREFORD, Hartlebury Castle, Hereford and Worcester County Museum.

KING'S LYNN, Houghton Hall, Houghton, Norfolk, PE31 6UE.

LECHLADE, Kelmscott Manor.

LEICESTER, Leicester County Museums, Art Gallery and Record Service, LE1 6TD.

LIVERPOOL, Merseyside County Museums, William Brown Street, L3 8EN.

LONDON, Bethnal Green Museum, Cambridge Heath Road, E2 9PA.
   British Museum, Great Russell Street, WC1B 3DG.
   The Embroiderers Guild, Apartment 41, Hampton Court Palace, East Molesey, Surrey, KT8 9AU. Full membership allows use of the library, collection and courses.
   Fenton House, Windmill Hill, Hampstead, NW3 6RT.

Gunnersbury Park Museum, Gunnersbury Park, W3 8LO.

Ham House, Richmond, TW10 7RS.

Horniman Museum, Forest Hill, SE23 3PQ.

Kensington Palace, W8.

Museum of London, London Wall, EC27 5HN.

Osterley Park, Isleworth, Middlesex, TW7 4RB.

RCA Textile School, Kensington Gore, SW7 2EU.

Victoria and Albert Museum, South Kensington, SW7 2RL.

Westminster Abbey.

William Morris Gallery, Forest Road, Walthamstow, E17 4PP.

MANCHESTER, The Gallery of English Costume, Platt Hall, Rusholme, M14 5LL.

Whitworth Art Gallery, University of Manchester, M15 6ER.

MONTACUTE, Montacute House, Nr Yeovil, Somerset, TA15 6XP.

MORPETH, Wallington, Cambs, NE61 4AR.

NEWCASTLE-UPON-TYNE, Laing Art Gallery and Museum, Higham Place, NE1 8AG.

NORWICH, Blickling Hall, Blickling, NR11 6NF.

Castle Museum, Norwich Castle, NR1 3JU.

Felbrigg Hall, NR11 8PR.

Strangers' Hall Museum, Charing Cross, NR2 4AL.

NOTTINGHAM, Castle Museum and Art Gallery, The Castle, NG1 6EL.

Museum of Costume and Textiles, Castle Gate, NG1 6AF.

OXBURGH, Oxburgh Hall, Nr King's Lynn, Norfolk, PE33 9PS.

OXFORD, The Ashmolean Museum, Beaumont Street, OX1 2PH.

PADIHAM, Gawthorpe Hall, Nr Burnley, Lancashire, BB12 8UA.

PRESTON, Harris Museum and Art Gallery, PR1 2PP.

PULBOROUGH, Parham Park, West Sussex.

READING, Museum of English Rural Life, University of Reading, Whiteknights, RG6 2AG.

SEVENOAKS, Knole, Kent, TN15 0RP.

STAMFORD, Burghley House, Lincolnshire, PE9 3JY.

ST DOMINICK, Cotehele, Nr Saltash, Devon, PL12 6TA.

TICKNALL, Calke Abbey, Derbyshire.

WELLS, Cathedral, Somerset.

Museum, Cathedral Square (samplers).

WHALLEY, Stoneyhurst College, Lancashire.

WINCHESTER, Chilcomb House, Hampshire County Museum.

WOLVERHAMPTON, Wightwick Manor, Wightwick Bank, WV6 8EE.

WOODSTOCK, Oxfordshire County Museum, Woodstock, Oxfordshire, OX7 1SP (smocks).

YORK, Castle Howard, Nr York, North Yorkshire.

Castle Museum, The Mound, YO1 1RY.

Ireland

BELFAST, Richard Atkinson & Co., Ltd. Donegal Road, BT12 6HT.

Ulster Museum, Botanic Gardens, BT9 5AB.

DUBLIN, National Museum of Ireland, Kildare Street, Dublin 2.

HOLYWOOD, Ulster Folk Museum, Cultra Manor, Co. Down, BT18 0EU.

Scotland

EDINBURGH, National Museums of Scotland, formerly National Museum of Antiquities of Scotland, Queen Street, EH2 1JD.

National Museums of Scotland, formerly Royal Scottish Museum, Chambers Street, EH1 1JF.

Palace of Holyroodhouse, Lothian.

GLAMIS, Glamis Castle, Tayside, DD8 1RJ.

GLASGOW, Art Gallery and Museum, Kelvingrove Park, G3 8AG.

The Burrell Collection, Pollok Country Park, 2060 Pollokshaws Road, G43 1AT.

GORDON, Mellerstain, Berwickshire, TD3 6LG.

INNERLEITHEN, Traquair House, Peeblesshire, EH44 6PW.

PAISLEY, Museum and Art Galleries, High Street, PA1 2BA.

PITLOCHRY, Blair Castle, Perthshire.

Wales

CARDIFF, Welsh Folk Museum, St Fagans, CF5 6XB.

CLWYD, Erddig, Nr Wrexham, LL13 0YT.

Europe

Austria

SALZBURG, St Peter's Abbey.

VIENNA, Kunsthistorisches Museum.

Museum für Angewandte Kunst.

Schatzkammer, within the Hofburg (Kunsthistorisches Museum).

ZWETTL, Monastery.

Belgium

BRUSSELS, Musées Royaux d'Art et d'Histoire.
GHENT, Musée d'Archéologie de la Byloke.

Bulgaria

SOFIA, Ethnographic Institute.

Czechoslovakia

CHEB, Municipal Museum.
PRAGUE, National Museum.

Denmark

COPENHAGEN, Danish Folk Museum.
Dat Danske Kunstindustrimuseum.

Finland

BORGA, Town Museum.
HELSINKI, National Museum of Finland.
VAASA, Historical Museum of Pohjanmaa.

France

BAYEUX, Centre Guillaume le Conquerant.
CHARTRES, Cathedral Treasury.
EVREUX, Musée Municipal.
HAUTE GARONNE, Cathédrale de St Bertrand de Comminges.
LYONS, Musée Historique des Tissus.
MULHOUSE, Musée de l'Impression sur Etoffes.
PARIS, Musée des Arts Decoratifs.
Musée du Louvre.
Musée Jacqremart-Andre.
Musée National des Thermes et de l'Hotel de Cluny.
VAR, Church of St Maximin.

Germany

BADEN-BADEN, Staatliche Kunsthalle.
BAMBURG, Diocesan Museum, Cathedral Treasury.
DRESDEN, State Art Collections.
HAMBURG, Museum für Kunst und Gewerbe.
KARLSRUHE, Badisches Landesmuseum.
KREFELD, Textilmuseum.

MUNICH, Bayerisches Nationalmuseum.
Residenzmuseum.
Stadtsmuseum.
NUREMBERG, Germanisches Nationalmuseum.
STUTTGART, Wurttemburgischen Landesmuseums.

Greece

ATHENS, Benaki Museum.
Museum of Greek Popular Art.

Hungary

BUDAPEST, Hungarian National Museum.
Museum of Applied Arts.
Museum of Fine Arts.

Iceland

REYKJAVIK, National Museum of Iceland.

Italy

ANAGNI, Anagni Cathedral.
ASCOLI, Palazzo Communale, Ascoli Piceno.
ASSISI, Treasury of San Francesco.
BOLOGNA, Museo Civico Medievale.
FLORENCE, Industrie Femminili Italiane.
Museo degli Argenti.
Museo de St Maria del Fiore.
Museo Nazionale.
Palazzo Davanzati.
PIENZA, Capitolo della Cattedrale de Pienza.
ROME, Pinacoteca Vaticana.
Vatican Library Museum and Treasury.
TRENTO, Cathedral Treasury.
VENICE, Maria della Salute.

Netherlands

AMSTERDAM, Rijksmuseum.
Stedelijk Museum.
ANTWERP, Rockoxhuis.
ARNHEM, Nederlands Openluchtmuseum.
HAGUE, Costume Museum.
LEEUWARDEN, Fries Museum.
NIJMEGEN, Gemeente Museum.
ROTTERDAM, Museum Boymans-Van Beuningen.
Rotterdam Kunststichting
UTRECHT, Arrtsbisschoppelijk Museum.

Norway

OSLO, Kunstindustrimuseet.
  Norwegian Folk Museum.
TRONDHEIM, Nordenfjeldske Kunstindustri Museum.
  Videnskapsselkapets Oldsaksamling.

Poland

CRACOW, National Museum.
WAWEL, Cathedral Treasury.

Portugal

LISBON, Nacional de Arte Antiga.

Romania

BUCHAREST, Museum of Art.
PUTNA, Monastery.

Spain

BARCELONA, Apparel Museum-Rocamora Collection.
  Chapel of St George of the Generalitat.
  Museum of the History of the City.
  Textile Museum.
GERONA, Cathedral Treasury.
MADRID, Institute of Valencia de Don Juan.
  Madrid Museum.
TOLEDO, Cathedral Treasury.
VICH, Museo Episcopal de Vich.

Sweden

SKARA, Cathedral.
STOCKHOLM, Nordiska Museet.
  State Historical Museum.
UPPSALA, Cathedral Treasury.

Switzerland

BASLE, Historisches Museum.
BERNE, Bernisches Historisches Museum.
LUCERNE, Ursuline Church.
ZURICH, Bellerive Museum.
  Kunstgewebemuseum.
  Schweizerisches Landes-Museum.

Yugoslavia

BELGRADE, National Ethnographic Museum.
ZAGREB, Ethnographical Museum.

United States of America and Canada

Canada

MONTREAL, QUE, McCord Museum, McGill
  University, 690 Sherbrooke Street West.
  Montreal Museum of Fine Arts, 1379 Sherbrooke
  Street West.
SAINT JOHN, N.B., The New Brunswick Museum, 277
  Douglas Avenue.
TORONTO, ONT, Royal Ontario Museum, 100 Queen's
  Park.

United States of America

BALTIMORE MD, The Baltimore Museum of Art, Art
  Museum Drive.
  The Walters Art Gallery, 600 North Charles Street.
BLOOMFIELD HILLS MI, Cranbrook Academy of Art,
  500 Lone Pine Road.
BOSTON, MASS, Museum of Fine Arts, 465 Huntington
  Avenue.
  SPNEA, Harrison Gray Otis House, 141 Cambridge
  Street.
CAMBRIDGE, MASS, Busch-Reisinger Museum, Harvard
  University, 29 Kirkland Street.
CHICAGO, ILL, The Art Institute of Chicago, Michigan
  Avenue at Adams Street.
CLEVELAND, OHIO, The Cleveland Museum of Art,
  11150 East Boulevard.
CONNECTICUT, Historical Society.
CRANBROOK, Academy of Art.
  Cranbrook House.
DEARBORN, MICH, Henry Ford Museum, Greenfield
  Village.
DEERFIELD, MASS, Historic Deerfield Inc, Route 5.
DENVER, COL, The Denver Art Museum, 100 West
  14th Avenue Parkway.
DETROIT, MICH, The Detroit Institute of Arts, 5200
  Woodward Avenue.
HARTFORD, CONN, Wadsworth Atheneum, 600 Main
  Street.
INDIANAPOLIS, IND, Indianapolis Museum of Art, 1200
  West 38 Street.
LAWRENCE, KANSAS, University of Kansas Museum of
  Art, University of Kansas.
LOS ANGELES, CAL, Los Angeles County Museum of
  Art, 5905, Wilshire Boulevard.
MINNEAPOLIS, MINN, The Minneapolis Institute of
  Arts, 102 East 24 Street.

NEWARK, N.J. The Newark Museum, 43–49
   Washington Street.
NEW YORK, The Cloisters.
NEW YORK CITY, The Brooklyn Museum, Eastern
   Parkway, Brooklyn.
   Cooper-Hewitt Museum of Design, Smithsonian
   Institution, Fifth Avenue at 91st Street.
   F.I.T. Design Laboratory, 27th Street and Seventh
   Avenue.
   Metropolitan Museum of Art, Fifth Avenue and
   82nd Street.
   Museum of Contemporary Crafts, 29 West 53rd
   Street.
PALM BEACH, FLA, Henry Morrison Flagler Museum,
   Whitehall Way.
PHILADELPHIA, PA, Philadelphia Museum of Art,
   Parkway at 26th Street.
RICHMOND, VA, Valentine Museum, 1015 East Clay
   Street.
ST LOUIS, MO, The St Louis Art Museum, Forest Park.
WASHINGTON, DC, Memorial Continental Hall,
   Daughters of the American Revolution Museum.
   National Museum of History and Technology,
   Smithsonian Institution.
   The Textile Museum, 2320 S Street NW.

WILLIAMSBURG, VA, The Colonial Williamsburg
   Foundation, Drawer C.
WINTERTHUR, DEL, Henry Francis du Pont Winterthur
   Museum, Route 52.

Rest of the World

AUSTRALIA, Art Gallery of South Australia, Adelaide.
   National Gallery of Victoria, Melbourne.
CHINA, Hunan Province Museum.
   Jingzhou Area Museum, Hubei Province.
   National Palace Museum, Taipei.
EGYPT, Cairo Museum, Cairo.
HONG KONG, Museum of Art.
JAPAN, Chion-in Temple Collection, Kyoto.
   Enkaku-ji Temple Collection, Kamakura.
   National Museum, Kyoto.
   Shuzen-ji Temple Collection, Shizuoka.
KOREA, Museum of Korean Embroidery, Seoul.
NEW ZEALAND, Dominion Museum, Wellington.
USSR, Hermitage Museum, Leningrad.
   The History and Art Museum, Zagorsk.

FURTHER READING

General

ALFORD, LADY M., *Needlework as Art* (first published 1886), reprint E.P. Publishing 1975

BRIDGEMAN, H. and DRURY, E., *Needlework, an Illustrated History*, Paddington Press, 1978

BRIGGS, A., *A Social History of England*, BCA London 1984

BUCKLE, M. and DAY, L.F, *Art in Needlework*, Batsford 1901

CHAPMAN, S.E., *Historic Floral and Animal Designs for Embroiderers and Craftsmen*, Dover Pictorial Archive Series 1977

CLABBURN, P., *The Needleworker's Dictionary*, Macmillan 1976

CLABBURN, P., *Masterpieces of Embroidery*, Phaidon Press 1981

DEAN, B., *Church Needlework*, Batsford 1990

DEAN, B., *Ecclesiastical Embroidery*, Batsford 1958

DEAN, B., *Embroidery in Religion and Ceremonial*, Batsford 1981

FINCH, K. and PUTNAM, G., *The Care and Preservation of Textiles*, Batsford 1985

HIBBERT, C., *The English, A Social History 1066–1945*, Grafton Books 1987

HONOUR, H. and FLEMING, J., *A World History of Art*, Macmillan 1982

HUGHES, T., *English Domestic Needlework, 1660–1860*, Lutterworth Press 1961

JOURDAIN, M.A., *English Secular Embroidery*, Kegan Paul 1910

KENDRICK, A.F., *English Embroidery*, Batsford 1913

MASTERS, E.T., *The Gentlewoman's Book of Art Needlework*, Henry and Co.

MAYO, J., *A History of Ecclesiastical Dress*, Batsford 1984

NEVINSON, J., *Catalogue of English Domestic Embroidery*, HMSO and Victoria and Albert Museum 1938

ROTHSTEIN, N., (ed.), *Four Hundred Years of Fashion*, Victoria and Albert Museum/William Collins 1984

SNOOK, B., *Needlework at Parham* (available at Parham)

SWAIN, M., *Figures on Fabric, Embroidery Design Sources and Their Application*, A and C Black 1980

SWAIN, M., *Historical Needlework, a Study of Influences in Scotland and Northern England*, Barrie and Jenkins 1970

SYNGE, L., (ed.), *Book of Needlework and Embroidery*, Collins 1986

WILTON, The Countess of, *The Art of Needlework*, Henry Colburn 1844

Early Techniques

Classical Korean Embroideries, Korea-British Centennial Committee 1983

ANDERSEN, S.H. and JORGENSEN, L.B., 'Ancient Cloth', *Skalk* No. 1, 1985

BAKER, M. and LUNT, M., *Blue and White Cotton Embroideries of Rural China*, Charles Scribner's & Sons, USA 1977 and Sidgwick and Jackson, London 1978

CHUNG, Y.Y., *The Art of Oriental Embroidery*, Bell and Hyman 1979

NOMA, S., *Japanese Costume and Textile Arts* Vol. 16, Weatherhill/Heibousha 1974

SOAME-JENYNS, R., *Chinese Art*, Phaidon 1981

STUART, *Funeral Tent*, 1882

WATSON, W., (ed.), *The Great Japan Exhibition*, Royal Academy of Arts, London 1981

WILSON, V., *Chinese Dress*, Victoria and Albert Museum 1986

YARONG, W., *Chinese Folk Embroidery*, Thames and Hudson 1987

Early English Embroidery

BROHOLM, H.C. and HALD, M., *Costumes of the Bronze Age in Denmark*, Nordisk Forlag, Copenhagen 1970

BUDNY, M. and TWEDDLE, D., 'The Maaseik Embroideries', *Anglo-Saxon England* Vol. 13, Cambridge University Press 1984

BUDNY, M., and TWEDDLE, D., 'Early Medieval Textiles at Maaseik, Belgium', *The Antiquaries Journal* Vol. LXV, Part II, pp.353–89

BURNHAM, D.K., 'Coptic Knitting, an Ancient Technique', *Textile History* Vol.3, Pasold Research Fund 1972

COLLINGWOOD, P., *Textile and Weaving Structures*, Batsford 1987

HALD, M., *Ancient Textiles from Bogs and Burials*, National Museum of Denmark 1980

KOCH, J., 'Skefning-Needlbinding', *Skalk* no.2, 1976

WILSON, D., *The Bayeux Tapestry*, Thames and Hudson 1985

Opus Anglicanum

Opus Anglicanum, English Medieval Embroidery, The Arts Council 1963

CHRISTIE, A.G.I., *English Medieval Embroidery*, Clarendon Press 1938

KOVACS, E. and LOVAG, Z., *The Hungarian Crown and Other Regalia*, Corvina, Budapest 1980

LEITHE-JASPER, M. and DISTELBERGER, R., *The Kunsthistorisches Museum, Vienna*, Philip Wilson Publishers Ltd 1982

Embroidery and Tapestries of the Fifteenth Century

FILLITZ, H., *Der Schatz des Ordens Vom Goldenen Vlies*, Residenz Verlag, Vienna 1988

LEITHE-JASPER, M. and DISTELBERGER, R., *The Kunsthistorisches Museum, Vienna*, Philip Wilson Publishers Ltd 1982

VERLET, P., FLORISOONE, M., HOFFMEISTER, A. and TABARD, F., *The Art of Tapestry*, Thames and Hudson 1965

WEIGERT, R.A., *French Tapestry*, Faber and Faber 1962

WINGFIELD-DIGBY, G., *The Devonshire Hunting Tapestries*, Victoria and Albert Museum and HMSO 1971

The Embroidery of the Tudor Era

ARNOLD, J., *Patterns of Fashion, c.1560–1620*, Macmillan 1985

BOYNTON, L. (ed.), *The Hardwick Hall Inventories of 1601*, The Furniture History Society 1971

EISENBERG, E., *The Captive Queen in Derbyshire*, Derbyshire Heritage Series 1984

GIROUARD, M., *Hardwick Hall*, The National Trust 1976

LEVEY, S.M., *The Hardwick Embroideries*, National Trust 1988

STRONG, R. and TREVELYAN-OMAN, J., *Elizabeth R*, BCA 1971

SWAIN, M., *The Needlework of Mary Queen of Scots*, Van Nostrand Reinhold Co. 1973

WINGFIELD-DIGBY, G., *Elizabethan Embroidery*, Faber and Faber 1963

Seventeenth-century Embroidery

The Mary Bellis Collection, Christie's sale catalogue 1987

ARNOLD, J., *Patterns of Fashion, c.1660–1860*, Macmillan 1964/72

MAYORCAS, J.D., 'English stumpwork', *The Connoisseur* Vol.188, No.758, 1975

WORDEN, B., (ed.), *Stuart England*, Guild Publishing 1986

Needlemade Laces

LEVY, S., *Lace, a History*, Manet and the Victoria and Albert Museum.

VINCIOLO, F., *Renaissance Patterns for Lace, Embroidery and Needlepoint* (originally *Singuliers et Nouveaux Pourtraicts*, 1587), Dover Publications 1971

The Migration of European Embroidery to North America

BETTERTON, S., *American Textiles and Needlework*, American Museum in Britain

BURNHAM-HOWE, M., *Early American Embroideries in Deerfield, Massachusetts*, reprint Historic Deerfield 1963

CHURCHILL-BATH, V., *Needlework in America, History, Designs and Technique*, Mills and Boon 1979

FENNELLY, C., *Textiles in New England, 1790–1840*, Old Sturbridge Village Booklet Series 1961

POLLARD-ROWE, A., *Crewel Embroidered Bed Hangings in Old and New England*, Boston Museum Bulletin Vol.LXXI, Nos 365 & 366, 1973

SAFFORD, C.L. and BISHOP, R., *America's Quilts and Coverlets*, Studio Vista 1974

Embroidery of the Eighteenth Century

ARNOLD, J., *Patterns of Fashion, c.1660–1860*, Macmillan 1964/72

BRIMLEY-JOHNSON, R., *Mrs Delany*, Stanley Paul 1925

BUCK, A., *Dress in Eighteenth Century England*, Batsford 1979

DE SAINT-AUBIN, C.G., *Art of the Embroiderer* (originally *L'Art du Brodeur*, published 1770), reprint David R. Godine 1983

Nineteenth-century Embroidery Techniques

Victorian Church Art, Victoria and Albert Museum 1971

ARNOLD, J., *Patterns of Fashion, c.1660–1860*, Macmillan 1964/72

ARNOLD, J., *Patterns of Fashion, c.1860–1940*, Macmillan 1966/72

CAULFEILD, S.F.A. and SAWARD, B.C. (eds.), *Dictionary of Needlework, 1882*, reprinted as *Encyclopedia of Victorian Needlework*, Dover 1972

GIBBS-SMITH, C.H., *The Great Exhibition of 1851*, HMSO and Victoria and Albert 1981

KLICKMANN, F., *The Cult of the Needle*, Girl's Own Paper and Woman's Magazine

KLICKMANN, F. *The Home Art Book and Fancy Stitchery*, Girl's Own Paper and Woman's Magazine

MORRIS, B., *Victorian Embroidery*, Herbert Jenkins 1962

PROCTER, M.G., *Victorian Canvas Work, Berlin Wool Work*, Batsford 1972

Whitework and Imitation Laces of the Eighteenth and Nineteenth Centuries

CAMPBELL-PRESTON, D., *Needlemade Laces and Net Embroideries*, The Woman's Magazine Office 1938

SWAIN, M., *Ayrshire and Other Whitework*, Shire 1982

SWAIN, M. *The Flowerers, the Origins and History of Ayrshire Needlework*, W. and R. Chambers 1955

WARDLE, P., *Victorian Lace*, Herbert Jenkins 1968, reprint Ruth Bean 1982

The Influence of the Arts and Crafts Movement

May Morris, 1862–1938, William Morris Gallery 1989

ADAMS, S., *The Arts and Crafts Movement*, Apple Press 1987Adburgham, a., *Liberty's, a Biography of a Shop*, George Allen and Unwin 1975

ANSCOMBE, I. and GERE, C., *Arts and Crafts in Britain and America*, Academy Editions 1978

ASLIN, E., *The Aesthetic Movement, Prelude to Art Nouveau*, Ferndale Editions 1981

BUFFET-CHALLIE, L., *Art Nouveau Style*, Academy Editions 1982

DUFTY, A.R., *Morris Embroideries, the Prototypes*, The Society of Antiquaries 1985

MACFARLANE, F.C. and ARTHUR, E.F., *Glasgow School of Art Embroidery 1894–1920*, Glasgow Museums and Art Galleries 1980

MACLEOD, R., *Charles Rennie Mackintosh, Architect and Artist*, Collins 1968

PARRY, L., *Textiles of the Arts and Crafts Movement*, Thames and Hudson 1988

PARRY, L., *William Morris Textiles*, Weidenfeld and Nicolson 1983

A Summary of the Embroidery of the Early Twentieth Century

A Background to NDS Needlework, NDS (Needlework Development Scheme)

Experiment in Embroidery Design, Hand and Machine Embroideries created from the Original Drawings of Mary Kessell, Needlepoint Development Scheme.

Needlework Development Scheme, NDS 1951

The Overlord Embroidery, Overlord Embroidery Trust 1978

ARNOLD, J., *Patterns of Fashion, c.1860–1940*, Macmillan 1966/72

ARTHUR, L., *Kathleen Whyte, Embroiderer*, Batsford 1989

BLOOM, U., *The Inspired Needle*, Hurst and Blackett 1959

DOUGLASS, M., *Discovering Embroidery*, Mills and Boon 1955

DOUGLASS, W., *Embroidery*, Mills and Boon Craft Note Book Series No. 1, 1959

DOUGLASS, W., *Let Me Embroider*, Mills and Boon 1960

DREW, J.H., *Embroidery and Design*, Isaac Pitman

EDWARDS, J., *Chronicle of Embroidery 1900–1950*, Bayford Books 1981

HARRIS, K., *Church Needlework, Altar Linen*, Embroiderers Guild

HOGARTH, M., *Modern Embroidery*, The Studio Ltd. 1933

HOWARD, C., *Twentieth Century Embroidery in Great Britain to 1939*, Batsford 1981

HOWARD, C., *Twentieth Century Embroidery in Great Britain 1940–63*, Batsford 1983

HOWARD, C., *Twentieth Century Embroidery in Great Britain 1964–77*, Batsford 1984

HOWARD, C., *Twentieth Century Embroidery in Great Britain from 1978*, Batsford 1986

LILEY, A., *The Craft of Embroidery*, Mills and Boon 1961

LILEY, A., *Embroidery, a Fresh Approach*, Mills and Boon 1964

MACBETH, A. and SPENCE, M., *School and Fireside Crafts*, Methuen 1920

MONTAGUE, B., *The New Forest Embroidery*, New Forest Association 1981

NICHOLSON, J., *Contemporary Embroidery Design*, Batsford 1954

PESEL, L., *Historical Designs for Embroidery*, Batsford 1956

SIMPSON, H.M., *And Sew to Sew*, Needlework Development Scheme 1955

WINDSOR-FRY, G., *Embroidery and Needlework*, Pitman 1946

Samplers

One Man's Samplers, The Goodhart Collection, Embroiderers' Guild 1983

CHRISTIE, A., *Samplers and Stitches, a Handbook of the Embroiderer's Art*, Batsford 1920

CLABBURN, P., *Samplers*, Shire Publications 1977

COLBY, A., *Samplers*, Batsford 1964

EDWARDS, J., *Sampler Making 1540–1940*, Bayford Books 1983

HUISH, M., *Samplers and Tapestry Embroideries*, Longmans 1900, reprint Dover Publications 1970

HUMPHREY, C., *English Samplers at the Fitzwilliam*, Fitzwilliam Museum, Cambridge 1984

KIND, D., *Samplers*, HMSO and Victoria and Albert Museum 1960

Needlework Tools

GROVES, S., *The History of Needlework Tools and Accessories*, Country Life Books 1966

JOHNSON, E., *Needlework Tools*, Shire Publications 1978.

ROGERS, G.A., *An Illustrated History of Needlework Tools*, John Murray 1983

WHITING, G., *Old-Time Tools and Toys of Needlework*, Columbia University Press 1928, reprint Dover Publications 1971

INDEX